DISCARD

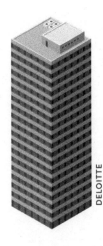

DELOITTE

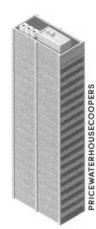

PRICEWATERHOUSECOOPERS

ERNST & YOUNG

KPMG

# THE BIG FOUR

The Curious Past and Perilous Future
of the Global Accounting Monopoly

## IAN D. GOW
## STUART KELLS

LA TROBE
UNIVERSITY PRESS

IN CONJUNCTION WITH BLACK INC.

Published by La Trobe University Press
in conjunction with Black Inc.
Level 1, 221 Drummond Street
Carlton VIC 3053, Australia
enquiries@blackincbooks.com
www.blackincbooks.com

9781760640637 (hardback)
9781743820285 (ebook)

A catalogue record for this
book is available from the
National Library of Australia

Cover design by Kim Ferguson
Text design and typesetting by Tristan Main
Cover image © enjoynz / Getty Images

Printed and bound in Great Britain by Clays Ltd, St Ives plc

# CONTENTS

# SCIENCE, MAGIC AND THE PREHISTORY OF THE BIG FOUR

Founded in the nineteenth century as the world's first national accounting body, the Institute of Chartered Accountants in England and Wales quickly established a dining club, sports clubs and a library. Among the library's first acquisitions was a copy of Luca Pacioli's ground-breaking Renaissance book of practical mathematics, *Summa de Arithmetica* (1494).

*Summa de Arithmetica* explains how to manage ledgers, inventories, liabilities and expense accounts. As well as pioneering the use of Hindu–Arabic numerals in Europe, it helped popularise double-entry accounting. 'For every credit in a ledger,' Pacioli wrote, 'there must also be a debit.' The enlightened author encouraged entrepreneurs to stop consulting astrologers and recluses for advice about this or that venture; all a merchant needed to succeed, Pacioli counselled, was access to cash, a good bookkeeper and an up-to-date system of accounts.

Pacioli belonged to a noble tradition of scholarship. Bookkeeping – along with cartography, perspective and ballistics – was one of the first sciences of the scientific revolution. The German polymath Johann Wolfgang von Goethe considered double-entry bookkeeping 'amongst the finest inventions of the human mind'.

Curiously, the careful counting of money preceded the careful measurement of lunar movements and accelerating cannonballs. The physical sciences, such as astronomy and physics, drew heavily on fiscal precedents: several pioneer physicists and cosmographers had also learned economics and accounting. Copernicus, for example, wrote on monetary reform as well as on the planets. Galileo taught bookkeeping, and learnt much from the field.[1] In 1696 Sir Isaac Newton was appointed Warden of England's Royal Mint.[2]

In the early days of science, numbers were put to all manner of purposes, practical and impractical. The first Latin and Italian books on arithmetic also instructed their readers on conjuring, astrology, thaumaturgy, games, jests, curses and black magic. As we look back with modern eyes, the line between early mathematics and magic appears strikingly fine; indeed, the relationship between math and the occult has a long history. Early in the fifth century, St Augustine issued a warning: 'The good Christian should beware of mathematicians and all those who make empty prophecies. The danger already exists that mathematicians have made a covenant with the devil to darken the spirit and confine man in the bonds of Hell.'

When, in the thirteenth century, Roger Bacon advocated the adoption of the Hindu–Arabic numerals, the church accused him of practising magic and condemned him to life in prison. Long after those strange-looking numerals arrived in Europe, they were still seen as exotic, even disreputable. The numerals, though, were a boon for Western culture. Much more practical and versatile than the Roman ones, the Asian numerals opened the way for modern mathematics, and hence modern accounting.

---

1   He also taught the new mathematics of fortification, such as how to build 'star forts' to withstand artillery.
2   The mathematician Carl Friedrich Gauss is said to have pointed out an error in his father's financial calculations – at the age of three.

Double-entry bookkeeping rests on a tautology: the value of an organisation's assets must equal the claims of creditors and owners to those assets. This was a new idea. Earlier financial records reflected a very different philosophy. The Domesday Book of 1086, for example, is a set of simple lists that assert King William's property rights, ecclesiastical rights, legal privileges, taxes and commitments. It is not a balanced schedule of debits and credits. Absolute rulers were more interested in counting their gold than in tallying their debts – that is, in reckoning what they owned rather than what they owed. The rise of double-entry among bankers and merchants in the late medieval period reflected the tectonic social, political and economic changes of the age, and the shift of power to the men and women who energised the Renaissance.

The Pacioli volume became one of the most valued possessions of the Institute of Chartered Accountants, both for its ground-breaking content and for its worth on the rare book market. An 'incunabulum' (meaning it was printed before 1501), the book is today appreciated as one of the earliest printed volumes about numbers. Another copy, finely bound in vellum and recently found in an old cupboard, sold at a Milan book auction for 530,000 euros. These volumes are rare survivors: most other copies from the 1494 edition were read to pieces by teachers, students, bookkeepers and merchants.

The institute's other treasures include *Nieuwe Instructie* (Antwerp, 1543), a work whose translation into French and English helped spread double-entry accounting to Western Europe (the author was Jan Ympyn Christoffels, a travelling silk trader), and the only surviving complete copy of *The maner and fourme how to kepe a perfecte reconying* (London, 1553), written by James Peele and adorned with elegant sample ledgers.

The institute's collection would be described in 1966 as the world's most complete library devoted to accounting and allied subjects. It is a monument to a powerful principle: that sound bookkeeping is the foundation of success in statecraft and in commerce. The modern accounting profession was built upon this principle. Firms promised to guide their clients through a perilous terrain, and towards a noble goal. The four largest accounting and audit firms have profited spectacularly from widespread confidence in this idea. How well founded is that confidence? How fit are the big firms as trustworthy guides? And how stable is their position as the heirs to Pacioli and Christoffel and Peele?

# INTRODUCTION

Stretching back centuries, the history of Deloitte, EY, KPMG and PwC is a fascinating story of wealth, power and luck. In many profound ways, the so-called Big Four accounting and audit firms have influenced how we work, how we manage, how we invest and how we are governed.

The firms have been called many things. High priests of capitalism. More powerful than sovereign states. Protectors of the public interest. The conscience of the free market. Heroes of corporate integrity. Benign watchdogs. Toothless lapdogs. A necessary evil. An institutionalised oligopoly. Corporate sweatshops. Accountants of fortune. Skilled enablers of white-collar fraud. Each of the Big Four is a case study of corporate triumph – and drama. Underneath their polished images are colourful tales of commercial success, but also of ethical compromises, professional angst, botched ventures, debauched parties, scandalous marriages, disreputable interests and arcane rites.

In a field that is seen as somewhat beige and lacking in prestige, the Big Four are the glamour boys, the glowing success stories of their field. In 2011 their total revenue broke emphatically through the US$100 billion mark. Since then it has kept on rising, surpassing US$130 billion in 2016. In that year, before a regrettable incident at the

2017 Oscars, PwC ranked alongside Disney, Nike and Lego as one of the ten most 'powerful' brands in the world.

With almost 1 million staff operating worldwide (not counting subcontractors), the Big Four are collectively one of the world's top employers. They directly employ more staff than there are active personnel in the Russian military. The number of people who have worked for a Big Four firm is much larger still. Many are now in other professional services firms, or senior roles in industry or government. In their work, they operate according to a 'Big Four style' – or in arch reaction against it.

Paul Gillis, a former PwC partner, described the Big Four as 'supranational organisations, substantially unrestrained by national borders, transcending nationalistic claims and state based attempts to regulate them'. The firms are formally – and seemingly intractably – integrated into the functioning of the modern financial system and modern democracies. They enjoy growing connections, too, with less democratic governments in the developing and recently developed worlds. In China, for example, the firms have become agents of the economic boom, and hot targets for regulatory control.

The four firms dominate several key markets for accounting, tax and audit services. Nearly all the largest businesses in the United States and the United Kingdom, for example, are audited by one or more of the firms. Of the 500 companies in the S&P 500 index, 497 used a Big Four auditor in 2017. Nearly all those businesses also buy management consulting services from the Big Four. In 2017, PwC alone claimed to provide services to 422 of the *Fortune* Global 500. Modern economies simply cannot function, it seems, without accountants, auditors and management consultants.

The Big Four got to where they are today through a complex process of commercial marriages and tie-ups – a process so elaborate and repetitive it is suggestive of fractal biology. Corporate mergers on a colossal scale (and with questionable rationales) were a feature of the business world in the 1980s. Examples from America include Pan Am's acquisition of National Airlines, Standard Oil's purchase of Kennecott Copper, and the Campeau Corporation's hostile takeover of Federated Department Stores – a transaction that *Fortune* magazine called 'the biggest, looniest deal ever'. Accounting firm mergers also reached a crescendo in that decade. In 1986 Peat Marwick and the mostly European firm KMG came together to create KPMG. In 1989 Ernst & Whinney and Arthur Young combined to become Ernst & Young. In the same year Deloitte Haskins & Sells merged with Touche Ross to form Deloitte & Touche. With the latter two mega-mergers, the Big Eight became the Big Six.

Five years earlier, Deloitte Haskins & Sells had come close to a merger with Price Waterhouse. There was much to recommend the marriage. The firms shared a common history, stretching as far back as the sector's early days in London. Both had advised England's railway companies, for example, and helped build the professional prestige of accountancy. The merger promised to create a modern powerhouse. In America alone, Deloitte at the time had 103 offices and 8000 employees; Price Waterhouse's American footprint encompassed ninety offices and 9000 employees. But internal opposition to the merger was strong. Naysayers claimed the two firms had starkly different cultures. In fact, the cultures were not really divergent, but considered in the context of the overall sameness of accounting practices, small differences loom large. When put to an international vote among partners, the merger option was rejected.

In 1989 Price Waterhouse again found itself in merger talks, this time with Arthur Andersen, the raging upstart founded by a former Price Waterhouse employee. Those talks also failed; Price Waterhouse would have to wait another nine years before finally consummating a union – with Coopers & Lybrand, thereby forming PricewaterhouseCoopers and reducing the Big Six to five.

Soon after, Ernst & Young and KPMG flirted but did not reach third base. (Speaking about the difficulty of consummating a merger, the chairman of Ernst & Young in China lamented that such exercises were 'like wooing a pretty young lady – one may lose for no reason at all'.) Even so, the Big Five did become the Big Four – and in a way that no one expected. Arthur Andersen's rapid and spectacular exit in 2002, in the wake of scandals involving Enron, WorldCom and Waste Management, left behind four majors. Such was the market concentration of the accounting industry now that another top-tier merger was impossible.

Since that time, the firms have been remarkably stable, and remarkably successful. So successful, in fact, that regulators and commentators have raised concerns about the monopoly power of the Big Four. Accountancy is notably less competitive than other professions, such as law and engineering. Competition is especially weak in the market for audit services. In 2016 the editor of London's *Financial Times* called for greater competition in that market: 'Four big firms are too few, not least because their very scarcity makes the application of strict regulation more difficult.'

Monopoly concerns were raised even before Arthur Andersen's exit. In 1997 Christopher Pearce, finance director of Rentokil and chairman of a group representing the finance directors of FTSE 100 companies, told the *Economist* that the merger of Price Waterhouse and Coopers & Lybrand would 'reduce the choice for auditing services and increase the conflicts of interest'. As early as 1976, the US Senate's Metcalf Report worried that '[t]he Big 8 are so large and influential in relation to other CPA firms that they are able to control virtually all aspects of accounting and auditing in the US'. The economic literature on monopoly and oligopoly is well established. Faced with a captive market, the monopolist raises prices, works inefficiently and shirks on quality. With the Big Four operating under a valuable monopoly concession in auditing, observers have noticed the commoditisation of audit services, and an erosion of their scope and reliability.

On the surface, the accounting and auditing industry has reached a state of cosy equilibrium. The firms collaborate in industry forums;

staff move regularly between them; the firms match each other's market presence and service lines, and copy each other's pricing, outputs and marketing strategies. Cosy or not, though, things are about to change. Today, the firms have a very uncertain future. They are on the cusp of a new era. In this book, which looks both backwards and forwards in time, we describe explosive pressures in each of the major service lines of the Big Four firms. Examples are the technological innovations that are rapidly making traditional forms of audit obsolete, and new sources of competition. Taken together, these pressures for change have an inexorable power, such that the industry will not be the same in five years' time.

The transformation may well arrive sooner than that – and it might be messy. Since the 1970s, the major accounting firms have endured recurring crises and have been sued thousands of times. Some of the suits, particularly those against the Big Four as auditors, have been perilously large. In 2011 the Association of Chartered Certified Accountants published its concern that audit firms would see 'potentially catastrophic litigation'.

As recently as 2016, PwC narrowly escaped the financial equivalent of what astrobiologists term an 'extinction-level event' (ELE). Taylor, Bean & Whitaker (TBW) was a US mortgage company. Lee Farkas, the company's chair and majority owner, masterminded a fraud that bankrupted the company and its major subsidiary (and main lender), Colonial Bank, one of the twenty-five largest banks in the United States. The fraud involved cash transfers and fake mortgages that massively inflated the assets of TBW and Colonial. Soon after the FBI raided TBW's grand headquarters, the two businesses declared bankruptcy. The collapse of Colonial – the biggest bank failure of 2009, the third-biggest since the beginning of the financial crisis, and the sixth-biggest in US history – cost the Federal Deposit Insurance Corporation (FDIC) around US$3 billion. A thousand employees lost their jobs, and multiple lawsuits were launched.

Federal prosecutors described Farkas as a 'consummate fraudster'. Others called him a 'burly college dropout' and a 'pathological liar' who was 'as generous as he was vicious'; employees on the receiving end of his office tirades referred to having been 'Farkased'. He and his co-conspirators were accused of submitting materially false financial data to the Securities and Exchange Commission and the Government National Mortgage Association (Ginnie Mae). In 2011 Farkas was found guilty of misappropriating US$3 billion and trying deceptively to obtain US$570 million in taxpayers' funds from the Troubled Asset Relief Program to prop up Colonial. Farkas used the money to buy caviar, holiday homes, classic cars, a private jet, a seaplane, strip clubs and a portfolio of Brazilian and Asian-fusion restaurants. Sentenced to thirty years, Farkas began his imprisonment at a medium-security jail in North Carolina – where Bernie Madoff was a fellow inmate. Paul Allen (TBW's former CEO), Delton De Armas (its former CFO), and Desiree Brown (its former treasurer) also received prison sentences.

PwC had audited Colonial's holding company, Colonial BancGroup, every year from 2002 to 2008. TBW's bankruptcy trustee accused PwC of failing to detect an unmissable fraud, and of certifying the existence of more than a billion dollars of Colonial assets that were in fact worthless, or were not owned by the company, or never actually existed at all. The ensuing legal action – the biggest claim ever made against an audit firm – sought US$5.5 billion from PwC.

In August 2016 PwC settled the lawsuit. The value of the confidential settlement is closely guarded but is believed to be one of the largest ever in the history of the Big Four. The TBW–Colonial fraud and its consequences featured in an episode of the television series *American Greed* – agonising watching for the auditors. And the agony is not over yet. At the time of writing, PwC is still involved in TBW-related litigation launched by the FDIC. That agency has also gone after Colonial's former internal auditor, Crowe Horwath.

In 2005 KPMG faced its own ELE when the US government accused the firm of knowingly selling tax shelters that gave the finger to the Internal Revenue Service (IRS). The shelters, it was claimed, generated more than US$100 million in fees for KPMG, and deprived the public of billions in tax revenue. In an enormous stroke of luck for KPMG, the government decided not to indict. A conviction, the government feared, would destroy the firm – and the current system of corporate auditing. Without KPMG, the lawmakers worried, the Big Four would become the Big Three, and there would not be enough large accounting firms to audit America's corporations. Terrifyingly for KPMG, though, the decision could easily have gone the other way. KPMG barely escaped a fate similar to that of its former Big Five rival Arthur Andersen.

The other firms have also had their share of trouble. In the early 1990s, for example, EY had to pay out more than US$400 million for failures relating to the savings and loan crisis. The firm was forced to publish full-page newspaper advertisements to rebut rumours that the payouts would send it into bankruptcy. In 2010 EY was again in strife, accused of 'a broad pattern of negligence and complicity' after a series of further lawsuits and calamities. And all four firms were deeply and controversially implicated in the 2008 financial crisis, the largest financial upheaval since the Great Depression. Deloitte, for example, had audited TBW in the years leading up to Colonial Bank's collapse; Deloitte paid to settle three related lawsuits in 2013.

Just as dangerously, the Big Four have been drawn into a toxic series of tax scandals, including LuxLeaks and the Paradise Papers. Ours is a new era of transparency and digital disruption, and in no area of Big Four services are those forces more intense than in taxation advisory.

The firms have come so close to the abyss that regulators and legislators have recommended that they prepare 'living wills'. A dismal concept borrowed from banking, such wills set out contingency arrangements for the orderly transition of clients and contracts; for ring-fencing of viable business units; and for the rapid winding-up of unviable ones. They also include agreements with regulators on how assets, staff and funding would be dealt with in the event of a calamitous failure.

The demise of Arthur Andersen provides a vivid case study of what such a failure looks like. Convicted in 2002 of obstruction of justice, the firm shrank from 85,000 employees to a rump of 200. (Late in 2001, Andersen's global CEO Joe Berardino had toured overseas offices and reassured staff that 'everything would be OK'.) In the months before the firm collapsed, it had become a laughing stock. In January 2002, for example, at the Alfalfa Club dinner in Washington DC, President George W. Bush joked that he'd just received a message from Saddam Hussein. 'The good news is he is willing to let us inspect his biological and chemical warfare installations,' Bush said. 'The bad news is that he insists Arthur Andersen do the inspections.'

The aftershocks of the firm's troubles reverberated far and wide. Fewer top students thought of joining the major accounting firms. Opinion poll respondents rated accountants low on professional integrity. The firms were subjected to increased government scrutiny, mainly via the *Sarbanes–Oxley Act*. The greatest impact fell on the former Andersen staff, the vast majority of whom 'had nothing to do with Enron but lost their jobs nonetheless'. They'd all been Enroned.

According to author Robert B. Reich:

> Some senior partners moved to other accounting or consulting firms. Joseph Berardino ... got a lucrative job at a private equity firm. Some other senior partners formed a new accounting firm. But many lower-level employees were hit hard. Three years after the conviction, a large number were still out of work.

Partners and staff lost much of their retirement benefits. When the Supreme Court later reversed the conviction that had led to Andersen's collapse, a former 'Android' wrote on the website for Andersen alumni: 'Does this mean we can bring a class action against the DOJ for ruining our lives?'

*

Much of the literature on business and economics has a particular type of firm in mind: an industrial company that produces physical goods. That type of firm, though, is becoming less and less representative of the modern economy. Firms that deliver *services*, and that trade in intellectual property, have prospered spectacularly. The Big Four are an example of this, indeed an exemplar. How they deviate from the stand-ard picture of enterprises is of much practical interest for the study of economics and business.

The Big Four provide a rare opportunity to study service firms in detail. That opportunity, though, has not been taken up in a wholly satisfactory manner. Despite the importance and success of the Big Four, and despite the precarious position in which they find themselves, they are surprisingly under-documented. Remarkably little has been written about them or their conduct. Most of the studies that do exist have a particular flavour. In large part, the academic literature on audit and accountancy consists of narrow and ahistorical studies whose attitude towards the Big Four is typically reverential, or at least non-confrontational. Moreover, as Cooper & Robson (2009) observed, most accounting firm histories are 'whiggish in their perspectives and orientations. They tend to focus on those who led the firm and construct events as the accomplishment of professional ideals through the response to client and market demands'. Burrage (1990) similarly criticised much of the historical work on the professions:

> [Historians] tended to concentrate on the elite of the profession and the issues that came to the attention of their governing bodies. They rarely sought to study the working practice of the rank and

file members of the profession, rarely referred to other professions, rarely sought to relate changes in the profession to changes in the wider society and rarely therefore found any reason to criticize the profession. Their main task was to recount the success story of responsible leaders coping with the problems that faced the profession.

There is another difficulty, too, for people wishing to look upon a true picture of the accounting profession: much of the extant history of the Big Four was commissioned by the firms themselves. In their marketing and corporate communications, the firms promulgate a safely homogenised version of their past. As the histories of many major companies show, however, there is often a big difference between the public narrative and the true story. In our Big Four research, we've found just such a difference. The true history is much more colourful, and more fascinating, than the manicured versions.

This book is our attempt to understand the past, the present and the likely future of the Big Four. Reflecting our personal interests and backgrounds, we've adopted what we believe is a novel approach. Robert Skidelsky wrote in 2016:

> Today's professional economists … have studied almost nothing but economics. They don't even read the classics of their own discipline. Economic history comes, if at all, from data sets. Philosophy, which could teach them about the limits of the economic method, is a closed book. Mathematics, demanding and seductive, has monopolized their mental horizons. The economists are the idiot savants of our time.

Skidelsky's critique, which applies equally well to many of today's accounting academics, is something we've tried strenuously to heed – by keeping a clear eye on accountancy's place in history and society.

# INTRODUCTION

Partners and staff in accounting firms use tools that depend on a series of innovations: Hindu–Arabic numerals, the invention of zero, the mathematics of fractions, the concepts of assets and liabilities, the genius of double-entry accounting, and the fraught practice of auditing, which has always meant different things to different people. Each of these innovations came from somewhere and someone. The histories of science, commerce and culture shed invaluable light on the current predicament of accountancy. For insight into the Big Four, we've looked far and wide. We've read the standard business texts, but also Dickens and Thackeray, Pacioli and Fibonacci, Darwin and Snowden. Our book is not a history of concepts or of organisations but of people, full-blooded and fallible.

The Big Four firms are culturally rich environments. Rainmakers. Beauty parades. Sales targets. Three-sixty reviews. Casual Fridays. Consistency meetings. Qualification meetings. Stand-up meetings. Hot-desking. Body shopping. Eating what you kill. Burning the code. Feeding the baby. Ranking and yanking. Upping or outing. Finders, minders, grinders. Golden handshakes, golden parachutes, golden cushions. Big Four partners and staff share a corpus of lore and trade-craft that is as rich as the fabled in-house traditions of stage playing, ice skating or the armed forces. Using our inside-outside perspective, we've tried to capture Big Four culture accurately, and to convey what life in the firms is actually like.

Authors deciding where to start a book on the Big Four are spoiled for choice. The firms' activities and services can be traced back through early-modern times to medieval, classical and even older precedents. Accountants are news today, and they've been news for millennia. In ancient Mesopotamia, for example, proto-accountants and auditors measured harvests, recorded royal purchases and checked the payment of tributes and taxes. Their activities are documented in clay tablets, books thousands of years older than *Summa de Arithmetica*. Bookkeepers can fairly claim to have invented writing and created the very first books.

We've elected to start with the Medici Bank of the late middle ages and the Renaissance. That illustrious bank's history contains lessons that are sharply relevant today. The bank's leaders established partnership structures and a professional legacy from which the Big Four were, in large part, born. Its history also parallels in intriguing ways the lives and passions of several pioneering accountants. So the Medici – along with Britain's railways – serve as a powerful lens through which we can examine the origins and destinations of the Big Four.

Those destinations include corporatisation, digital disruption and regulatory separation – such as into eight full-service accounting firms, or some other number of pure audit and pure consulting businesses. Whichever form it takes, the imminent transformation of the Big Four will have enormous implications for the firms' staff, partners and clients, and for our overall democratic and economic systems. One intention of this book is to help prepare us all for those implications.

We hope our book is timely. The Big Four tend only to come under significant scrutiny when something goes really badly wrong: a failed mega-audit, for example, or a botched mega-merger. Yet the pressures currently confronting the Big Four are just as dangerous and, potentially, as dramatic as those that precipitated the firms' worst disasters.

In a 1958 article for *Accounting Review*, Nicholas Stacey sought to explain why there were so few accountants in modern literature. Accountants, Stacey wrote, were 'innocent of romance'. We disagree. In this book we've endeavoured to capture some of the romance, grandeur and nobility of accountancy, and of the past, present and future of the Big Four.

*

The book is organised as follows. Part I, 'Infancy', investigates the economic and cultural history of the Big Four. We explore medieval and early-modern precedents of the Big Four's global partnership structures, examine the creation story of the modern accounting firm, and relate important episodes from the early days of the four firms' antecedent partnerships. The focus of this part is the pioneers, the founders and their milieu, and the dynamics of partnerships and professions.

Part II, 'Maturity', describes the Big Four in their modern incarnations: how they have defined themselves, their professional values and their boundaries, how they brand themselves, whom they hire. We attempt to understand how the modern Big Four culture emerged, and the predominant features of that culture.

Part III, 'The Difficulties of Adulthood', explores the hard challenges that the Big Four currently face across all their major service lines. A series of spectacular Big Four calamities can be traced to recurring causes, including fundamental conflicts between the service lines, and an apparent underinvestment in auditing – a service that is uniquely important to the value of the Big Four brands. In this context, the 'audit expectation gap' has emerged as a key battleground for the Big Four. We examine that battleground, along with the fraught concept of 'audit quality'. In the field of taxation services, too, there is a surfeit of problems. We explore Big Four tax disasters, and how a new ethic of disclosure is undermining old models of tax avoidance. The part concludes with an examination of the rich suite of challenges facing the Big Four in their most important new market: China.

Finally, Part IV is concerned with obsolescence and endgames. We look ahead to the immediate future and what may well be the 'Twilight Years' of the Big Four. Much can be learned from the firms' challenges and calamities. We examine how a combination of old and new pressures is likely to force the firms into a radical transformation. These pressures include technological change, regulatory action and the arrival of disruptive competition. The likely impacts span all aspects of the firms – their people, ownership, structure, networks, services and methods. We also return to the late middle ages and the Renaissance to explore how everything can go wrong for an international, diversified, networked organisation. We conclude with an examination of the Big Four's legacy.

# PART I

# Infancy

Antecedents of the Big Four can be found in surprising places – including late-medieval Florence. The modern history of the firms contains remarkable echoes of the pre-modern and early-modern history of the Medici Bank. How that bank was structured and staffed – and how its staff worked and lived – would be repeated centuries later in curious ways. We therefore explore in this part the Medici Bank as a Big Four antecedent; in later chapters we trace some of the echoes, before returning to the Medici Bank in detail in Chapter 14 to understand possible Big Four endgames.

The foundations of the Big Four were also laid in early financial scandals, during the Industrial Revolution but particularly amid the rapid development of Britain's railways in the nineteenth century. We examine those foundations in this part, along with the firms' key founders, and the beliefs and convictions that guided how they worked.

# 2

# GLORY, NOT INFAMY

## The Medici Bank as a precursor to the Big Four

### The merchant state

Piero de Medici – known as 'Piero the Gouty' ('Piero il Gottoso') – was born in 1416. In 1464 his father died and Piero inherited, at the age of forty-eight, a famous institution that was exceptionally profitable and well-run. Piero's father – the illustrious Cosimo de Medici – and his grandfather – Giovanni de Medici – had built the family business into Europe's most important private enterprise: the greatest bank in the world.

The Medici Bank was based in Florence, the capital of Tuscany. In the late middle ages, Florence was a substantial and prosperous city and the centre of global finance. A large gold coin, the florin, was first issued and named there; its widespread use throughout Europe added to the city's financial prestige.

Unlike most cities and countries in late medieval Europe, Florence was ruled by a mercantile family, the Medici. The activities of the Medici Bank were intertwined with those of the Florentine state, to such an extent that the boundary between bank and state was conspicuously fuzzy. Upon Cosimo's death, Piero became the head not only of the Medici Bank but also of the Florentine government.

Myth and rumour surround the bank's origins, but it seems to have begun as a criminal syndicate. 'Prior to the 1390s,' Niall Ferguson writes in *The Ascent of Money*, 'the Medici were more gangsters than bankers: a small-time clan, notable more for low violence than high finance.' After studying in detail the family's felonious origins, Gene Brucker found five instances in the mid-fourteenth century in which courts condemned Medici men to death for murder. Each time, the family used its wealth to buy its man out of trouble. Apart from the murders, Brucker also uncovered a rap sheet of other violent crimes committed by Medici men between 1343 and 1360.

Brutality and ruthlessness may have been two early causes of the Medici Bank's success, but another cause was less daunting: the adoption of double-entry accounting. If royal accounting is essentially feudal, double-entry is intrinsically capitalist. It is ideal for calculating and distributing profits among dispersed owners and claimants – such as the dispersed owners of Tuscan mercantile partnerships. That is why, in the late middle ages, Florentine merchants were critical to double-entry's development and use. Florentine enterprises adopted double-entry accounting as early as 1340.

In the Renaissance, no bank did more than the Medici's to spread double-entry accounting throughout Europe. One of the first international financial institutions, the Medici Bank knew to take seriously the various claims on its assets. Though exceptionally ugly (observers made note of his pale skin, uneven eyes, jutting chin, narrow lips and thin hair), Piero's father Cosimo had been highly popular among Florentines. He was also highly influential, both in Florence and abroad. From his father, Cosimo had learned the value of meticulous bookkeeping, and he built his own reputation as a wise banker and sound ruler.

A close relationship – more commercial than spiritual – with the Catholic church was crucial to Cosimo's success. He made astute loans to men on the rise – men who would later become bishops, cardinals and popes. When Tommaso Parentucelli was Bishop of Bologna, for example, Cosimo advanced him the requisite funds for climbing the ecclesiastical ladder. Giovanni de Medici had made similar investments, such as financing the rising cleric and extroverted Neapolitan, Baldassarre Cossa. A former pirate who retained piratical tendencies throughout his life, Cossa borrowed Medici money so he could buy his way into the office of cardinal. Parentucelli and Cossa both rose as far as pope. From that exalted office they would both reward the Medici Bank for its support.[3]

In this way, the Medici became the preferred bankers to the church, and ecclesiastical banking became the family's core business. The reach of the church was enormous, and its need for finance was large and stable: the Medici were in clover. Under the leadership first of Giovanni and then of Cosimo, the bank earned more than 50 per cent of its profits from Rome. Like his father before him, Cosimo managed borrowers with care and acuity; he knew when to be hard and when to be soft.[4] Through intelligent use of their power, the Medici built a business that was the envy of competitors near and far.

## Not puffed up

As well as ambitious clerics, Cosimo supported artists and men of letters. When the great bibliographer and calligrapher Niccolò de Niccoli 'ruined himself' by buying and commissioning too many books, Cosimo gave him unlimited credit. Upon Niccoli's death, his marvellous library

---

3   The Medici also used their power to block priests from advancement. In one notorious case, the bank stopped a young cleric from being made bishop. The block was lifted when the cleric's father, outwardly a celibate cardinal, paid his debts.

4   An example of Medici firmness: as security for the debts of unreliable Baldassarre Cossa, Giovanni de Medici kept hold of a richly jewelled papal mitre, along with pieces of gold plate from the papal treasury.

of manuscripts passed into Cosimo's hands. The banker gave 400 of them to the library of the convent of San Marco in Florence. Many of the others entered Cosimo's own library. Cosimo possessed both the financier's instinct and the collector's; commentators have since drawn parallels between those two urges. Tim Parks, the author of *Medici Money*, saw in the collecting habit an impulse towards 'control, order and possession' – an impulse that is fundamental to accounting and finance.

The collecting behaviour was also connected to another Medici craving. Despite the family's criminal past, or perhaps because of it, Cosimo and his kin hungered for respect and respectability. Cosimo could cut corners occasionally: in 1457, for example, he prepared false statements and – according to Raymond de Roover in *The Rise and Decline of the Medici Bank: 1397–1494* – 'ordered his agents to alter certain figures in the balances to be submitted to tax officials'. He was not the first businessman to keep two sets of double-entry books for tax purposes. And he skated deftly around the scriptural injunction against usury. But Cosimo took pains to be seen as an ethical businessman who gave back to society and treated his debtors well. Having learned from Giovanni the importance of an unsullied reputation, Cosimo advocated prudence and sobriety in business and in life. He detested gambling, for example, and demanded that his senior colleagues follow his abstemious example.

When wise Giovanni de Medici lay dying on 20 February 1429, he called the family together – his wife, his sons and their wives – and spoke his final words:

I leave you in possession of the great wealth which my good fortune has bestowed upon me … Speak not as though giving advice, but rather discuss matters with gentle and kindly reasoning. Be chary of frequenting the Palace; rather, wait to be summoned, and then be obedient, and not puffed up with pride at receiving many votes.

Have a care to keep the people at peace, and to increase the commerce of the city. Avoid litigation or any attempt to influence justice, for whosoever impedes justice will perish by justice. I leave you clear of any stain, for no evil deed has been committed by me. Thus I bequeath glory and not infamy to you as a heritage. I depart joyfully and with more happiness if you do not enter into party strife. Be careful not to attract public attention.

Cosimo lived by his father's advice, especially the part about staying out of the public eye. There were several reasons for this. One was his poor health. Late in Cosimo's life, there were rumours that he suffered from the plague; many Florentines were afraid to visit him. A more significant and longstanding reason, though, was that the Medici business depended on discretion; their power relied on an aura of mystery.

## An international concern

At its apogee, the bank maintained branches and agencies in Rome, Venice, Bruges, London, Pisa, Avignon, Milan, Basel, Geneva, Lübeck, Cologne, Ancona, Montpellier, Perugia and Rhodes. In late medieval times and during the Renaissance, the pope was the only European ruler with subjects in all corners of the continent. Those subjects – including people from as far afield as Iceland and Greenland – paid the tithes and taxes that funded the diverse activities of the church. The Medici were crucial in the discreet management of all these payments.

An itinerant branch of the bank followed the pope wherever he went, to tend to his financial needs. In 1437 and 1438, for example, the branch followed Pope Eugene IV to Bologna and Ferrara. The next year, the pope moved to a Dominican friary in Florence, where he presided over the council that attempted to merge the Roman Catholic and Greek Orthodox churches. The itinerant branch went to Florence, too, just as it had done years earlier, from February 1419 to September 1420, when Pope Martin V resided in the same friary – even though, in both these cases, the bank's Florence branch was still in operation. For the duration of the 1439 council, the roving branch operated near the convent and church of Santa Maria Novella – just a few blocks from the Florentine branch's general office, on the Via Larga.

An earlier church council – the 1179 Third Lateran Council – had officially excommunicated usurers. The Council of Vienne in 1311–12 confirmed that stance. Christian usurers, like prostitutes, could not receive communion. Unless they made restitution, they could not be buried on hallowed ground (because, tradition had it, the usurer's heart was in his coffers rather than in his body). Canto XVII of Dante's *Divine Comedy* (written circa 1308–21) described vividly the fate of usurers in Hell: 'Sorrow ... gushed from their eyes and made their sad tears flow ... About the neck of each a great purse hung, whereon their eyes seemed still to fix and feed.' The usurers shared a chasm with blasphemers and sodomites.

In the late medieval and early modern period, though, the appetite for debt finance was as strong as its prohibition. Merchants and manufacturers needed funds for trading ventures and new factories. Within the higher ranks of the church, too, the demand for financial services was robust. Officials were often short of money; at other times they were flush with cash, and eager for places in which to store it – or hide it.

The great councils and conferences that characterised the church in this period also created demand for what at the time were advanced banking services. Eminent and wealthy individuals attended these gatherings, and the banks opened up temporary branches to service them. The Council of Constance, which lasted four and a half years, is an example.

The council was convened in 1414 to mend the embarrassing schism that saw three concurrent popes vying for legitimacy. It necessitated a gigantic logistical effort, and drew an entourage that included scores of prostitutes, jugglers and bankers. The itinerant Medici branch set up in Constance for the duration.[5]

Apart from providing banking services to its participants, the Medici played a central role in the council itself. The Medici Bank funded several participants at the event, including one of the contending popes. Baldassarre Cossa – now styling himself Pope John XXIII – arrived at the council accompanied by several 'men of eminence', including Cosimo de Medici, then aged just twenty-six.

Despite the backing of the bank, though, Cossa failed to become sole pope. When his suit collapsed, he fled Constance disguised as a postman and flanked by a crossbowman. Soon captured, he was put on trial for piracy, rape, sodomy, murder and incest. He spent a few months as the Holy Roman Emperor's prisoner until, in 1419, Giovanni de Medici paid Cossa's ransom of 38,500 Rhenish guilders. The Medici had paid his way in; now they bought him out. Giovanni gave Cossa a home in Florence, and interceded on his behalf with the uber-pope, Martin V. His reputation somewhat restored, Cossa made amends with the pontiff, who absolved him and named him Cardinal-Bishop of Tusculum. A few months later, Cossa died. As executors of his will, the Medici commissioned Donatello and Michelozzo to build him a beautiful tomb in the baptistery of San Giovanni.

For banks like the Medici, trading in foreign currency was a clever way to circumvent the ban on usury. A bank could advance an amount in Rhenish guilders, say, then collect the debt in florins, inserting a profit margin – effectively a hidden interest rate – into the

5　The council entourage also included bibliophiles: men such as Poggio Bracciolini and Cosimo's friend Niccolò Niccoli, who had an insatiable appetite for old and rare books, preferably handwritten on vellum, and who would raid nearby monasteries for neglected texts. In his 2011 book *Swerve*, Stephen Greenblatt recounted Poggio's rediscovery of a work by the Roman poet Lucretius. *On the Nature of Things* would be copied many times, helping to turbocharge the emergence of modern science.

exchange rate. Today's multinationals do something similar when moving funds between national business units. The Medici did it on a massive scale, as well as providing insurance and letters of credit to similarly lucrative effect.

Over time, the Medici expanded their business, eventually dealing not only in money but also in goods. The family became key traders in commodities and merchandise such as alum, iron, fish, horses, tallow, pepper, ginger, almonds, olive oil, wool, silk, tapestries, furs, gems, relics and slaves. From Douai, Cambray and Bruges, the bank sourced castrated boys who could sing soprano in the choir of St John the Lateran in Rome. The Medici trading network stretched along the Silk Road to India and even China. The diverse business lines were risky but highly profitable. Margins were especially high when the business 'overcharged' the pope for silks, brocades and jewels.

Alum was an important product with many uses but few sources. The uses included degreasing wool, fixing textile dyes, tanning leather, making glass and concocting a variety of drugs. As well as trading in it, the Medici invested in its production, and led a cartel that sought to restrict its supply throughout Europe.

## The family

In the fourteenth and fifteenth centuries, Italy's slaves came from many lands, including Tartary, Russia, Circassia, Armenia, Bulgaria, the Balkans and the Levant. Most slaves in Florence were women who became domestic servants or concubines, although the line between these occupations was very fine. Venice and Genoa were among the main slave markets in Renaissance Europe. Those cities were where to go to buy an Adyghe or Abkhazian beauty. The Venetian branch of the Medici Bank participated actively in this trade. In 1466, for example, Filippo di Cino Rinuccini bought from the Medici Bank a Russian woman, aged about twenty-six, for seventy-four and a half florins.

Cosimo de Medici's personal tax declaration for the year 1457 listed four slaves in his household, all female and of different ages.

In 1427, at Venice's Rialto, Cosimo's agent Giovanni Portinari purchased a handsome Circassian woman. Aged twenty-one or twenty-two, she'd been appraised as 'a sound virgin, free from disease'. Cosimo gave her an Italian name – Maddalena – and she entered the Medici household as his servant. Within a year or two of her arrival, Maddalena and Cosimo had a son, Carlo – a half-brother to Piero. Despite his unfortunate face, money meant that Cosimo could still have a good time.

Italy's foundling hospitals were full of the offspring of slaves and their masters. Many such children, though, were acknowledged by their fathers as semi-legitimate. Cosimo was one father who faced up to his paternity and his obligations. Carlo would be raised in the Medici household. Maddalena sat at the family's main dinner table and remained in the household for two decades. Theirs was a very modern family.

No women worked in the Medici Bank, and nor would Carlo join the family business. Instead, his entry into the priesthood would further strengthen the bank's ties with the church. He became Abbot of San Salvatore at Vaiano, and at the end of his life was archpriest of Prato. A cultured man who emulated his father's collecting on a more modest scale, he died in Florence in 1492.

## Failsafe

For the history of accounting and corporations, one feature of the Medici Bank is especially important. The bank was actually a network of partnerships, each of which served a defined geographical territory and offered a defined set of services. With this structure, the Medici managed the fraught dynamics of a large and dispersed partnership organisation. Turf disputes between offices, or between partners of the same office. Arguments about the founding of new offices or new service lines. Arguments about the allocation of costs and profits. Retiring partners. Rogue partners.

These dynamics defined the bank's internal culture, as did the need to maintain strong systems and tight financial control over the bank's diverse activities and disparate offices. With no external accounting profession to call upon, the bank relied instead on scrupulous in-house accountants and auditors such as Angelo Tani and Rinieri da Ricasoli. Meticulously they examined which of the bank's transactions generated profits and which generated losses. From time to time, corrupt and incompetent managers overstated profits, understated defaults, accounted for loans as profits or perpetrated ever more creative frauds. Tani and Ricasoli had the job of keeping the managers honest and bringing the worst to account.

The Medici Bank's older rivals – such as the Peruzzi, the Bardi and the Acciaiuoli – had dominated Italian finance in the fourteenth century. The structure of those banks carried with it a critical risk, as the Florence-based Peruzzi Bank demonstrated. In 1331, outsiders were able to take that bank over because it was a single partnership in which Peruzzi family members held majority ownership. The Medici were determined to avoid that fate.

A key insurance policy was the franchise business model, which the family pioneered. A network of limited partnerships was much harder to take over; even more important, it legally and financially inoculated each branch from the others' losses. If one branch was sued for a breach of contract, for example, the other branches could avoid being implicated. As Jacob Soll notes in *The Reckoning: Financial Accountability and the Making and Breaking of Nations*, 'When Tommaso Portinari was sued over the defective packing of nine bales of wool, he argued successfully that the bales had been packed by the London branch and that the Bruges branch was therefore not responsible.' The franchise structure had another advantage: branch managers could be held accountable for the extent to which they made profits and avoided losses.

The Medici built several failsafes into their structure. They retained, for example, the right to regularly renegotiate the partnership agreements, or to dissolve them at any time. All partners were therefore at the mercy of the Florentine 'head office'. Unlike their earlier rivals, the Medici rewarded branch managers with a share of the profits, in addition to their salary. At the end of each financial year, head office dissolved the partnerships, went through the books, and made a reckoning and a distribution of profits. Profit sharing motivated the partners, but it also created a strong incentive for junior staff to perform well. Successful juniors could advance towards partnership and the promise of greatly enhanced earnings. More than any of their peers, the Medici were therefore responsible for creating the 'partner track'.

# 3

# TRANSPORTED

## How the Big Four began in the dangerous world of nineteenth-century accountancy

### Unsettled

Lombard Street in the City of London was named after the colloquial term for an Italian banker. By the nineteenth century, London had long supplanted Florence as the centre of global finance and the prime mover in financial innovation. All the Big Four trace their history directly to predecessor firms that began in nineteenth-century London, such as Deloitte & Greenwood, Cooper Brothers, W.B. Peat & Co. and Marwick, Mitchell & Co. The nineteenth century was a boom time for accounting. It was also the profession's 'wild west' era, even more so than the 1980s. In 1811 the London trade directories listed twenty-four accounting firms. Seventy years later they would list 840.

Many of the men who were attracted to accountancy would quickly leave the field. Richard Le Gallienne, for instance, left the Liverpool-based accounting firm of Chalmers Wade & Co. to become a poet. (Other former accountants throughout history include the actor Randolph Scott, the author John Grisham, and the pistol designer Georg Luger.) But among those who remained were some now famous names. William Deloitte started practising in 1845; Samuel Price, in 1848; William Cooper, in 1854.

Nineteenth-century lawmakers rushed to catch up with the new reality of industrial capitalism and the limited-liability company, which was first introduced in Britain in 1855. Bankruptcy was one overwhelming feature of that reality. Between 1817 and 1869, the number of English bankruptcies increased fivefold. Bankruptcies were so common, and so damaging, they became a prominent theme in popular novels and plays. Business failures – more than 10,000 per year – were disastrous for many entrepreneurs and investors but a boon for accountants, whose work expanded rapidly as a result.

In the middle decades of the nineteenth century, accountancy as a profession was in flux. Even the meaning of the word *accountant* had not yet been settled. According to William Hazlitt, that label was adopted by a diverse range of moneylenders, bookmakers, spruikers and other shady operators. 'Accountants' were concerned with much more than accounts. In Charles Dickens' *Little Doritt* (1855–57), a moonfaced and cold-hearted Mr Rugg presents himself to the public, with calculated vagueness, as 'General Agent, Accountant, Debts Recovered'. Samuel Price started out similarly with Bradley and Barnard, a firm of 'public accountants, auctioneers and general agents to assignees and creditors in bankruptcies'. In 1874 an English chancer wrote to prospective clients: 'I take the liberty of enclosing my card. I have recently commenced business as Law Stationer, Law Bill Clerk, Public and Private Auditor and Accountant, House, Land and Estate Agent, Rent and Debt Collector, and Trustee in Bankruptcy.'

Bankruptcy and insolvency work was a risky business. Individual accountants took on personal liability for decisions they made as liquidators and trustees. This line of work was perilous, too, for another reason. It presented multiple opportunities for fraud and shady behaviour among accountants. Secret disposals of assets. Over-stating the costs of administering and disposing of estates. Theft. Yet it was the main business line for the accounting firms in their first decades, more important than auditing and general bookkeeping.

The incursion of accountants into the management of bankruptcies was not without resistance. A nineteenth-century judge lamented the entry of accountants as 'one of the grossest abuses ever introduced into law'. Solicitors, he said, were 'gentlemen', whereas accountants were 'ignorant'. Goethe's grand pronouncements about the nobility of accounting were far in the past.

Just as the definition of *accounting* was unsettled, so too its core terminology was in flux. One example: in the early years of the profession, other constructions of the word *accountant* had currency, such as *accomptant*. Varieties of *agent, clerk, cashier, notary, bookkeeper, valuer, reckoner* and *auditor* also vied as synonyms. As long ago as the thirteenth century, 'awdytours' had been appointed in England to 'verify the honesty of persons charged with fiscal ... responsibilities'. (A later proposal to replace or augment *accountant* with *cognitor* was defeated because the new word brought to mind unhelpful connotations: know-it-all-ism, but also 'a pterodactyl-type dinosaur swooping over the mountaintops'.[6]) Non-financial auditors were rich in their diversity. In the sixteenth century, for example, one variety was responsible for inspecting the virginity of potential brides and the virility of potential husbands. In the nineteenth century, another variety – the *number-taker* – spotted trains and checked their freight on behalf of the Railway Clearing House. *Turf accountant* was a better-sounding name for the humble bookie.

## Low practice

At this early stage, the prerequisite skills for accountancy were ill-defined. There were no qualifying examinations that served as a

---

6    Arthur W. Bowman, editor of *Bowman's Accounting Report* in Atlanta, described the term that way in 2001 when speaking to Jonathan D. Glater of the *New York Times*.

gateway to the profession.[7] For this and other reasons, the profession was viewed darkly by many prominent figures. Henry Brougham, Lord Chancellor from 1830 to 1834, described accountants drolly as those who 'could give no proper account of themselves'. For many early practitioners, the activities we regard today as accounting services were merely a sideline.

Some of those practitioners were largely untrained, some were unsuccessful businessmen, others failed lawyers. Robert (later Sir Robert) Hardy was a co-founder of the firm that eventually became EY. He took up accountancy after failing as a hatter. As the nineteenth century progressed, though, the accounting trade gradually adopted a recognisable shape. The charlatans and incompetents were mostly weeded out. Consistent methods and standards were adopted. In 1880 several accounting societies came together to form, by royal charter, the first national professional association of accountants: the Institute of Chartered Accountants in England and Wales (ICAEW). Accountants had won professional status, but only just.

In the eighteenth century, the new professions of medicine and law had had to endure all manner of ridicule and satire. A 1718 tract, *Hell in an Uproar*, captured lawyers' contemporary reputation 'for low practice and high charges':

> *I think no men on earth live more profane,*
> *Than students in the Law, in vice they reign;*
> *They drink and whore all night; i'th morning rise*
> *To cozen, swear, and tell a thousand lies*
> *As long as clients can feed us with the gold.*

As for doctors, they were just as bad as Chaucer's physician:

---

7   In England, written exams for chartered accountants did not begin until 1882; they'd been introduced in Scotland some years earlier.

*We come not nigh; but for the gentry; who*
*Have golden hooks to bait, we gallop to*
*Their houses fast enough, both night and day,*
*We make a coach and horses dance the hay;*
*Through thick and thin we go, through cold and heat,*
*To smell their urine, feel how pulses beat,*
*These we can cure, if money comes apace,*
*We keep them backward, things which are more base*
*We act, young heirs that want their fathers' wills*
*Fee us to rid them with a dose of pills.*[8]

By the nineteenth century, though, doctors and lawyers were well entrenched in their professional spheres, whereas accountants attained only the lower, 'underprivileged' rank. In his 1857 *The Choice of a Profession*, H. Byerley Thomson defined the 'privileged' professions as those with legally restricted membership: priests, barristers and physicians, all of whom received 'a superior education' and came from 'a superior class'. Less exalted and less well educated, accountants ranked alongside painters, sculptors, architects, civil engineers, civil servants, teachers and actuaries – the statisticians of death. These professions, Byerley observed, lacked a legal restriction on entrance and so deserved less respect. From the very beginning, then, accountants had to fight for standing and recognition. Not until 1991 was an image of an accountant mounted in Britain's National Portrait Gallery.

## Felons and heroes

In the nineteenth century, Britain's economy ceased to be based predominantly on farming and instead became much more urbanised,

---

8    The tract's author, Richard Burridge, was tried in 1712 for blasphemy.

industrial and capital-intensive. (There were more sheep in Britain at the start of the nineteenth century than at the end, for instance.) This shift released workers from agricultural production, and saw growth in capital markets and in the size and complexity of businesses. Legislatures in Britain and the United States passed the first modern corporations law statutes. Hitherto, corporate structures had mostly been used for one-off ventures – like sea voyages – or time-limited ones. Now they came to be used on a large scale for business entities that were intended to exist perpetually, and that would undertake a range of activities under a broad mandate.

Naturally, the early profile of the accounting firms' activities reflected the economy of Victorian Britain. Working for the India trade. Servicing the burgeoning banking and finance sector. Handling, occasionally, the affairs of princes and dukes. And helping to steer those dominant, archetypical Victorian businesses, the railway companies.

Built upon whaling and slave trading, the South Sea Company was the most celebrated enterprise of the first decades of the eighteenth century. Everyone who could do so rushed to acquire a slice of the action. And then, in 1720, the bubble burst and the company collapsed catastrophically. This was the world's first great financial scandal. Thereafter, the British government restricted the raising of capital by joint stock companies. Railways, though, were granted special status: until 1860 they were one of the few types of company – along with banks and some insurers – permitted to raise capital from more than five people.

Late in the eighteenth century, James Watt had made the steam engine much more efficient, and commercially viable. His innovations set the scene for the railway mania that gripped Britain in the first half of the nineteenth century. By 1848 almost 8000 kilometres of track had been laid across the country. More than three-quarters of England's total route mileage was built between 1830 and 1875.[9] Around two-thirds of the main lines had been built by 1854. There were so many railway schemes underway that Britain experienced critical shortages. There were not enough engravers, for example, to produce the elaborate share certificates. In the face of such demand, the profitability of engraving soared. Other beneficiaries of the railway boom included newspapermen (thanks to the demand for advertising), stonemasons, foundries, lawyers – and accountants.

The economics of rail transport posed a thousand puzzles for the rail companies, and for their accountants. How should capital investment and maintenance be funded and accounted for? How should profits be calculated once the initial big expenditures on track, bridges, warehouses, depots and rolling stock had been made? How should the release of dividends to shareholders be profiled over the life of the company and its investments? Founded in 1842, the Railway Clearing House handled the tangle of payments between the multiplying railway businesses which used each other's track. The Clearing House became a classic archetype of bureaucratic complexity, and was one of several frustrating models for Charles Dickens' famous Circumlocution Office.

The railway companies were the principal clients of the leading accountants in their formative years. The companies adopted iconic and picturesque names, such as the Shropshire Union Railway & Canal Co.; the Ware, Hadham & Buntingford Railway; the Isle of Wight Railway Co.; and the London and North Western Railway Co. (LNWR). One of Britain's largest nineteenth-century enterprises, LNWR operated at a size and with prestige commensurate with that of today's British Airways. Doing business on such a scale at such a time necessitated sophisticated corporate strategies and governance. As much as

---

9   The railway network reached its apogee in the Edwardian period, and shrank thereafter.

the old cuttings and stations and engines, those corporate features were the companies' legacy. James Meek noted in the *London Review of Books*, 'The way big corporations around the world are run today – owned by shareholders, with directors making strategy and managers running day to day operations – came out of the British railways.'

For accountants, though, this was a treacherous industry. The rail companies were a breeding ground for crooks and rogues. Misleading and fraudulent practices were rampant: the understating of liabilities, the over-issuing of debt, engaging in cartel behaviour, paying dividends from capital, playing around with depreciation and outright fraud. The prospectus for the Somersetshire Midland Railway claimed 'the greater portion of it will be perfectly level', whereas much of the proposed line was in fact very steep, 'as it climbed on to and through the Mendips'. Railway company secretaries and treasurers regularly absconded with funds. The companies were vulnerable, too, to Ponzi-like scams. According to rail historian Christian Wolmar, the sole purpose of some investment schemes was 'to pay the bills on previous projects drawn up by the same promoters'. At the height of the rail mania, memories of the South Sea Bubble came flooding back.

Scepticism about railway investment was intense. As Marjorie Whitelaw noted in her 1958 article on 'The Lunacy of Railways':

> In the 1820s, you could invest in balloon companies which would carry passengers through the London air at forty miles an hour, or in coaching companies which were going to run coaches on relays of bottled gas instead of horses. Or you could lose your money in a railway run by steam.

Just as bankrupts had, railway scoundrels entered popular culture. In Trollope's *The Way We Live Now* (1875), unscrupulous financiers and speculators hijack a great railway linking Salt Lake City and Veracruz. The novel's villain is the enigmatic financier Augustus Melmotte.

The hero is the accounts clerk, Croll, who refuses to witness a forged signature and who discovers other frauds perpetrated by Melmotte.

In real life, too, the hero of the railways boom was the man whom *The Bookkeeper* called in 1896 'the foe of deceit and the champion of honesty': the professional accountant. The leading accounting firms took pains to understand how railway businesses should operate. By making such investments in idiosyncratic expertise, accountants positioned themselves as the men who would protect Victorian England from the pitfalls of big commerce: from the opportunists, frauds and other malefactors who sought to exploit the Industrial Revolution. In this role, accountants shared with teachers, doctors, lawyers and priests a responsibility to the wider community. They were the foot soldiers of integrity.

William Deloitte, for example, discovered a major fraud perpetrated on the Great Northern Railway. A former bankrupt, Leopold Redpath became share registrar at GNR. In that role he perfected a clever scam, forging deeds that transferred GNR shares to himself. Thus receiving a generous flow of dividends – up to a quarter of a million pounds – he bought a grand house opposite Regent's Park and set himself up as a gentleman and, perversely, a philanthropist. He served, for example, as governor of Christ's Hospital. The company's internal auditors noticed a discrepancy between GNR's dividend payments and its authorised capital, yet they continued to declare that the company's accounts were satisfactorily presented.

A few years earlier, William Deloitte had successfully investigated fiscal misbehaviour at the Great Western Railway. Now, the owners of Great Northern called on him for help. The internal auditors had never thought to inspect the share registry. After examining the registration books, Deloitte unravelled the deception and exposed its extent. Convicted of felonious fraud, Redpath was transported in 1858 to Fremantle, Western Australia.

Other rail companies rushed to engage Deloitte to check their share registers. Edwin Waterhouse, too, was paid to unearth frauds. He and

Deloitte and their partners helped clean up the railway industry. Thanks to these victories, public opinion was now on the accountants' side. The leading accountants were now in such a position of trust that the government began looking to them for advice about the legislation that would help keep the railways on track. Deloitte and Waterhouse, for example, contributed to the 1868 *Regulation of Railways Act*. That act mandated double-entry accounting and prescribed the form in which half-yearly accounts had to be published and filed with the Board of Trade. A landmark in public accounting, that form of accounts would prevail for two generations, until the 1911 *Railway Companies (Accounts and Returns) Act*.

In 1921 an era came to an end when Britain's parliament passed the 'grouping act', which amalgamated many of the country's 120 railway businesses into four enormous consortia (known thereafter as the 'Big Four'): Great Western Railway; London, Midland and Scottish Railway; London and North Eastern Railway; and Southern Railway. Deloitte's and Waterhouse's firms were prominent among the new mega-companies' auditors. Price Waterhouse also had the unenviable task of auditing the circular, tangled, mind-straining activities of the Railway Clearing House.

# 4

# A CURIOUS MATCH

## The remarkable founders
## of the Big Four

### Collaboration

Dining together, playing golf together, going to church together – the routines of partnership created a sense of brotherhood and common purpose among accountants. The profession's self-confidence grew, just as its boundaries became more distinct.

To the extent that there was any competition between the major accounting firms, it was decidedly mild and gentlemanly. The partners collaborated at the ICAEW and in other professional bodies. They moved in the same clubbish circles. Freemasons were prominent in the profession's early years; George Sneath of Price Waterhouse and Sir Arthur Whinney of Whinney, Smith & Whinney, for example, were both leading members of the Chartered Accountants Lodge. Firms refrained from poaching one another's staff and clients. They even traded jointly when delivering services abroad.

In 1911, for example, the rival firms Price Waterhouse and W.B. Peat & Co. merged their Egyptian businesses. They traded in Cairo and Alexandria as Messrs Peat, Waterhouse & Co. Other collaborations would soon follow. In St Petersburg (from 1916) and Rotterdam (from 1919) Waterhouse and Peat traded together as Price, Waterhouse, Peat

& Co. The Russian office was inevitably short-lived. When the revolution came, the partners were lucky to escape with their lives; they left behind the firm's books and petty cash. From 1920 the two firms adopted the same form of joint representation in Calcutta, Johannesburg and Buenos Aires. That same year the firms also extended their European collaboration to cover the whole of the Continent.

These collaborations worked so well that further tie-ups were contemplated. But in 1924 the firms' international collaboration came to an end when W.B. Peat & Co. fell for another suitor: Marwick, Mitchell & Co. James Marwick and Sir William Peat, both Scotsmen, settled upon that merger while consuming brandy, cigars and 'superb cuisine' on a transatlantic ocean liner. In the ensuing decades, mergers between major accounting firms would become commonplace.

## Colourful

What do we mean when we say someone 'looks like an accountant'? The popular image is of a greyish man in a grey flannel suit – think Keith Bishop or Kevin Malone from *The Office*, or Oscar Wallace in *The Untouchables*. The first leaders of the accounting profession, though, were surprisingly colourful. An Australian Price Waterhouse partner at the turn of the nineteenth century, Edwin Flack competed successfully in the first modern Olympic Games in athletics and tennis. At the medal ceremony in Athens in 1896, with Flack having won the 800-metre and 1500-metre finals, the confused hosts raised the Austrian flag.

Sir Albert Wyon was another character. A dyed-in-the-wool bachelor with a fondness for chorus girls, he had another claim to fame: he scuppered, almost single-handedly, the mooted 1920–21 merger between Price Waterhouse and W.B. Peat & Co. There was much to like about the merger proposal. Sir Harry Peat and Sir Nicholas Waterhouse were friends, and their families had become close.

The firms had collaborated successfully abroad. And joining together would bring greater size and market clout. Wyon, though, feared the merger would kill the golden Price Waterhouse goose. For him, professional services depended on personal relationships and individual responsibility, as he later explained in a piece for *The Accountant*:

> What methods assure to a large accounting organisation, composed for the most part of salaried employees, the same sense of professional responsibility as that attained by an individual practitioner or small group of practitioners working together as partners? [Remaining small would] secure uniformity of standards and the preservation of traditions, ideals and a high sense of responsibility.

To save the goose, Wyon killed the deal – by whipping up strident internal opposition, and becoming its spearhead.

Many of the Big Four pioneers were religious non-conformists and social outsiders. A rule-breaking, lumbago-suffering oddball, Samuel 'Sammy' Price often found himself in trouble. In 1848 he entered what English law regarded as an incestuous marriage. Emma Nutter Price was his niece – the eldest daughter of his half-brother Thomas. To avoid legal strife in Britain, Samuel and Emma married in Denmark. The marriage produced a daughter, and much consternation. That same year, Price left the firm of Bradley, Barnard & Co. to establish a new partnership with William Edwards. The partnership, unlike the marriage, lasted only a year. In 1849 Price set up business as a partnership of one.

Price came from a family of potters. (Remarkably, Prices were still potting as late as 1961.) In other respects, too, he was good with his hands. A fan of prize fights, streetfights and indeed any kind of fight, he was not averse to joining in himself. Junior staff regarded him as a somewhat threatening character. In 1865, with Edwin Waterhouse and William Holyland, he founded Price, Holyland & Waterhouse. (Holyland would retire in 1871.) Edwin's son Nicholas shared the following recollection of a childhood visit to the firm's offices:

> We stood waiting by the commissionaire's box for my father to come down. My father and Mr Price came down and I was introduced ... There was a little whistle on the commissionaire's speaking tube – that was the horrible contraption before house telephones were invented. Mr Price removed the whistle and put the tube to his ear, and a voice belonging to someone upstairs, who thought he was addressing the commissionaire, was distinctly heard to say, 'Has Old Sammy gone yet?' Mr Price replied, 'I'll come up and "Sammy" you', and up the stairs he went as fast as his legs could carry him.

Edwin Waterhouse was the youngest of seven children. His brother Alfred became a famous architect. Another brother, Theodore, would found the London law firm Waterhouse & Co.[10]

## Friends

Edwin was a member of the Religious Society of Friends, also known as the Quakers. This is most likely how Waterhouse met Holyland, who also seems to have been a 'Friend'. So named because its adherents were said to tremble or quake before God, the Quaker movement was a radical and persecuted offshoot of the Church of England – one of a proliferation of Protestant sects that also included the Ranters, Baptists, Moravians, Muggletonians and Fifth Monarchists.

10  Yet another famous nineteenth-century Waterhouse, a more distant relative, was the painter John William Waterhouse.

The Quaker movement first emerged in the seventeenth century. Its members worshipped in austere surroundings; the 1675 meeting house at Briggs Flats looked like a farmhouse and was furnished with plain benches. Edward Burroughs' 1659 foundational Quaker text contained strange echoes of Giovanni de Medici's 1429 deathbed advice: 'We are not for Names, nor Men, nor Titles of Government, nor are we for this Party, nor against the other, because of its Name and Pretence; but we are for Justice and Mercy, and Truth and Peace, and true Freedom, that these may be exalted in our Nation.'

By 1660, thanks in part to Burroughs' noble words, the ranks of Quakers had grown to about 50,000. By the mid-eighteenth century, though, there were one-fifth fewer Friends. By the time Sammy Price set up his accounting firm, the number of Quakers had slumped further still, to about 20,000. The 1860s, however, saw a revival in the movement, thanks to galvanising causes such as prison reform and the abolition of slavery. A rule change also helped make Quakers more prominent in the nineteenth century: Friends who married non-Quakers were no longer automatically 'disowned'.

Sombrely dressed and teetotal, Quakers were sceptical of hierarchies and ideologies. They preached modesty and self-control, embraced pacifism and simple living, and professed to value all people equally. The foundation of Quaker morality was conscience. On the basis of these and other precepts – including conservatism, caution and a belief in individual action – Friends became prominent in banking. Writing for the *BBC News Magazine* about the history of Quakers in the British confectionary industry, Peter Jackson called them 'natural capitalists'.

Quaker entrepreneurs – men such as Edward and Joseph Pease – were prominent in the development of the railways. Strict Quaker managers brought a distinctive operating style to that industry. They encouraged members of the public, for example, 'to report any speeding or other misdemeanours by the drivers ... directors were known to patrol the line themselves, seeking out miscreants who had to appear before a disciplinary committee to explain their actions'. Passengers hoping to travel on the very first railways 'had to give their name, address, age, place of birth, occupation and reason for travelling'. The Quaker Thomas Edmondson reduced ticket-office fraud by proposing that tickets be consecutively numbered.

Quakers' emphasis on personal responsibility and conscience also made them natural auditors. The inner experience of an ever-present, ever-watchful God was a helpful attribute for those charged with the careful, often solitary work of checking the integrity of accounts. The role of the guiding inner voice in auditing is occasionally called out explicitly. In 1933, for example, a US Senate hearing considered whether external certified practising accountants (as opposed to internal auditors and 'controllers', or a government agency) should be given an exclusive concession to audit public companies. The senators grappled with the age-old question: who would watch the watchers?

SENATOR BARKLEY: Is there any relationship between your organization with 2,000 members and the organization of controllers, represented here yesterday with 2,000 members?

MR CARTER [President of the New York Society of CPAs]: None at all. We audit the controllers.

SENATOR BARKLEY: You audit the controllers?

MR CARTER: Yes; the public accountant audits the controller's account.

SENATOR BARKLEY: Who audits you?

MR CARTER: Our conscience.

The lawmakers greeted Carter's response with scepticism, but granted the concession anyway.

Edwin Waterhouse's Quakerism helped him find clients and staff. One of his first jobs was to develop a costing system for John Fowler, a Quaker manufacturer and inventor of the steam plough. Quakerism also shaped his approach to accounting and auditing. He saw himself as a 'Christian gentleman' responsible for delivering an important social service. Three authors recently found in Waterhouse's Quaker ethics the basis of a 'fiduciary logic' that helped guide the early accounting profession's practices and enhance their legitimacy. This was especially timely in the aftermath of the South Sea Bubble, the railway frauds and other investment scandals that had shaken gravely the public's confidence in the apparatus of capitalism.

## A generous share

A branch line of the South Eastern Railway had made Surrey more accessible to rich Londoners, who quickly established picturesque estates there. Having fallen in love with the Surrey countryside, Edwin Waterhouse bought his Surrey estate, 'Great Inholme', in 1877. He built a fine house and gave it the romantic name 'Feldemore'. The house, which overlooked the village of Holmbury St Mary, would include an excellent library and a billiard room lit with electric light.

Edwin's Surrey neighbours included the merchant banker Sir Frederick Mirrielees, and the author and former colonial officer Colonel Thomas H. Lewin. A British archetype, Lewin was one of the thousands of 'dull Victorian souls' who, according to Frank McLynn in the *Independent*, 'served their time in India, married money, retired and then spent forty years in rather pointless retirement'. 'So strait-laced that he regarded most actresses as prostitutes', Lewin had a reputation for 'going native'. On the Subcontinent, for example, he'd adopted the name Thangliena, a crudely Indianised version of Tom Lewin. The Lewins named their eldest daughter Everest.

Edwin had his gardeners pick up litter in Holmbury St Mary so the village would be 'spick and span' when his guests visited on weekends. He penned a long memoir of his life in Surrey and London – a document that Michael J. Mepham called, in the *Accounting Historians Journal*, 'the only complete autobiography of a founder of one of the major international accounting firms'. Spanning the period from Edwin's birth in 1841 to his death in 1917 – he was buried in a modest grave in the churchyard of St Mary the Virgin in Holmbury St Mary – the memoir gives fascinating details of his clients and of the 'labyrinthine frauds' he uncovered. Unknown and unregarded in the Price Waterhouse archive for almost seventy years, the memoir was rediscovered by an archivist in 1985; an edited version was published three years later.

Despite his Quaker ethos, Edwin Waterhouse had been as moody and intolerant in the office as his partner Samuel Price. In 1904 Edwin was sixty-three when his fellow partners – Fowler, Sneath and Wyon – contemplated pushing him out of the firm. What motivated the conspirators? Over and above his difficult personality, there was the question of money. As the only surviving founding partner (Price had passed away in 1887), Edwin was entitled to an annoyingly generous share of the firm's profits.

The coup plotters circulated a document, not for Waterhouse's eyes, that set out their plans, whereby Waterhouse would resign immediately and the partnership would be reconstituted under the old brand but with new leadership. (That document, too, is in the Price Waterhouse archive, bearing the innocuous heading 'The suggestion that E.W. should retire from the firm'.) The insurrection, however, failed. Waterhouse worked on, towards a retirement date of his own choosing. Along the way, he implemented his own succession plan.

## Generational change

Edwin's son Nicholas had been so unhappy at school that he wrote home to his mother, Georgiana, in his own blood. Given this fact, it is not surprising that, at university, he preferred medicine to economics or law. Cutting up bodies was especially fascinating. According to his personal reminiscences, he spent many hours in Oxford University's dissecting rooms. At his father's urging, however, Nicholas ultimately chose to study jurisprudence, 'being the discipline closest to accountancy'.

After coming down to London, he joined his father's firm as an articled clerk in 1899. He passed, barely, the accounting exams in 1903. His father wrote to him: 'My dear boy, though you are pretty hopeless in your work, for goodness sake be one of the first in the queue every morning so at least my partners will think you are trying.' Just three years later he was admitted to the partnership; Nicholas himself called his elevation a 'blatant example of nepotism'. He was now a leader in a firm and a profession not much to his liking. (Apart from cadavers, collectable postage stamps were far preferable to ledgers and quarterly reports.) Neither diligent nor meticulous, he did, however, manifest a gentlemanly charm and 'country-club etiquette'. Using those attributes, Nicholas Waterhouse pioneered what is now a Big Four archetype: the partner who is better at schmoozing than doing.

That picture is not entirely fair. Nicholas eventually rose to the top of his profession, and he made good a dynastic succession that at first had looked even less promising than the transition from Cosimo de Medici to his son Piero. An injured knee prevented Nicholas from serving in the First World War, but he did contribute – as Director of Costings at the War Office, and as a member of the Disposals Commission and the liquidation committee that closed out the outstanding War Office contracts after the war. On the strength of Nicholas's charisma, plus his contribution to accountancy and his impact on the war effort, King George V knighted him in 1920.

46

Lady Waterhouse was born Audrey Hale Lewin in 1883, the second daughter of the Surrey retiree Tom 'Thangliena' Lewin. Like her father, Audrey married money, wedding Nicholas Waterhouse in 1902. Vain, fashionable and given to conspicuous displays of her new wealth, she was usually surrounded by what the English biographer Charlotte Breese called 'a cloud of Turkish cigarettes and Chanel No. 5'. Breese claimed Audrey refused to have children 'for fear of losing her beautiful figure'.

Nicholas may have been thoroughly respectable by day, but out of hours he and his wife joined the 'faster' crowd between the wars. They gave each other nicknames: Nicholas was 'Nicky' or 'Docker', and Audrey 'Mauve' or 'Mov'. With other nicknamed friends, such as the Bohemian pianist Leslie 'Hutch' Hutchinson, the Waterhouses embraced the swinging, flapping 1920s. At parties that climaxed in 'scenes of open debauch', Mauve and Docker entertained their decadent friends at their stylish London home at 2 Swan Walk, Chelsea.

Drugs as well as sex were a feature of the parties. Hutch seems to have experimented with a veritable pharmacopeia of drugs, including cocaine – all very un-Quaker-like. Sometimes Nicholas would join in the debauch, but at other times he would seek refuge elsewhere. Maintaining his passion for stamp collecting, he assembled several prized collections of pre-stamp covers, Postmaster Provisionals, General Issues, Carriers, Locals, Departmentals, Proofs and Essays, and wrote two books on philately, including a major handbook on US stamps, *A Comprehensive Catalogue of the Postage Stamps of the United States of America* (1916).

Charlotte Breese describes one Swan Walk party at which Nicholas and fellow philatelist George V played with stamps in the basement, while the guests above, 'stimulated by drink and cocaine at Nicholas's expense, chanted, "Hey, Hey, Let Nicky Pay!" Hutch and Mauve, armed with a musical saw, used to sing and vigorously enact, "Let's Do It". King George bore a striking resemblance to his cousin Tsar Nicholas of Russia. (Apart from Nicholas Waterhouse, George also befriended other Big Four royalty, including Nobuzo Tohmatsu, Japan's naval attaché to the United Kingdom from 1934 to 1936, and future founder of a firm that became part of Deloitte Touche Tohmatsu.)

Rare stamps and raucous parties were not the only outlets for the Waterhouses' wealth. Audrey first encountered literary and artistic circles through her father, who knew George Meredith and Sir Edward Burne-Jones. Now, she and her husband supported artists and men of letters, just as Cosimo de Medici had done.

The author, painter and provocateur Wyndham Lewis relied on the Waterhouses for many years. Nicknamed 'Professor' in the Waterhouses' circle, he was a misanthrope and a leech, a sexually ambitious misfit with fascistic tendencies. Few of his friendships survived his personality. Litigious, ruthless and intrigued by magic – as well as by feng shui, occultism and lesbianism – Lewis was always in a dispute with someone about a perceived slight, a question of ideology or the failure of some grandiose project. The Waterhouses subsidised not a few of those projects, including Lewis's irascible book *The Apes of God*, and his equally fractious journal *The Enemy*. Lewis's biographer David Trotter tells how, at the end of 1923, 'well-wishers established a joint fund to provide Lewis with a stipend of £16 a month for as long as he might remain in need of it'. On one occasion, a delay in the cheque elicited from Lewis an ungracious response: 'WHERE'S THE FUCKING STIPEND?'

Audrey Waterhouse died in 1945. Samuel Price had married his own niece; now, Nicholas Waterhouse, late in life, in another curious echo of the Medici, married his housekeeper. Her name was Louise How. Nicholas, characteristically, gave her a nickname, Tim. He was seventy-six, she forty-six. Some people thought an explanation was in order. To the wife of his successor at Price Waterhouse, Nicholas wrote:

I think you realise what my forty-two years of married life were to me and the desolation that came on me eight years ago, but I am not one who can face living alone and 'Tim' ... is such an old friend of ours and has so devotedly looked after me.

Neither of Nicholas's marriages produced children. He continued to support Wyndham Lewis through illness and financial crises until the artist's death in 1957. (In at least one of Lewis's disputes, the legal Waterhouses – Waterhouse & Co. – acted for the other side.) Nicholas also provided for Lewis's long-suffering widow, Gladys, until his own death in 1964. After Lady Louise Waterhouse died in 1988, she was buried alongside her late husband and his parents at the church of St Mary the Virgin in Holmbury St Mary, Surrey.

# PART II

# Maturity

In Part II we focus on the post-war years, the time when today's international accounting firms assumed their current shape. This period saw the emergence of a recognisable relationship between the big firms and governments; the evolution of strongly commercial attitudes to advertising and branding; and the adoption of a profile of activities in which tax and advisory services became increasingly important. The big firms claimed an ever-expanding turf, and worked hard to protect it. A central feature of this period was the emergence of the Big Four culture, which was forged in a clash of values.

# 5

# MERE AUTOMATA
## Staking out the Big Four's turf

### Accountancy megatrends

In one of his notorious purges, Henry Ford famously sacked his accountants *en bloc*. 'They're not productive,' he said. 'They don't do any real work. I want them out of here today.' That story cannot be the whole truth; Ford's enterprise would've collapsed without in-house bookkeepers and financial controllers. But the anecdote helps illustrate a wider twentieth-century trend, that of large industrial companies electing to outsource their accounting services. Corporates that had maintained significant in-house accounting units – such as IBM and Unilever – would decide it was preferable to buy those services from the marketplace.

This trend, unsurprisingly, helped spur and transform the accounting firms, as did other twentieth-century shifts: diversification of the firms' activities, particularly into 'management consulting' or 'advisory' services; cosying up with governments; benefiting from the 'audit explosion' and the rise of the 'audit society'; and, like modern Medici, spreading out internationally, with networks of branded franchises in which each national practice was a separate legal entity.

The second half of the twentieth century would prove to be a golden era for accountancy. In Britain, for example, the number of people working in financial and business services grew from 637,000 in 1951 to 4,276,000 in 1998. Within that category, according to the *Cambridge Economic History of Modern Britain*, 'specialist firms supplying professional services like accounting and computer systems mushroomed'. In the United States, finance and business services accounted for 4.4 per cent of total employment in 1950, and 12.2 per cent in 1995. In aggregate, 'services' became the largest employer of men and women in the United States, the United Kingdom and other advanced economies, such as Canada and Australia. The accounting firms were perfectly positioned to enjoy the best of this services boom. Accountancy's decades of prosperity, though, were also the time in which the seeds of future calamities were sown.

## Invasion

Price Waterhouse established its first foothold in the United States through an agency arrangement with a New York–based Welshman by the name of Lewis D. Jones. Business was soon coming in thick and fast – from railways, ferries, brewers, threshers and grain elevators. Jones appealed to the London office for help. Not wanting Americans to examine the accounts of British companies operating abroad, the firm stipulated that any new personnel had to be Englishmen, though preferably with some American experience. This rule was almost immediately relaxed when the London office sent out W.J. Caesar, a Scotsman.

Having begun as offshoots of the British firms, the major US accounting practices were soon making their own weather. Deloitte opened its US office in 1893. A short time after, it began auditing the soap and candle manufacturer that became Proctor & Gamble, which would remain a client for more than a century. Price Waterhouse's US agency quickly became an office in its own right. After a fitful start, it built lucrative relationships, including a crucial one with the financier and bibliophile J. Pierpont Morgan (whose fabulous library on Madison Avenue included a copy of Luca Pacioli's *Summa de Arithmetica*). Marwick, Mitchell & Co. also earned Morgan's trust, advising him on the solvency of the Knickerbocker bank. During the financial panic of 1907, Morgan famously took charge, hosting tense overnight meetings in his library. According to Walter E. Hanson, a former chair of Marwick, Mitchell & Co., 'The work our firm did contributed, however modestly, to Morgan's strategy for ending the panic and laid the groundwork for greater business acceptance of the accountant's role in industry.'

Accountants had made it to the American big league. Soon, most US public companies would choose to have their accounts scrutinised by external auditors. Independent accountants became part of the furniture of modern capitalism.

The aftermath of another financial calamity was even more of a boon for accountants. In the wake of the Wall Street crash of 1929, the *Securities Act* of 1933 and the *Securities Exchange Act* of 1934 required all new and continuing registrants to have their financial statements audited by independent certified practising accountants (CPAs). This legislation stimulated the long boom in accounting and audit services. Just as the American accounting profession had begun as an offshoot of the English profession, so, too, the regulation of accounting and auditing in the United States was based significantly on British precedents.

## Unwelcome developments

During the world wars, accountants became an integral part of the national economy. In Britain during the First World War, masses of accountants joined up as officers and soldiers, but also served as officials helping to manage purchasing, inventories, nationalised assets and wartime laws against profiteering. Nicholas Waterhouse was not the only prominent accountant to be recognised for his service; Gilbert Garnsey, for example, was knighted for his work as Controller of Munitions Accounts.

For the accounting firms, these investments in the national effort bore fruit. As well as deepening their standing as fighters for integrity and the public good, there were immediate and practical benefits. As Edgar Jones noted with respect to Price Waterhouse, 'government work introduced the firm to many leading civil servants, industrialists and politicians and demonstrated to them the value of the accountant's skills'. New relationships created new leads and new clients. Government networks became as important as religious ones had been in the firms' early days.

Throughout the twentieth century, the accounting profession maintained a complex relationship with government. Again like latter-day Medici, the big firm partners were the ones to whom presidents and prime ministers turned for counsel. The firms provided advice and services in support of infrastructure investment, healthcare policies, defence procurement, the design of regulations, and nearly every other aspect of public administration. Feasibility studies for airports and rail systems. Advice on pension schemes and shrinking the public debt. At the same time, they spent millions lobbying bureaucrats and elected officials in order to shape the legal environment in which they operated.

The firms were called upon to help write important pieces of commercial legislation, just as they had done with the 1868 *Railways Act*. After the Wall Street crash, for example, accountants designed the Securities and Exchange Commission forms for filing financial statements. George O. May of Price Waterhouse helped write the Generally Accepted Accounting Principles (GAAP). Taking opportunities such as these was good business and great strategy: apart from the direct fees, working alongside governments helped burnish the firms' brands – and, perhaps most importantly, allowed them to fashion their own playing field.

Accountants used professional and quasi-regulatory bodies – such as the Auditing Practices Board in the United Kingdom and the Accounting Principles Board in the United States – to remove from the political agenda what Professor Prem Sikka termed 'unwelcome developments' – especially those that had 'the potential to dilute firm income'. As recently as 2013, PwC was accused of administering the Corporate Reporting Users Forum, ostensibly an accountability lobby group but whose actual aim, according to James Moore in the *Independent*, was 'to block reforms of the accountancy profession'.

Several foundational statutes – in areas such as bankruptcy, tax, insurance, securities and corporations law – helped bring the modern profession into being. The major firms acted to protect the legislative provisions to which they owed so much: provisions that helped raise standards of commercial conduct, and that had the side benefit of making business more complex, and accounting and audit services more marketable. The firms were supportive, too, of legislation that gave accountants and auditors a formal role in corporate governance, and that solidified the boundaries of their profession.

But the firms relentlessly opposed legislation that would direct how they did their work. The ICAEW, for example, opposed laws that its president argued in 1932 would reduce auditors to 'mere automata' who must 'obey audit programmes laid down by statutes'. In an 1888 address to the institute, Frederick Whinney remarked:

I think we should say a company must be honestly and ably managed; and if it is wound up it must be honestly and ably wound up. Now comes the question as to how you can secure that a company shall be dealt with in the course of its existence in such a manner, and I have no drastic measures to labour for you. I think it is impossible in the very nature of things to do so. I consider it impossible to lay down any legislative enactments which will deal successfully in detail with the management, inception, and perhaps the winding up of these companies. We must not have that which at the Banker's Institute was designated as 'grandmotherly legislation'. We must not have anything which will interfere with freedom of contract. We must not have anything which will incite people to say 'we did not exercise our own judgement, in giving into this company, but relied upon the report of the government inspector'.

Most of all, the profession opposed statutory changes that would increase firms' liability for failed audits and other fiascos. James Landis was a key architect of America's 1933 *Securities Act*. Looking back on the development of the act, Landis observed:

> Despite the fact now generally recognized that the registration requirements of the *Securities Act* have introduced into the accounting profession ethical and professional standards comparable to those of other recognized professions, the then dean of the accounting profession, George O. May, of Price, Waterhouse & Co. was strangely opposed to our proposed requirements for independent accountants.

The reasons for May's vehement opposition were not strange at all. The proposed legislation reduced the accounting profession's role in the making of accounting standards, and gave accountants joint and uncapped liability for a wide range of losses arising from defects in prospectuses and other investment documentation. May championed a counterattack that achieved, a year later, significant amendments to the original act, including a reduction in the 'excessive liabilities' placed on accountants. Today, the Big Four adopt a strongly commercial posture, but their current incarnation owes much to a series of decisions by governments and legislatures. Modern accountancy is intertwined with the modern state.

## Baffled

As well as to buttress the professional perimeter and contain their professional liability, the large accounting firms used their links with regulators and standard-setters to co-produce a coded, excluding but otherwise benign professional language that is rich with acronyms, jargon and euphemisms. No intelligent amateur could any longer make sense of the arcane professional standards, company accounts and audit reports.

Audit standards, for example, came to be populated with definitions – of terms such as 'positive assurance', 'negative assurance', 'reasonable assurance' and 'limited assurance' – that bordered on nonsense and confounded outsiders. Just as 'the conjuror's patter seemed contrived either to confuse or to mislead', the first modern doctors and lawyers had similarly been accused of using 'incomprehensible jargon' that only baffled laymen. The following definition, from the 2014 *Australian Standard on Assurance Engagements Other than Audits or Reviews of Historical Financial Information* (ASAE 3000), is a good example:

> Limited assurance engagement: An assurance engagement in which the assurance practitioner reduces engagement risk to a level that is acceptable in the circumstances of the engagement, but where that risk is greater than for a reasonable assurance engagement, as the basis for expressing a conclusion in a form that conveys whether, based on the procedures performed and evidence obtained, a matter(s) has come to the assurance practitioner's attention to cause the assurance practitioner to believe the subject matter information or subject matter is materially misstated. The nature, timing and extent of procedures performed in a limited assurance engagement is limited compared with that necessary in a reasonable assurance engagement but is planned to obtain a level of assurance that is, in the assurance practitioner's

professional judgement, meaningful. To be meaningful, the level of assurance obtained by the assurance practitioner is likely to enhance the intended users' confidence about the subject matter information or subject matter to a degree that is clearly more than inconsequential.

While it is fun to ridicule passages like this, there is a serious issue beneath the tortured syntax, waffling clauses and foggy vocabulary. Over the past century or so, laws, regulations, standards, guidelines, practice notes and templates for accounting and auditing have become ever more specific and prescriptive. The Australian standards on assurance engagements, for instance, require that audit reports must have a title page and a contents page, and that auditors must write down their clients' instructions. And yet all the effort to pin down precisely the conduct and standards of accountants and auditors has probably had the opposite effect. Being now rules-based rather than principles-based, the regulatory instruments have become less effective by allowing conduct that adheres to the letter of the laws and standards but that tramples on principles of good governance. A large truck may comfortably be driven through many of the current standards.

The Big Four use their regulatory relationships to shape accounting standards, but may have a poor understanding of how users of financial reporting information actually operate. The setting of standards is based on a complex process involving appeals to ill-defined terms – such as the 'conceptual framework' – which provide little practical direction for most accounting issues. The firms have also used their relationships and advocacy to claim new turf. In the legal services market, for example, they've petitioned governments and regulators for permission to undertake quasi-legal work, and to extend advisory services into areas traditionally occupied by lawyers.

## The Big Four and Big Law

In accountancy's early days, lawyers and accountants often belonged to the same associations and moved in the same circles. There was commonality, too, in the nature and conditions of their work, and in the types of men who did that work. Recall how members of the Waterhouse family co-founded both Price Waterhouse and the law firm that is now Field Fisher Waterhouse. Most accountants offered some types of paralegal assistance, while lawyers offered accounting-flavoured services in areas such as tax and insolvency.

Gradually, though, in a process that resembles biological speciation, the two professions became more defined and more divided from each other. Accountants did accounting and lawyers did law. Fast-forward to the present day, though, and the species are interbreeding: boundaries have again become blurred. PwC operates a major global legal practice equipped with 2400 lawyers in eighty-three countries. Deloitte has 1300 lawyers in fifty-six countries. EY and KPMG also maintain substantial legal practices. Traditional law firms have noticed this encroachment into their professional pastures, and they're not pleased.

Accountants in quasi-legal markets have walked a long road to get where they are. In 1924 the US Board of Tax Appeals determined that no professionals except lawyers and CPAs could practise before it. The inclusion of CPAs was highly irritating for the lawyers, who were of course seeking to protect their territory; it was a case of 'top-tier' professionals trying to keep an 'underprivileged' profession in its place. Since then, large accounting firms have been accused of the 'unauthorised' or 'surrogate' practice of law.

The market for legal services is highly regulated by statutes, local practice rules and ethics requirements. Several jurisdictions, for example, limit the extent to which lawyers can share fees with non-lawyers. Critics of the Big Four's move into the law complain the accounting firms are sneaking under or over these regulatory barriers, and are less restricted than law firms (and other professions, such as doctors) in their ability to advertise and otherwise to conduct business. In India, for example, after a complaint from the Society of Indian Law Firms, the Bar Council served notices to the Big Four, alleging a breach of registration requirements relating to law practice. In Australia, some leading law firms have suggested they might reduce the amount of work they refer to the Big Four, who used to be complementary but are rapidly becoming competitors.

In defence of their turf, lawyers have argued that accountants cannot offer the same breadth of client protections, such as the legal privilege of confidentiality. Law firms have also sought the safety of scale, grouping together to form the mega-partnerships that together are known as 'Big Law', in direct opposition to the Big Four. The accounting firms, though, are not retreating. Envisioning a lucrative future in legal-style work, the firms are using their public-sector relationships to protect the gains they've made so far, and to pave the way for further advances.

They are fighting other battles, too. The firms' most emphatic foray has seen them enter the diverse field of 'management consulting'.

## The move into 'advisory'

That accountants would enter the field of consulting was not immediately obvious. Nor was it without resistance, even from within the accounting profession itself. Arthur Lowes Dickinson, an early senior partner at Price Waterhouse, thought accountants ought not advise businesses on how they should be run; they should stick to making sure clients' accounts were accurate. Dickinson's views remained influential for many years. Arthur Andersen's first foray into systems advice was branded a folly. Stephen A. Zeff, in his 2003 paper 'How the U.S. Accounting Profession Got Where It Is Today: Part I', describes how, in 1979, Arthur Andersen's chairman and chief executive was forced to take early retirement after suggesting that the firm be split into two businesses, audit and consulting.

The first steps into consultancy were tentative ones. In 1963 Price Waterhouse elevated its systems department and renamed it 'Management Consultancy Services', reflecting how some of the firm's competitors were presenting such services to the market. (Arthur Andersen, which had begun consulting in the 1950s, had called its systems department 'Administrative Services Division'.) Price Waterhouse's new department provided a set of outputs that today seems narrowly prescribed: 'periodic reviews of management organisation; advice on the form and content of statistical information (management accounts) ...; reviews of administrative systems; advice on the organisation of office procedures; and proposals for mechanising accounting procedures and the use of computers.' Any misgivings about consulting, however, were destined to be overridden, and the scale and ambition of advisory services grew. The firms were soon developing and implementing improvement strategies for car makers, defence departments, agribusinesses, Big Oil, Big Pharma, Big Government. Arthur Andersen, Price Waterhouse and their main competitors thrived in this emerging market.

Apart from creating profitable new business lines for accountants, the sale of advisory services helped solve the perennial problem of seasonality in bookkeeping and audit workloads. As the Price Waterhouse partner Paul Grady noted in 1945:

> The curse of public accounting in the past has been the tremendous stress and strain on all personnel during the first quarter of the year, accompanied by the large numbers of temporary workers ... the basic causes of the old peak season are still with us and they must be conquered as a condition precedent to satisfactory progress by the profession.

In the early years of Price Waterhouse, August was always a season of slack. Nicholas Waterhouse recalled that 'it was so quiet that staff on holiday were sometimes told to stay away "for another week or even two"'. In stark contrast, the year-end peak was chaotic. In the 1910s, some American accounting firms adopted a radical solution: hiring non-accountant blow-ins such as teachers and even farmers, who could serve as casual labour during the worst of the peak.

For labour-intensive accounting firms, troughs in demand are even worse than peaks. The firms deal in staff hours, not in widgets that can be stored as inventory and sold later. Unutilised staff are a dead loss. Apart from the annual cycles, the firms face cycles in overall economic activity and in those service lines that are more strongly tied to booms or recessions. Insolvency specialists, for example, prosper when the rest of the economy does not. How might the firms make the best of the cyclicality? The sale of advice – which is subject to fashions but is intrinsically non-seasonal and non-cyclical – offered a solution.

Even in the nineteenth century, selling advice had been a routine part of traditional audit, tax and general bookkeeping services. Clients asked the firms for guidance about management systems and the presentation of accounts, for example. But advisory was not a distinct service, and nor was it an area of emphasis in training or recruitment. What share of revenue came from the provision of advice? It is impossible to know for sure, as the boundaries between service lines were ill-defined, but a figure of 5 per cent seems plausible. Whatever the number, it was certainly not enough to smooth the peaks and troughs.

From that modest base, though, the revenue share of advisory would rise, reaching around 20 per cent in the late 1970s. By that time, six of the then Big Eight accounting firms would rank in the top ten US management consulting outfits. (Arthur Andersen topped the list in 1983.) Throughout the 1980s, the share of consulting crept ever upward. By 1990 it accounted for around 25 per cent of revenue for all the Big Six firms – except Arthur Andersen and Andersen Consulting, for which the share had reached 44 per cent. By the end of that decade, advisory was coming close to earning half the total revenue of all four firms.

A few years later, three of the Big Four would make a dramatic retreat from advisory – sparking the creation of BearingPoint, Capgemini and Monday – and then plunge back into that sphere with even greater gusto. In 2013, for the first time, a Big Four firm's advisory revenue surpassed that of its traditional accounting practice. Deloitte achieved that milestone 168 years after William Deloitte had opened his accounting practice in London.

## Liberation

What is startling about the history of Big Four advisory in the twentieth century is not so much its novelty as its diversity and its rate of growth, a rate such that the Big Four quickly rivalled the 'pure' strategy firms including the 'Elite Three': McKinsey, Bain and Boston Consulting Group. They continued to win the juiciest engagements, but the Big Four generated comparable advisory revenues by tilling away at the less sexy end of the market. A new equilibrium was reached in which everyone had a place. As Vinod Mahanta wrote in 2013 for the *Economic Times*, 'Usually the white-shoe consultants [such as the Elite Three] feel the Big 4 consultants are competent but more suited for nuts and bolts kinds of engagements. And the Big 4 consultants … believe that the strat guys are good but … overrated.'

The expansion of advisory services liberated the major accounting firms from the more limited fields of audit, bankruptcy and tax. Advisory services can be sold to any kind of client: public and private corporations, but also political parties, policy units, ginger groups, regulators, churches, societies and individuals. In the latter part of the twentieth century, the firms saw spectacular growth in services for government as well as for creative industries and non-profit entities, such as hospitals, nursing homes, universities, religious institutions and other charities. For the Big Four, the non-profit sector turned out to be surprisingly profitable.

Advisory services were also liberating in their breadth. The accounting firms could diagnose client issues, make recommendations about how to address the issues and then help implement the solutions. Managing transactions and improvement projects (via the ubiquitous 'project management office' or 'PMO') became core businesses for the Big Four. The firms were no longer just trusted advisers; they were now doers and managers. Many years would pass before the firms properly understood how this shift changed their risk exposure. As just one example, Deloitte was recently caught up in the botched implementation of a payroll system, the failure of which delayed the wages of thousands of employees.

The twentieth century was a time of methodological innovation for accountancy. New technologies caused successive waves of transformation: the typewriter, the duplicator, the calculator, the computer. The decades after the 1960s saw a great flowering of invention and sophistication in advisory services. Those services came to encompass corporate finance, systems advice, IT advice, internal audit, forensic audit, probity audit, economic advisory, economic modelling, financial modelling, efficiency reviews, program reviews, sector reviews, business cases, legal services, real-estate advisory, project management, investment logic mapping, cost-benefit analysis, valuations, evaluations, investigations, public relations, public affairs, employment advisory, executive search, restructuring and much more besides.

If Big Four advisory is 'all things to all people', then it is also a case of 'back to the future' for the accounting profession, recalling the early days in which 'accountants' were also law bill clerks, auctioneers and general agents ready to do pretty much anything. In the profession's youth, bodies such as the ICAEW took great pains to define and limit the field of accounting and auditing services. Auctioneers, law clerks, estate agents, debt collectors and general agents could by no means be allowed to call themselves accountants. Now, though, the pendulum of professional diversity within the Big Four firms has swung the other way. To maintain the current assortment of advisory services, the firms have had to assemble workforces as diverse as Hutch's illicit pharmacopeia.

## All comers

Fewer and fewer Big Four staff now refer to themselves as accountants. Fewer and fewer pursue formal chartered or CPA qualifications. All-comers are welcome as providers of advisory services. The profile of disciplines and service lines is as diverse as it was before the profession began to organise itself. A Big Four director recently encapsulated this diversity: 'In one team I worked in, there were accountants, auditors, actuaries, economists, engineers, psychologists, counsellors, social workers, architects, scientists, geologists, geographers, demographers, recruiters, marketers, managers, financiers, estate agents, literature majors. Plus a few generalists.'

The new arrivals have brought multiple professional cultures and different disciplinary languages. Each of the Big Four firms has taken steps to build a consistent 'advisory identity', analogous to the identities of tax and audit. Inevitably, though, the new arrivals are invested to differing degrees in the overarching Big Four culture, and in the allure of the partner track. The firms' efforts at cultural integration have therefore only been partly effective.

Other intrinsic problems have cropped up during the push into advisory. For one thing, specialisation in staff capabilities is expensive. Apart from the direct costs of idiosyncratic recruitment and bespoke training, there is an indirect cost for the Big Four in not being able to move staff seamlessly between service lines according to the work demands of the time. Investments in specialised services and capabilities are lumpy and create friction in Big Four teams, and in the firms' internal labour markets. Specialisation in advisory has undermined the original rationale for branching out into management consulting: the ability to move staff around in order to de-cycle the flow of work. It is impossible to fill shortages of auditors with geologists or social workers, for example. Specialisation is also unstable. All four firms have experienced the pain of assembling gun advisory teams, only to see them poached or cherry-picked by rivals.

## The hugger-mugger advisory toolkit

To deliver services across the diverse threads of advisory, the Big Four have had to assemble a mixture of tools that is as eclectic as the people who use them. To pinpoint the sources of those tools, scholars have searched near and far. Buddhist temples in Sri Lanka. The funding of the Crusades. Italian merchant finance. The Dutch East India Company. English manor-house accounting. Nineteenth-century business administration. Taylorist scientific management. Keynesian public finance. Nineteen-seventies management theory. Neoclassical economics. Thatcherism. New Public Management. Nineteen-eighties corporate finance. Japanese *kaizen* management and just-in-time manufacturing. Systems engineering. Drucker, Porter, Schumpeter. Ford, Galbraith, the Rand Corporation. Many of these sources did indeed feed the advisory toolkit. Perennially magpies, the Big Four have plucked their methods from all over the place.

Now a mainstay of Big Four advisory practices, efficiency reviews are an example of the eccentric history of advisory methods. Josiah Wedgwood pioneered such reviews in his eighteenth-century porcelain factories. The grandfather of Charles Darwin, Wedgwood was himself a genius, and one of the world's first and most thoughtful practitioners of cost accounting.

Apart from techniques such as double-entry accounting and financial audit, the firms have adopted tools that are not fiscal in character, or even quantitative: examples are mission statements, communication strategies, investment logic maps and cultural improvement programs. Equipped with their eclectic toolkit, the firms rode the twentieth century's grand cycles of industrial diversification and specialisation, of nationalisation and privatisation, and of deregulation and re-regulation. In the finance sector, for example, the firms helped banks merge with insurers under the glamorous label 'bancassurance'; when the promised synergies failed to materialise, they helped unravel the mergers on grounds of efficiency, focus and risk management. Advisers don't get rich telling their clients to remain the same.

A paradox of advisory services is that the idiosyncratic history of the tools is invisible to readers of written advisory outputs. All the borrowed tools are rebadged and shandied together. The resulting outputs are bland and ahistorical, bulked out with a mixture of common sense, conventional wisdom and motherhood statements, dressed up with chevrons and roundels and circumflexes, and dumbed down with safely moronic terms such as 'incentivise', 'impactful', 'bottom-up', 'top-down', 'stakeholder engagement' and 'learnings'.

All the written advisory outputs of the Big Four have a family resemblance that manifests in similar structures, disclaimers, graphics, typography and heft. The bulkiness of advisory letters and presentations and reports – known as the 'thud factor' – is curiously important. It actually helps determine what revenue is earned, as accounting firms sometimes base their pricing on the number of pages produced (or they base the number of pages on the price they intend to charge). A satisfying thud helps a client feel good about his or her purchase.

## The contentious value of advisory services

This brings us to an uncomfortable truth. The 'quality' of advisory services is an elusive concept. Advisory products are ostensibly about solving problems, but as much as anything they are actually about creating a state of mind in the client. Management consultants are purveyors of the mysterious endorphins that flow from being seen to properly tackle a problem – from answering the need to 'do something'. Through sophisticated surveys and interviews, the Big Four take pains to measure the states of mind their products create. Will the client be a source of repeat work? Will he or she recommend us to others? Has this output enhanced our brand in the market? The responses to these questions shape the future outputs of the firms, and the future prospects of partners and their teams.

Many advisory services are easy to deliver. Advisory teams use generic methods wherever they can, and applying a generic method to a specific problem is always cheap, even if the outcome leaves something to be desired. Advisory services are also much less risky (and less regulated) than accounting products such as tax services and financial auditing. Tax and audit bring all sorts of potential pitfalls and are subject to all manner of attempted mitigations. Advisory services, by contrast, are provided in a carefree, *laissez-faire* environment. Doctors, architects, engineers and many other professionals confront real dangers every day. In advisory, though, what can possibly go wrong? If the advice is ill-timed or ill-suited or just plain silly, those shortcomings rarely come to light. If a client acts on a piece of advice, there is no 'counterfactual' against which the action and its consequences can be compared – that is, there's no alternative universe in which the advice was not acted upon. A hundred different factors might determine whether a given strategy succeeds or not, and many are far beyond the control of the client and his or her advisers. For these and other reasons, verifying that a particular piece of advice was objectively harmful, and holding advisers to account for that harm, is all but impossible.

Advisory products, moreover, are highly caveated. Advisory reports and letters contain disclaimers that are often brazenly wide-ranging. 'No warranty is made of the quality of this advice.' 'No liability is assumed if someone acts on this advice.' 'It is not our fault if everything you told us was wrong.' Advisory disclaimers are a bureaucratic art form, a curious species of faux-legal anthropology.

## The scientific basis of advisory work

In the early modern era, accounting and bookkeeping sat very much in the sphere of science. Can the same be said of advisory outputs?

Underneath all the disclaimers and chevrons and Arial and Times Roman, advisory outputs are founded on empirical and quasi-empirical methods that have an intellectual basis. Yet that basis is seldom questioned. When it is, the picture is a sorry one. Advisory reports overflow with meaningless analyses and specious correspondences. Many staples of corporate advisory – mergers and acquisitions, equity-based compensation, independent directors, and various forms of outsourcing, downsizing and restructuring – have been shown to have only a weak correlation, or no correlation, with corporate success. The outputs adopt the trappings of rigour and science, but those trappings are little more than a veneer.

Indeed, many advisory products – particularly those that purport to predict a company's prospects – fall into the category of what statisticians call 'spurious specificity', and what the economist J.K. Galbraith called 'sophisticated ignorance', 'essential error' and 'fraud'. The advisory service line is where accountancy has most visibly decoupled from science.

# 6

# AN INJUDICIOUS CHANGE

## Adventures and misadventures in Big Four branding

### What's in a name?

Branding was key to how the Medici Bank flourished. From Scotland in the west to China in the east, the bank's brand was immediately recognisable as a signifier of safety and integrity. And it served a more local purpose, too, helping keep ambitious junior staff in line. A manager in a hurry could strike out on his own and establish a rival enterprise using Medici methods, but he could not claim to be part of the trademarked Medici Bank: the right to use that name was an exclusive privilege of the partnership.

Despite the family's criminal origins, and all the twists and turns in the Medici story, the name is still one to conjure with – an all-time great brand. Even today, it is used in European banking. The current Big Four names, too, are among the most recognisable worldwide brands, and so are among the firms' most valuable assets.

Early in the twentieth century, fans of Britain's magnificent Great Western Railway called it 'God's Wonderful Railway'; detractors called it the 'Great Way Round'. The first large-scale mergers among railway companies were remarkable for their anguished deliberations about corporate titles. Whose brand would have the greatest prominence in the new name? Whose heritage would come first? The same anguish has since featured in mergers of large accounting firms.

In 1989, for example, the failure of delicate discussions about branding was one reason why the mooted merger between Price Waterhouse and Arthur Andersen did not go ahead. (Another claimed reason was that the firms had 'wildly differing cultures'.) Each party to these discussions thought its own brand should prevail in the new entity. One negotiator on the Price Waterhouse side argued for retaining 'the subliminal marketing value of "price" in the name, for cost-conscious clients'. Such subliminal associations were in fact diametrically opposed to the premium image the firm had aspired to create. (Had Samuel Price been alive, he would've run upstairs and given that negotiator a walloping.) The discussions almost landed on the acronym 'PWA', a compromise that would've been close to the current brand, if without the strange capitalisation.

(During the recession of the early 1990s, Price Waterhouse reportedly offered a 40 per cent reduction in its audit fees – as a 'loss leader' to woo financial services behemoth Prudential as a client. The loss, so the reasoning evidently went, could be made up through the sale of lucrative non-audit services. According to the editors of the *Evening Standard*, writing under the headline 'A Cutting Sense of History at PwC', the discount, when it came to light, 'caused such a stink that it took several years for the firm to shake off the tag Cut-Price Waterhouse'.)

PwC, and the long-form name PricewaterhouseCoopers, betray the careful merger negotiations between Price Waterhouse and Coopers & Lybrand. These featured tortuous deliberations about letter spacing (or the lack thereof) and upper- and lower-case characters. Officially, the 'w' of Waterhouse now appears in lower case both in the firm's new full name and in the new acronym. The effect is a brand that looks inelegant and temporary. How, we wonder, would Edwin and Nicholas Waterhouse have viewed this odd compromise?

The acronym has been the subject of much fun in the industry. 'Pricks With Calculators', 'Proceed With Caution', 'People Working Cheap', 'People Working Constantly', 'Partners Without Class' – all have currency, as does the unfortunate homonym 'Pee-WC', another reason for the capitalisation. Although the firm is still called PwC, its latest logo has done away with capitalisation altogether.

Price Waterhouse was refining its typography long before its merger with Coopers & Lybrand. In 1940 the comma was dropped from Price, Waterhouse and Co. That decision, in the context of wartime austerity, prompted a newspaper columnist to joke that the change was an economy measure 'designed to save ink'. In 1981 the 'and Co.' was also jettisoned. (The 'Co.' stood for 'co-partners', not 'company'.)

For five of the firm's early years, Price and Waterhouse were in partnership with William Holyland. When the partners got around to commissioning a brass nameplate for their premises, Waterhouse worried that, if the plate were split-mounted across the swing doors, passers-by might read, on the first open door, 'Price, Holy Water', and on the second, 'land and house'.

When Price died in 1887, there were two remaining partners: Edwin Waterhouse and George Sneath, the bright and likeable son of a yeoman farmer. Waterhouse offered to change the firm's name to Waterhouse, Sneath and Co. but Sneath astutely demurred. There was too much value, he argued, in the established label. Things could easily have been different, which provokes an intriguing thought. Would PwC have become an international powerhouse as WaterhousesneathCoopers?

An oft-repeated story about Cooper Brothers concerns their original London premises in Gutter Lane, off Cheapside. As the firm grew, the street name became more and more of a bugbear. According to the story, the partners wrote to the municipal authorities suggesting a new name for the thoroughfare: Coopers Lane. The authorities are said to have countered with the suggestion that the firm change its name – to Gutter Brothers.

The acronym KPMG was adopted when Peat Marwick merged with the European firm KMG, which stood for Klynveld Main Goerdeler. The partners settled upon an ordering of letters that had no alphabetical basis, but that carried a helpful echo of the British honour KCMG. The acronym permitted just as much play as PwC. Apart from the challenge of remembering what the letters actually stood for (most employees still fail at this), there was play with creative alternatives such as 'Keep Playing More Golf', 'Keep Partners' Money Growing' and 'Keep Pulling Money from Government'.

Officially, the firm formerly known as Ernst & Young is now just two letters, EY. But it is still widely referred to by its old name. A significant minority of people also insist on pronouncing (and writing) Ernst as 'Ernest' – or even as 'Earnest', a not unhelpful connotation for an audit firm. Informal variants of the name include 'E-Why?' and 'Ernie' (as in Bert).[11]

Deloitte's stylised, pared-back logo reflects careful evolution. Many dollars were spent on the typography, right down to the green full stop, which is meant to connote innovation, not stopping. Prior to becoming a single-word brand, the firm was styled Deloitte Touche Tohmatsu, which is still the full title of the international group's principal legal entity, a company limited by guarantee. The surname Deloitte is a lightly anglicised French name that came down to William Deloitte from his grandfather Count de Loitte, an aristocrat who escaped revolutionary France.

Sir George Touche, a Scotsman and later a baronet, was born George Touch. His family pronounced their surname as 'toch', as in 'loch'; it rhymed with neither 'such' nor 'douche'. George added the 'e' to further distinguish his name from 'touch', a word that, for an accountant, is as bad as 'earnest' is good. In the Darwinian battle for Big Four brand presence, Touche was doomed to perish. Other 'lost' Big Four names include Whinney, Garnsey, Plender and Kettle. Those belonged

---

11   *EY! Magateen* is a raunchy South American magazine.

to partners who did as much as any others to build the major firms and the wider profession. It was largely a matter of chance that other men's names prevailed in the Big Four brands.

The current brands convey a reassuring aura of British integrity, British prudence and British law. Three of the four firms are based in the United Kingdom (KPMG is based in Amsterdam; Deloitte is a British entity, even though its headquarters are in New York). But in their ownership and sources of revenue, the firms have long ceased to be mostly British. Today, for example, the firms have far more personnel in Asia and North America than in the United Kingdom. China alone is poised to surpass Britain as the home of more Big Four staff. For many years, the peak organisation in Deloitte's global network was a Swiss-based entity known as a *verein* – what Andrew Clark in the *Guardian* rightly called 'an obscure ... membership structure originally intended for sports clubs, voluntary organisations and unions'. KPMG was also formerly a Swiss *verein* but is now a Swiss association.

The Big Four have become truly global businesses. Mr Sneath would've been proud.

## Uninvited solicitation

The culture in the early days of the profession was that accountants should not 'tout' for work. Instead, they were expected to come into contact with clients through formal and informal networks, or to rely on them coming through the door. Accountants, after all, were engaged in a profession, not mere commerce. Favoured strategies for meeting new clients and winning new work included sitting on charitable boards, joining country clubs and glad-handing at lodges, societies and chambers of commerce. Selling was low-key and a long game.

'It was a gentleman's profession,' according to Rick Connor, managing partner of KPMG's Denver office in 2002. 'Full-time salespeople were unheard of,' Connor told the *Wall Street Journal*. Active selling was antithetical to the public mission and professional authority of accountants, who, in the words of Ianthe Dugan, were 'the conscience of capitalism'. As late as the 1960s, the idea of a 'marketing campaign' for new clients simply did not exist in the profession. In the earlier years of the ICAEW, rules against advertising were enforced with the vigour and strictness of a medieval guild.

In 1881, for example, a member of the institute was formally censured for distributing postcards soliciting bankruptcy work. Other more subtle forms of marketing could also land members in hot water. According to Sir Harold Howitt in his 1966 history of the ICAEW, 'The secretary of the Institute was authorized, in all cases in which advertisements issued by members of the Institute came under his notice, to communicate with such members and to inform them that the Council considered such advertising to be unprofessional.'

Attitudes were broadly the same in the United States as in Britain. In 1922, the American Institute of Accountants banned member firms from advertising and certain other forms of self-promotion. Men such as Alwin Charles Ernst, however, could not resist the opportunities provided by the print media and other modes of marketing. He is credited with having created, in 1917, the accounting profession's first sales and marketing department, which he called 'Business Development'. Ernst & Ernst, a national firm in the 1920s, marketed its services overtly in newspaper ads with headings such as 'A National Service in the Interest of Better Business' and 'Where Knowledge Is Bliss and Ignorance Is Folly'. The American institute was unimpressed. In 1923 it accused Alwin and two of his fellow partners of violating the rules against soliciting and advertising. Pointedly choosing marketing over compliance, the three men resigned their institute memberships.

In the face of changing values and market realities, all these restrictions were doomed to fade away. An author writing about the *Crisis in Accounting Ethics* noted how advertising, soliciting and other modes of commercial competition became the new normal of accountancy:

In 1972, the Institute gave in to [the Department of Justice] by removing the ban on competitive bidding from its code of ethics. By 1979, Justice and the FTC compelled the Institute to drop its rules prohibiting direct, uninvited solicitation and advertising that is purely informational ... These amendments to the Institute's code of ethics, particularly on competitive bidding and direct, uninvited solicitation, profoundly changed the climate in which audit firms conducted their affairs. Competition among firms came to be signified more in the idiom of commerce – the aggressive pursuit of profit – thus placing strains on professional values.

Today, touting for work is the bread and butter of the Big Four, especially for advisory work, but also for tax and audit. A large proportion – often as much as half – of the daily work of partners and staff is spent preparing pitch documents and ferreting out new projects. More polite words, though, are used to describe this effort – terms such as 'market engagement' and Alwin Ernst's 'business development', now universally known as 'BD'.

Once the shackles were off, many Big Four offices quickly forgot any level of professional subtlety. Some took selling to an uncomfortable extreme. In 1983, amid strong competition for pension accounting services, Touche Ross & Co. issued a booklet promoting its wares. The firm offered to help clients 'prepare an effective and persuasive response' to the Financial Accounting Standards Board, by which the firm 'would assist your company in evaluating the effects, developing empirical supporting evidence, and identifying the economic consequences of the positions your company supports and rejects'. Touche Ross was accused of selling out its integrity and of being 'willing to become a blind advocate for its clients'.

Similar criticisms were levelled in 2011, when Deloitte entered a risky engagement with the peak body of the Australian tobacco industry. In the context of a political controversy about legislation that would mandate plain packaging of cigarettes – legislation the tobacco companies ardently opposed – the industry commissioned Deloitte to prepare a report on illicit tobacco, known as 'chop chop'. Officials from a federal agency, the Australian Customs and Border Protection Service, called the report 'potentially misleading' and questioned the 'reliability and accuracy' of its data. Deloitte released a second report, on counterfeit cigarettes; this Brendan O'Connor, a federal minister, described as 'baseless', 'deceptive' and 'bogus'. Criticism came, too, from the health sector and other advocates of plain packaging.

At the same time that Rick Connor of KPMG in Denver was speaking to the *Journal* about gentlemanly selling, his KPMG colleagues in Indiana were setting up a call centre from which telemarketers cold-called prospective clients to push the firm's tax products. A June 2000 memo instructed employees on how to get around 'Sticking Points and Other Problems', such as hesitant and reluctant customers. The memo suggested techniques such as the 'Get Even' approach (contacting clients with large tax payments due – clients who were likely to be 'extremely irritated') and the 'Beanie Baby' approach (telling clients the firm had put a cap on the shelter sales, which would soon be reached). Clients who thought the offers were 'too good to be true' were told that the products had been reviewed extensively – including by former IRS staff who now worked for KPMG.

## Retreat and advance

In the early 1990s all the Big Six firms ranked in the top seven consulting firms worldwide. As their consulting revenues began to rival their traditional accounting and auditing revenues, the firms began to market themselves as 'multi-line professional service firms' – business consulting organisations rather than accountants or auditors. There is more than one way for a major accounting firm to make money from advisory services. The firm can sell the services or, better still, it can sell an advisory business.

In 2002, in the wake of the Enron scandal and in the shadow of the *Sarbanes-Oxley Act*, KPMG and PwC fled from the advisory market. Via an initial public offering, KPMG sold KPMG Consulting, which became BearingPoint. For US$3.5 billion in cash and shares, IBM bought PwC Consulting, PwC's global management consulting and technology services business. EY had already sold its consulting arm, Capgemini, in 2000.

These carve-outs posed all sorts of challenges for the partner model and for Big Four ethics. In the grey zone between running a practice and dressing it up for sale, the firms faced incentives that were decidedly mixed. Disposals caused practical problems in the market, especially when major firms exited advisory only to re-enter it a few years later. KPMG, PwC and EY all did this. By the time any non-compete clauses had run their course, the firms were back in advisory with a vengeance. Deloitte had only sold parts of its advisory business, retaining the bulk of it, and was thus in an exceptionally strong position during the rush back into advisory. All this coming and going raised an important question: what of the clients?

The rush was emphatic and at times chaotic. In Australia, PwC rebuilt its advisory business by going on a shopping spree, acquiring one after another smaller strategy businesses, such as GEM Consulting, The Difference, Walter Turnbull, Ashley Munro and Mainstreet Corporate. These were grand times for the owners of small firms. In Australia and the United States, Deloitte vacuumed up boutique advisory practices and teams. Booz Allen Hamilton sued Deloitte in 2014, claiming the firm had stolen proprietary information in order to 'lift out' a specialised team of Booz employees.

Until 2008, Booz Allen Hamilton owned the strategic advisory business Booz & Co. In 2013 PwC acquired the business, which it renamed Strategy& (again with the awkward spacing), although it retained its focus on cyber security and risk services. The new name was designed to avoid legal strife and market confusion over the use of the Booz brand, which was well known in strategic advisory circles. The original carve-out agreement included a specific provision that the Booz name or variants of it could not be used in conjunction with a new entity. Booz Allen Hamilton continued to be a major provider of strategic services to governments and the defence sector. After the expiry of a three-year non-compete provision between Booz Allen Hamilton and Booz & Co., Booz Allen Hamilton expanded its consulting practice in areas such as technology integration and security.

Strategy& would prove as much a branding blunder as 'cognitor' and 'Monday', the latter being the name given to PwC's consulting arm prior to the IBM takeover. Immediately, the 'Monday' brand mobilised a coalition of opponents who disliked clever-dick consultants – and Mondays. The brand was launched online at www.introducingmonday.com. The launchers, though, had omitted to register www.introducingmonday.co.uk, which was instead snapped up by pranksters. Visitors to the hoax site were greeted by a crude animated donkey. 'This made me laugh,' one observer wrote. 'Fancy calling your company Monday – then the website made me laugh even more.' The folly of accountants dabbling in marketing was once again demonstrated. The brand was soon dropped. The donkey passed into Big Four legend.

# 7

# PORN STAR

## The culture of the Big Four

### Leverage

The day-to-day correspondence of the Medici Bank reveals men concerned with external matters such as the alum mines, the wool and silk markets and the creditworthiness of monarchs. But they were also concerned with internal matters. Were the bank's systems strong enough to detect fraud and prevent financial disaster? Who was ready for a pay rise and a promotion? Were the young men graduating from the abacus schools up to Medici standards?

Angelo Tani, Rinieri da Ricasoli and Cosimo de Medici all understood 'leverage', which in partnerships means growing the business by hiring junior staff to complement and extend the capacity and capability of partners. The Medici Bank was one of the first large partnerships to grapple with the underlying equation of leverage: the incontrovertible calculus that profit per partner is equivalent to margin times hourly rate times utilisation (the extent to which staff are busy) times the number of staff per partner. Bringing on more staff was one of the few ways in which the bank could pursue higher profits.

In this respect, the Medici Bank retained an artefact from its prior incarnation as a criminal syndicate. Italian crime families consisted of dispersed networks in which 'made' men ran crews and worked territories. Earnings flowed from the most junior thug upwards, through five other rungs of felon. The Big Four firms have adopted the same six-level hierarchy, though they give different names to the rungs: consultant, senior consultant, manager, senior manager, director, partner. The titles may differ but the way it works – with turfs and ranks and earners – is strikingly similar.

Leverage involves sending out less experienced staff to do the work that has been sold by directors and partners. Clients complain that those sellers – so engaging and compelling in the pitch meeting – usually vanish soon after the sale is complete, never to be seen again. The success of the Big Four may have been built on the backs of juniors, but institutionalised reliance on inexperienced staff can lead the Big Four into danger. In the TBW–Colonial case, for example, it was claimed that a PwC intern was in charge of checking billions of dollars' worth of collateral, and that the intern's supervisor was another junior, who thought his duties were 'above his pay grade'.

But juniors are the heroes of accounting scandals as often as they are the villains. In the Centro case in Australia, shareholders launched a class action to recover investor value lost as a result of a A$4.9-billion black hole in the company's financial statements. PwC was the auditor. Stephen Cougle led the firm's Centro account. In court he said junior audit staff – some of them recent university graduates – were responsible for the errors in the audit. In fact, however, one of those juniors had discovered mistakes, but Cougle allegedly failed to follow them up with 'a full review of the accounts'. The Australian Securities and Investments Commission (ASIC) banned him from auditing for two and a half years. PwC paid out approximately A$66 million of a settlement worth A$200 million.

Leverage drove growth among the Big Four, just as it had powered the expansion of Florentine commerce. Branding, too, was a cause of Big Four growth. As the four businesses became better known, clients gravitated towards them, creating a reinforcing current. Size conferred market power on the firms, and offered real or perceived benefits from diversification. Professional rules further encouraged the rush for bigness. In the 1970s, for example, the ICAEW directed that no audit practice could accept a client that represented more than 15 per cent of its revenue. In light of this and other strictures, most second-tier firms merged into what were then the Big Eight: Arthur Andersen, Arthur Young McClelland Moores & Co., Coopers & Lybrand, Deloitte Haskins & Sells, Ernst & Whinney, Peat Marwick Mitchell, Price Waterhouse and Touche Ross Bailey & Smart. When the major firms were ranked according to revenue, after the Big Eight there was daylight.

## Partner rewards

The Big Four brands include the names of ten men. Three of these (Cooper, Deloitte and Price) passed away in the nineteenth century. Two of them (Deloitte and Price) were among the twelve initial members of the pioneering Council of the Institute of Accountants in London, a predecessor of the ICAEW. Nine of the men passed away before 1949. The tenth man, Reinhard Goerdeler – the 'G' of KPMG – passed away in 1996. Since that time, no living Big Four partner has had his or her name or initial on the door. Instead of brand fame, partners have had to rely on other motivations: pay, perks, power and prestige.

The Big Four are owned and funded by their partners. Apart from retaining a quantum of profits, the firms finance themselves by calling on partners to contribute working capital, typically calculated as a proportion of annual earnings. It is common for new partners to fund this contribution by taking out a personal loan, and to structure their affairs to reduce their risk exposure (such as by establishing family trusts and transferring assets to a spouse or relative). Apart from supplying working capital, partners may be called upon to pay for commercial insurance and to provide personal guarantees – such as for the firms' current debts – that can be called upon in times of financial need.

Partner salaries include an 'at risk' component, the size of which depends in any given year on the performance of the individual, his or her division, and the whole office. Matters such as compliance and quality are also taken into account in the setting of this figure, but commercial performance is paramount. Approaches vary from country to country – Deloitte Australia, for example, has conventional partners as well as 'salaried partners', who own no equity in the firm – but the typical model is for partners to hold equity and to participate in profits based on the number of shares or units or 'partner points' they hold. (Non-equity partners are not expected to make the same contributions to working capital, insurance and so on.)

## The partner: A species

Thus remunerated, Big Four partners perform a multiplicity of roles. Workflow manager. Policeman. Life coach. Therapist. Custodian of secret wisdom. Champion of ideology. Lay philosopher. Guru. Snake charmer. In the 1970s the accounting firms formalised their processes for selecting and nurturing potential partners. All four firms now run versions of the 'Partner Acceptance Course' (PAC), in which potential partners are put through the ringer during the day, before repairing to the bar or spa of an evening. Partner selection is based on a curious mixture of personal attributes: stature, appearance, personality, charisma, aggression, ruthlessness, swagger. All these are measured at a PAC in real-time test scenarios that feature paid actors playing the parts of clients and colleagues. Not all candidates make it through this surreal filter. Those who do share an indefinable something, even a similar look: tanned skin, largish head, straightish nose, inquiring eyes, well-styled hair. It's an odd blend of preppiness, nerdiness and clubbability.

Anyone who has worked in accountancy knows the exotic anthropology of partnership, and the lurid taxonomy of partner subtypes. There is the Lifer, who joined the firm as a graduate and rose through the ranks. The Lifer is part of the furniture, inseparable from and ardently protective of the culture, or at least some nostalgic version of it. Some Lifers are also Technicians, who maintain encyclopaedic knowledge of standards and precedents. Mark Stevens is an investigative journalist who wrote a series of gritty volumes about accountancy. According to Stevens, the Technician looks as though he has been 'locked in a library ever since puberty'. For the Technician, 'the old image of the accountant with his head stuck in the stacks of ledgers – the Caspar Milquetoast with an obsession for numbers – rings true'.

A new breed is the Super Partner, who has risen to godlike stature by turning an unpromising turf – such as advising the defence forces or hospitals or aged-care facilities – into a goldmine of fees. Partners who grow their small patch into a $50-million or $100-million business in five years or so can write their own ticket. They can also get away with all sorts of things. Hiring their children. Bending or rewriting internal rules about filing and training and purchasing. Making diva-like demands, such as the installation of better phone reception at holiday resorts. Playing a lot of golf. The Super Partner is invincible.

Then there is the Parachuted Partner, a so-called 'lateral hire' plucked from an eminent role in defence or industry or government; 'lateral' because the partner has entered the hierarchy sideways rather than from below. In the Big Four culture, 'lateral hire' is a loaded term. A former Big Four director defined the term this way:

> It means you've leapfrogged internal candidates who had their
> sights on your role. It means you haven't done the hard yards as a
> graduate and a junior. It means you haven't paid your debt to the
> culture. It means you're an unwanted competitor, one more mouth

to feed, one more obstacle on the road to partnership. Lateral hires are cultural lepers.

A few more types round out the taxonomy. There are the Perfectionists, who cannot finish a job; there is always a bit more to do. The Vampires, who, once let inside a client's premises, will never leave. The promiscuous Jumpers, who bounce between the Big Four firms, often resigning just after bonuses are paid. And the Comedians, one of whom was responsible for the following recent incident:

> Our team's partner was always pulling pranks that skated close to the edge. In a tender to which we were responding, the client – a university – asked for details of how our firm was doing positive things for the natural environment. In our tender response, which adopted a serious, professional tone, the partner wrote that we'd participated in a greenhouse energy trial of the 'HMATS' technology. If the client's tender evaluators had googled 'HMATS', they would've found a page describing the Human Methane Automotive Transport System, along with a bogus schematic diagram of a car in which a pipe, leading from the driver's seat, used the driver's farts to power the vehicle.

And then there is the Octopus, who can't keep his hands to himself.

## No dice

In 1456, as head of the Bruges branch of the Medici Bank, Angelo Tani had to sign a partnership agreement that imposed strict conditions on his conduct. He could only leave Bruges to visit the fairs of Antwerp and Bergen op Zoom, or to make unavoidable business trips to London and Calais and Middelburg. He was barred from entertaining women and boys, and equally stringent limits were placed on his living arrangements and business activities. An early appendage of the ICAEW, the Chartered Accountants' Dining Club, established similarly severe rules for the conduct of its members. Lady guests were barred, and gambling was a strict no-no. 'No dice or game of hazard shall on any account be permitted,' the rules insisted, 'nor shall any higher stake at whist than one shilling points be played for.'

Today, rumours of partners behaving badly are legion. Insider trading. Being forced into early retirement (or death) due to alcoholism. Entertaining girlfriends, boyfriends, mistresses and hookers – and charging the expenses to clients. Downloading porn on work computers. Or, worse still, uploading it. Some rumours begin as whispers and evolve into public scandals, court cases and sanctions. It is hard to know how seriously to take the others; certainly some of them are just scuttlebutt, the social lubricant of a competitive, inward-looking culture. Juicy rumours help define the texture of life in a Big Four firm, where respectability and compliance are perennially defined by reference to their opposites.

## Unfair share

For their first hundred years, the major accounting firms resembled gentlemen's clubs in their atmosphere and decor – and their membership. In 1940 only 175 of the 16,000 CPAs in the United States were women. Colleges actively discouraged women from majoring in accounting. And if a woman did graduate with an accounting qualification, she found it difficult to find a position in a leading firm. Arthur Andersen waited till 1965 before hiring female accountants. When women did break in, they were mostly confined to junior or administrative roles – secretaries, stenographers, comptometrists and subsidiary ledger posting clerks – and they had to leave when they married.

In professional journals and at professional get-togethers, male accountants opined gravely on the question of women, and of what they might be able to do. Those opinions oddly foreshadow today's conversations about the digital automation and commoditisation of accounting services. Accountants said about women what they now say about robots. The 1942 editorial of the *Journal of Accountancy* is an example: 'To relieve men for audit work, women accountants might well do such tasks as report reviewing, statistical analysis, and office management. The feminine virtues of patience, perseverance, attention to detail, and accuracy on top of sound training in accounting would fit them admirably for such a career.'

Women would eventually scale the profession's heights, but the pace of advancement was frustratingly slow. In 1888 the ICAEW refused Mary Harris Smith's membership application on the grounds of her gender. Not until 1919 did the *Sex Disqualification (Removal) Act* make such refusals illegal. Harris Smith then re-applied and became the first female chartered accountant in history. A succession of milestones would follow. By 1945 there were enough female members of the ICAEW to found a dining club that rivalled the men's: the Women Chartered Accountants' Dining Society. In 1983 Rayna Dean of Manchester became Price Waterhouse's first female partner. In 1999, neatly 111 years after Harris Smith was first shut out, Baroness Noakes became the first female president of the institute.

Deplorable episodes punctuated the rise of women in the profession. In 1990, for example, a US federal judge ordered Price Waterhouse to offer a partnership and almost $400,000 in back pay to Ann B. Hopkins, who alleged she'd been denied promotion to the partnership on grounds of sexual discrimination. After Hopkins' partner candidacy had been put on indefinite hold, she resigned and sued the firm for occupational sexism, arguing that her lack of promotion followed pressure to walk, talk and dress more 'femininely'.

A certain type of maleness has long been part of the Big Four wallpaper, as one employee recounted:

The partner I worked for always had his mind in the football locker room. He would greet male clients by telling them they looked like porn stars, then launch into X-rated anecdotes about his own sex life and the fun he was having with women he met at the gym, or bars, or the supermarket. This was his everyday verbal currency. When the firm started hiring senior women who'd worked in high-integrity environments in government and blue chip corporations, the culture clash was inevitable, and spectacular.

In 1981 Mark Stevens quoted a retired auditor:

> In my day, lunchtime was a relaxed affair. A good meal and good conversation with men of your own ilk. Now, if you want to tell a joke, you have to look around the table first. One of your partners may be a Negro, Spanish, a Jew, or a woman. You know how sensitive they are.

Things have moved on since Stevens captured that snapshot. The firms have adopted progressive policies aimed at cultural diversity, affirmative action and LGBTIQ inclusion. On the strength of its 'inclusiveness commitment' and efforts to create 'a work environment where lesbian, gay, bisexual, transgender and intersex professionals can be their authentic selves at work', EY Australia ranked third in the Top 20 at the 2016 Australian Workplace Equality Index awards. Deloitte Australia established 'GLOBE', a gay, lesbian, bisexual, transgender and intersex leadership forum and member community, which it described in this way:

> GLOBE's vision is to create an inclusive work environment where our LGBTI people can be their authentic selves and set out to achieve their career goals regardless of how they identify. GLOBE's

activities support Deloitte's overall goal of building an environment in which all our people feel valued and accepted. The GLOBE
working group meets monthly to coordinate activities, training
and awareness sessions throughout the firm.

In 2000, Deloitte created 'Inspiring Women', a firm-wide strategy aimed
at 'getting our unfair share of female talent'. The strategy focuses on
building an inclusive culture, investing in women's progression, and
overcoming structural and societal barriers to that progression.

Steps such as these are positive and laudable. In some offices,
though, traces of the old monoculture and retrograde attitudes remain:

> My practice group invited Laura Liswood from Goldman Sachs to
> speak at a staff meeting. A champion of workplace diversity, Laura
> taught us about how language can exclude minorities. After the
> meeting, I went straight to a seminar at which our white, Anglo-
> Saxon HR manager made excruciating fun of a young woman and
> her Indian surname that he said was unpronounceable.

In 2013, after a young Texan auditor named Glory resigned in a dramatic fashion from PwC – her hashtag-filled resignation email went
viral – she was attacked online for being a 'diversity hire'. In another
recent and well-publicised incident, a receptionist at PwC's London
office was sent home for not wearing high heels. In 2014 Erik Pietzka
won a sex discrimination case against PwC on the grounds that his
requests to work part-time for family reasons had been rejected, and
had damaged his prospects for promotion. In other incidents, notorious Octopuses have been promoted rather than censured, and their
prey seemingly paid off with plum assignments to New York or Monaco
or Barbados. And there is an ongoing flow of court cases concerning
harassment and other breaches of the firms' espoused values. The path
to enlightenment is a long one.

## Unwritten laws

As early as 1945 the senior staff of Price Waterhouse were concerned that 'an atmosphere of insularity' had developed inside the firm. W.E. Parker, newly admitted to the partnership, wrote of his view that the firm had become 'too wrapped up in its own affairs'. His colleagues regarded their office life as 'the be-all and end-all of existence'. They'd become caught up in an inbred, hothouse atmosphere, inwardly focused and keenly attuned to who was being promoted, who was on the fast track, what peers were earning and what other favours were being handed out. The culture was one of camaraderie and fellowship, but also of petty jealousies, bitter grudges and toxic resentments. Another symptom of the 'be-all and end-all' dynamic was a certain 'big firm arrogance', which was on display even in front of clients.

Parker's description highlights another Big Four paradox. The firms have strong internal cultures that tend towards insularity. But they also have high appetites for staff, and display an openness to recruit from diverse fields. These seemingly contradictory attributes are reconciled through a strong process of induction – some might say brainwashing. In *Final Accounting* (2003), Barbara Toffler quoted a new recruit beginning the Arthur Andersen training process in the 1990s: 'It is year Zero with the Khmer Rouge. You have just been born.' For some new hires, recruitment into a Big Four firm is not unlike penetrating the Church of Scientology, or the Moonies, or the CIA.

In the early years, the partners were an eclectic and colourful lot; remember Sammy, Flack and Docker. But by the mid twentieth century the pendulum had swung the other way. As the profession became more settled and the big firms more dominant, conformity was the order of the day. Even small deviations were pounced upon. Accounting luminary William Seatree drew criticism for capitalising the nouns in his reports. Worse still, he was divorced! Mark Stevens picked up on the strong culture of conformity: 'There are unwritten laws at [the big firms] designed to keep everyone looking and acting like everyone else.

The partnership exerts a collective pressure on those who stray from the norm, ostracising the more adventurous souls or cutting back on their share of the profits.'

A recent example, relayed by a Big Four director:

One of our partners was a Scotsman. Every now and then he turned up in the office or at a client site wearing a thickly woven orange tweed suit with a matching tie that looked as though he'd knitted it himself. On every such appearance, his outfit caused a discernible quiver of horror throughout the firm and the partnership.

The tacit rules go far beyond the dress code, though. Don't guard your turf too stridently. Don't collaborate with other divisions too eagerly. Don't come across as overly ambitious, or too lacking in ambition. Don't complain about all the time-sheeting and performance metrics. Don't complain when your practice group moves to open-plan seating. Don't bite your nails. Don't bring a cut lunch. Be flexible and available. Drive a decent car.

We hired a partner named Alex. He had a Greek background and a loud, flamboyant personality. His connections into the major banks were excellent, and he was good at turning these into billable engagements. The other partners recognised his peculiar way of doing things was part of what made him good at winning work, just one part of the whole 'Alex package'. Some parts of the package, though, were not to be borne. He insisted on driving an old battered Skyline. A senior partner pulled him aside for a talking to. The firm could live with all the gesticulating and bombast, but the car had to go. A few months later, a Porsche replaced the clunker in the partners' car park.

Mark Stevens relayed a story told by a PepsiCo executive about the partner from the big accounting firm who lived next door. At the height of summer, the partner-neighbour donned Bermuda shorts, stripped to the waist, picked up a Löwenbräu and mounted his ride-on mower. The next day at work he was hauled over the coals. An executive partner had been in the neighbourhood and had happened to see his colleague, thus attired, cutting his front lawn. The spectacle sent him into a rage. Lawnmower Man was told not to make such 'crude public displays'. He should never drink outside, and never wear less than a golf shirt. What if a client saw him? Stevens concluded his anecdote – an analogue precursor to the digital problem of posting embarrassing pictures online – with a saucy coda: 'Word has it he leaves his shirt on to make love. Never know who's under the bed.'

The culture of conformity, Stevens argued, was not simply 'conformity for conformity's sake'. It was a deliberate tactic, aimed at fulfilling what clients expected to see when they came across a senior accountant. Being an accountant was a performance. Andrea Whittle, an academic who used an 'ethnomethodological' approach to study the Big Four, corroborated Stevens' suspicion. She observed blank-faced, buttoned-up staff working 'cloaked behind a veil of blandness'. To be an auditor, she concluded, 'you have to convincingly act like an auditor, and put on a smooth public face'. You have to live up to the image. And you have to believe it: clients can smell a lack of self-belief as keenly as wolves can smell fear.

For Stevens, the accountant image was very specific. Brown briefcase. Wing-tip shoes. White shirt. Three-piece suit with pinstripes or no stripes. (In the sartorial history *A Gentleman's Wardrobe*, Paul Keers claimed, plausibly, that pinstripes were inspired by the lines on ledgers.) Most Big Four partners didn't dress ostentatiously; they looked like modestly paid bank supervisors or insurance adjusters. Clean-shaven was the rule, although it was sometimes broken. Ernest Cooper famously took to wearing a beard after visiting Greece early in his career. Much vexation and hand-wringing followed. Today, beards have become fashionable outside the Big Four, but are still frowned upon inside. Staff at one practice were recently told, in no uncertain terms, that wearing a beard would be a barrier to partnership. Beards are fine for economists and engineers, but not accountants.

In the present century, 'casual Fridays' are a fashion battleground for the Big Four, one that highlights the cultural tension between freedom and constraint. Partners laud the permission to wear casual clothes as an example of their cultural liberality – and at the same time doggedly regulate it via emails and broadsides on the unacceptability of muffin tops, flip-flops or tattoos. The regulators, after all, are the same people who roasted Lawnmower Man. Matthew Crawford has written insightfully about modern offices and modes of work. The typical Big Four office is an example of what he called 'a place of moral education, where souls are formed and a particular ideal of what it means to be a good person is urged upon us'. Casual clothes days are perilous: a hot zone of conflict between old paternalism and new managerialism.

# 8

# THE MOST AVERAGE GUYS IN THE ROOM

## Big Four professional values

### Not for sale

In his 1915 book *Of Human Bondage*, Somerset Maugham described the interior of a nineteenth-century accounting office: 'It was dark and very dingy. It was lit by a sky-light. There were three rows of desks in it and against them high stools. Over the chimney-piece was a dirty engraving of a prize fight.' The quality of furnishings conveyed status. At Price Waterhouse's offices, for example, partners had ornate fireplaces, mahogany desks and Turkish carpets. Clerks warranted none of these luxuries.

Viewed through modern eyes, the daily routines of nineteenth-century accounting firms look like quaint antiques. At the start of each day, commissionaires sharpened pencils, changed nibs and restocked pins and paperclips. Porters served bread and biscuits for afternoon tea. Auditors working in the field were expected to wear a top hat and either a tailcoat or a frockcoat. Bowler hats and short coats were acceptable for clerks in the office. In Cooper Brothers' early years, there was a clear division between partners and staff. After work, the latter would enjoy 'smoke concerts' at the local pub. The highlights of the concerts were irreverent songs about the foibles of the partners.

In that era, accounting services were delivered very much at the 'human scale'. Personal relationships were as important as personal judgement and individual decisions. To regulate the conduct of practitioners, the profession relied on shared values of prudence, respect, honesty, probity, collegiality, meritocracy, courtesy, humility, independence, objectivity, self-restraint and what Mark Stevens called, in *The Big Six*, 'a disdain for the trappings of commercial businesses'. The firms were defined by what they didn't do as much as by what they did. Ethics were inculcated slowly, through hands-on experience, and through such shared institutional traditions as Protestantism, Quakerism and Freemasonry. Accountants were for hire, but not for sale.

A source of pride, the firms' professional values guided the nature of the work they did and the conditions of their staff's employment. In the journal *Accounting Horizons*, Stephen A. Zeff explained how it all worked. As late as the 1960s, partners were assured, 'except in rare instances of substandard performance', of tenure till retirement. 'If a partner secured a new client, he was praised, but the rewards doled out to partners recognized the quality of audit service to one's clients.' If a partner stood up to a client over questionable accounting practices, the partner could expect to be backed by the partnership 'with its full resources'. Having made partner, an accountant would typically not leave to take up a role at a rival firm or in another industry. Partnership was seen as 'the pinnacle of one's career'.

## Role models

Inevitably, of course, much of this had to join the ban on advertising in the wastepaper basket of Big Four history. Just as they gathered advisory methodologies from all over the place, so too the large accounting firms would pluck cultural elements from many different fields – not just the law and the church, but also universities, think tanks, fast-food outlets and call centres. The Rust Belt, Madison Avenue, the City of London, the Admiralty. Wall Street, Whitehall, the West Wing. In the latter decades of the twentieth century, new values of ambition, commercialism and compromise would permeate the profession as thoroughly as the trust falls, accent walls and breakout spaces of Silicon Valley infiltrated the Big Four offices.

Acknowledging accountancy's tensions between public spirit and commercial drive, and between modesty and showiness, Harvard Business School professor David Maister made, in the 1990s and 2000s, a series of pleas for accountants to reconnect with their humble roots. Maister criticised the trend of Big Four mergers and appealed for a return to the old days of personability and human-sized relationships. He argued that the ideal firm consisted of 'effectively functioning, small-scale practice groups'. Echoing the advice of Giovanni de Medici – to avoid being 'puffed up with pride', and to 'speak not as though giving advice, but rather discuss matters with gentle and kindly reasoning' – Maister nominated an unlikely character as the ideal model of the professional adviser: Peter Falk's illustrious TV detective, Lieutenant Columbo.

Columbo's investigative approach is all about the subordination of ego. He wears a rumpled coat, smokes cheap cigars and drives an old Peugeot – even worse than Alex's Skyline. When he knows the solution – and he knows the solution to every crime – he wears this knowledge quietly and humbly. According to Maister, all accountants and consultants could learn a great deal from Columbo's example.

As well as lancing the egotism and arrogance of senior accountants, Maister's analogy is a polemic against Big Four standardisation and commoditisation. Columbo's approach is 'customized, one-off, situational'. How does he make criminals drop their guard? Falk's detective uses 'gut-feel and instinct' instead of official police methodology.

Though amusing and fascinating, the analogy suffers from fundamental problems. One is that it depends on the client adopting the role of murderer. (Most metaphors of the accountant–client relationship are drawn instead from the fields of seduction and romantic love, and are expressed with words like *flirtation*, *wooing* and *consummation*.) More importantly, the analogy is inconsistent with the reality of contemporary partnerism. As a group, modern-day accountants have largely ignored Maister's appeal and Columbo's example.

## Accountants turn tougher

In the battle against traditional values, commercialism has come out on top. As is clear from the plethora of audit and advisory controversies and extinction-level events, the principles of professional probity and independence have been tested again and again. But another of the professional values, self-restraint, proved to be the most difficult to preserve, as the accounting firms rushed headlong into spectacular expansion.

Under the headline 'Accountants Turn Tougher', a 1969 *Business Week* article announced the end of self-restraint: "'Some firms," says an unnamed senior partner of a big New York accounting firm, "say they draw the line against consulting that involves them in management decision making. But don't let anybody fool you. We take on any job."'

In advance of Hewlett-Packard's 1978 audit, ten accounting firms wrote asking to be given the engagement. In October 1980, at the annual meeting of the American Institute of Certified Public Accountants (AICPA), outgoing board chairman William Gregory remarked:

It seems that the effects of the phenomenal growth in the profession and competitive pressures have created in some CPAs attitudes that are intensely commercial and nearly devoid of the high-principled conduct that we have come to expect of a true professional. It is sad that we seem to have become a breed of

highly skilled technicians and businessmen, but have subordi-
nated courtesy, mutual respect, self-restraint, and fairness for a
quest for firm growth and a preoccupation with the bottom line.

The professional services climate had changed for good. In 1984 the
senior partner at Touche Ross said the big firms were reluctant to lose
a client over a matter of principle. The following year, J. Michael Cook,
chairman of Deloitte, reportedly remarked: 'Five years ago if a client of
another firm came to me and complained about the service, I'd immediately warn the other firm's chief executive ... Today I try to take away
his client.'

By 2003, according to Stephen Zeff, accountancy had all the hallmarks of an industry rather than a profession. Those hallmarks
included 'cut-throat competition, low-balling, cheap advertising, and
open solicitation by one CPA of another CPA's clients'. The rush to
commercialism made the accounting firms much bigger and more
profitable. But it also made their staff more susceptible to flexibility and
compromise when faced with awkward requests from clients. Rather
than hold companies to account, accountants looked for ways to say
yes. Zeff described how, in the 1980s, partners would huddle with technicians to find a way through:

> ... perhaps restructuring a major vehicle, reconfiguring a transac-
> tion, or straining to rationalize the application of a suitable
> analogy – to enable the firm to approve the accounting treatment
> sought by the client. The 'accommodation' or 'negotiation' mental-
> ity fostered by this important shift in focus may have led many
> audit partners to incline toward compromise rather than invoke
> their principles even in routine discussions with clients.

The same anxious huddles can be seen in any Big Four office today. As
the commercial focus intensified, senior partners noticed the tension

between the firms' old strategies and new imperatives. Some partners were eager to break out of the professional constraints altogether. In 1985 Ralph Walters of Touche Ross captured the dilemma:

> The major firms are on a growth treadmill that inevitably will stop, but each manager is determined to keep it moving ever faster during his regime. This has required diversification into many 'information-based' services. The aggregate effect of these diversifications is to change the balance of the professional mindset – moving farther from an audit mentality and toward a consulting mentality. The diversified service draws the firms increasingly into competition with other disciplines that have few or no professional/ competitive constraints, and our traditional professional standards of conduct are a competitive handicap.

## Are you my auditor?

Sneath, Wyon, Whinney and the Waterhouses would never have regarded their professional values as a 'competitive handicap'. Central to Walters' dilemma is the collision between audit and advisory, a conflict that roils at the heart of the cultural shift in accountancy. The growth of management consulting changed the role and focus of auditors and other professionals. Not only were they to check their clients' books, now they were also to look for opportunities to sell consulting services.

In 1984 Paul Bloom advised professional services firms on how they could convert 'doers' into 'sellers'. Traditionally, according to Bloom, the job of selling in professional services organisations had largely fallen to the handful of senior people who exhibited an interest and a flair for it: these were the 'finders'. In contrast, 'project management and technical tasks have been left to others ("minders" and "grinders"). But increasingly, these organizations are finding it necessary to get broader participation in selling. Clients and patients generally prefer to be courted by the persons who actually perform the services.'

Mark Stevens put this more bluntly, claiming that all the major accounting firms employed gun salesmen but were chary about mentioning their expertise. Why? 'Simply because it is deemed unprofessional for CPAs to wind up sales robots and send them off, smiles flashing to pitch accounts.'

For all personnel – not just the 'sales robots' – success at selling came to mean success as a Big Four employee. Several national practices adopted the McKinsey '8–4–2' approach. Under that approach, staff at all levels are accountable for targeted levels of sales, billable time and 'business development'. Specifically, they are expected to be on at least two active assignments, and to have at least four well-advanced proposals in train, and to have at least eight opportunity leads. These expectations are in marked contrast to the early days of Price Waterhouse, in which it was not unusual for a partner to have only one major engagement on the go at any one time.

Outside observers saw the imperatives of corporations and commerce replacing those of professionalism and the public interest. Clients, too, noticed the change. In 2002 Ianthe Dugan wrote in the *Wall Street Journal* about C. Anthony Rider, an audit Lifer at EY's Buffalo office. As a Big Four partner on a US$300,000 salary, Rider found himself at the sharp end of the new emphasis on selling and 'commercial outcomes'. EY gave him a US$3-million sales growth target, and put him and his fellow partners through training on how to cross-sell legal, structural and technological advice, as well as advice on insurance, financial planning and mergers and acquisitions – in fact, in Rider's words, 'anything under the sun'.

When Rider took his new approach into the field, a bemused client asked him, 'Are you my auditor or a salesperson?' Like many longstanding partners, Rider struggled with the new focus, or rather the new lack of focus. He did not achieve the sales target. First his salary was cut by 10 per cent, then he was let go. For the generation of consultants who grew up with 8–4–2, the historical origins of the Big Four – and the old professional values – are as alien as top hats and inkpots and frockcoats.

## Bulge bracket

As the old values have fallen away, the large accounting firms have looked to other industries as sources of commercial values to emulate. Prominent among those industries is the much freer-wheeling world of bulge-bracket investment banking – a world of steroidal commercialism that is the polar opposite of Quakerism and Lieutenant Columbo and the humble imprecations of Giovanni de Medici.

The history of investment banking has many parallels with the history of the Big Four. Firms in both sectors trace their origins back to the same innovations and mercantile partnerships of the late middle ages and the Renaissance, and similarly sized nineteenth-century professional practices. Firms such as Morgan Stanley and Merrill Lynch, for example, came from similar predecessors and faced similar challenges in the transition from gentlemanliness to rampant commerciality. Along that journey, investment banks have been implicated in similar scandals and disasters to those of the Big Four – sometimes the very same. The trajectories of the two universes, though, are far from parallel.

If leading accounting and audit partners were 'well paid … but not wealthy', successful investment bankers were very well paid indeed – and very wealthy. In the 1980s and '90s, Big Four partners routinely rubbed shoulders with investment bankers: they worked on the same transactions (for much lower fees) and drank at the same clubs, pubs and bars. Bankers are generously remunerated – often too generously – because they take colossal risks in a high-stakes game. The story of the

Big Four over the past four decades has been one of rising stakes: bigger offices, bigger engagements, more staff, greater risks. It is only natural that Big Four personnel have looked enviously at the bankers' salaries and bonuses and lifestyles, and imagined what life on the other side might be like.

The Big Four have borrowed more than 'living wills' from banking. Partners and staff in some divisions and offices have adopted investment banking–style titles, calling senior managers 'associate directors' and senior partners 'vice-presidents'. Within the Big Four, some service lines have come close to replicating the investment banking culture. Big Four corporate finance practices – with their compulsory ties, cufflinks and conceit – are a conspicuous example. From these and other divisions, some Big Four staff have jumped from pseudo-banking into the real thing. Big Four personnel moving into investment banks have always seen this as a promotion. Personnel going the other way have always had to endure jokes about raising the average IQ of both industries.

In emulating the ethos and methods of investment banking, some accountants picked up the worst aspects of banking culture: strippers in the office, cocaine after work and so on. The emulation, though, could only ever be half-done. The Big Four manage risks that are an order of magnitude smaller. The accounting firms lack the bankers' capital resources, working hours, analytical horsepower and commercial permission. The Big Four can only ever support a medium-octane culture. The strippers will always be less beautiful, the cocaine less pure.

## Maestros

The first modern accountants had trained in Florentine abacus schools, English grammar and Quaker schools, or the Dutch merchant schools of Rotterdam, Delft and Bergen op Zoom. Before the 1950s, there were few university graduates in the Big Four. Even today, top-ranking

students from well-known universities tend not to undertake vocational first degrees, and tend not to join accounting firms.

In the nineteenth century, employment in accounting firms was
modelled on that at other professional practices, such as law firms. In
place of university qualifications, junior staff completed articled clerk-
ships before advancing up the rungs of seniority. The great majority of
the early partners of Price Waterhouse – men such as Fowler, Halsey,
Sneath and Wyon – were trained within the firm and rose up the ranks.
None of them, except Edwin Waterhouse, arrived equipped with a university qualification. Waterhouse had studied at the middle-class
University College and left with what Edgar Jones called a 'good
second-class BA degree'.

The practice of 'growing their own' continued to such an extent
that, in 1995, Ian Brindle could call 'promotion from within' one of the
defining features of the Price Waterhouse culture. According to
Brindle, the other thing that defined the culture was the firm's lack of
experience with large-scale mergers: 'unlike most of our competitors,
we have grown internally without resort to major mergers'. Within
three short years, both features would cease to be part of the Price
Waterhouse culture.

Even in 1995, things were changing at Price Waterhouse.
Approximately half the partners and managers in the firm's UK tax
practice had joined from other organisations. Lateral hires were also
becoming important in management consultancy and, increasingly, in
audit. Other firms followed suit. 'By the 1990s,' Stephen A. Zeff wrote,
'non-CPAs were well represented in the top management of the Big 6.'

Most lateral hires have come from other accounting firms or from
nearby disciplines such as economics and finance. Some, though, have
come from far away indeed. Steve Samek, the US head of operations at
Arthur Andersen, hired a violinist so his auditors could better think of
themselves as 'maestros'. In December 2016 Russel Howcroft took on a
new senior role at PwC in Australia: 'Chief Creative Officer'. Howcroft's

background is in advertising and television. The scope of his new role includes advising senior marketing executives on brand strategy. Other Big Four offices have also appointed colourful non-accountants to senior roles. Deloitte's Australian innovation unit hired people with experience in IT, academia and circuses. Creativity in accounting used to be a bad thing.

The firms' creative aspirations now feature prominently in their corporate communications, and especially in their graduate recruitment collateral. PwC's 2017 recruiters, for example, trumpeted the chance to experience 'flexibility, creative work, new markets [and] innovative solutions' in 'a place where professional rigour plays with creativity in a fluid, fast-paced environment'.

The great majority of recruits, though, still follow more or less the old pathways through vocational accounting and commerce qualifications into graduate CPA programs. At a fundamental level, the firms are resistant to professional diversity, which poses a devil's dilemma for them. Appointing non-accountants to lead the firms into a non-accounting future promises freshness and innovation, but risks estrangement from their core businesses. In branching out, they risk losing sight of their trunks and their roots.

## Pigeons

There is also a disconnect between the creative rhetoric and the reality of daily life for juniors in the Big Four. Checking accounts. Testing controls. Collating data. Counting regulations. Transcribing interviews. Spending hour after hour in the arid uplands of Planet PowerPoint, Planet Word and Planet Excel. Only people of a certain disposition can endure all this for any length of time. This is how one Big Four manager described her experience:

> I was stuck in a *Dilbert*-esque nightmare. Just one example. I had
> to fill in a form for my personal development plan. The field where

I had to write my 'personal vision' permitted a total of twenty characters. My vision was too big. And I felt as though I was the one in the wrong.

Another wrote:

Working in the Big 4 is bureaucratic, even more so than in banking or government. In my Big 4 firm there are systems and targets for time recording, resource management, risk management, realisation reporting, utilisation reporting, utilisation forecasting, charge rates, engagement pricing, margins, delegations, purchasing, expenses, subcontractors, contract review, contract negotiation, document creation, file creation, file review, report clearance, performance assessment, onboarding, offboarding, talent identification, talent development, professional development, consistency, diversity, mentoring, compliance, culture, conflicts, environmental sustainability, community engagement, client feedback, quality control, quality assurance, team planning, business planning, strategic planning. We have four different types of rubbish bin. The process for appointing subcontractors has five separate approval steps. As I said, it's very bureaucratic.

In her famous viral resignation email, the 'diversity hire' Glory criticised her colleagues for working late to impress partners. Partners, she wrote, should not be treated like royalty: 'They are average Joes like you and I, only their pockets are a little bigger.' Her job, she said, involved 'filling out useless workpapers that won't really benefit anybody'. Auditing was 'for people who truly don't have any other options'. Her hashtag responses to coaching and partner meetings included #soforced, #thatissoawkward, #fakeconvosforfakeauditors, #waytoointimate-formytaste and #noidontwanttogazeintoyoureyesatatablefortwo.

Author and leadership scholar Gerard Seijts famously defined 'culture' as what happens when no one is looking. In the Big Four, though, someone is always looking. The national practices use overt and covert means to watch their staff, including video cameras in the ceilings of open-plan offices. All project files are formally reviewed: staff whose files consistently fail review can be fined or fired. Emails and social media posts are monitored, and restrictions are placed on the use of Hotmail, Gmail, Dropbox, Twitter, Facebook and Instagram (but not, it seems, LinkedIn). Some sites are banned on work computers during working hours; some are inaccessible altogether. Staff working in such conditions feel as over-regulated as those first railway travellers.

There is method, though, in the madness. The fog of objectives and targets and metrics serves a strategic purpose. Perpetual time pressure elicits greater effort – much of it out-of-hours and unpaid – and forces prioritisation of that effort. Assessing staff performance across multiple dimensions and with shifting and uncertain weightings has a similar effect to the dangling, uncertain reward of partnership: these are tried and tested means to achieve intense effort across multiple dimensions of action, including work output, organisational loyalty and adherence to firm values. The same impacts have been shown in psychological experiments with pigeons. When rewards are fixed and predictable, pigeons shirk effort, doing only the required minimum. But when the rewards are random and probabilistic, the pigeons work their hearts out.

## Gamesmanship

It is no surprise that the staff at Cooper Brothers sang at 'smoke concerts' about the foibles of their partners. In the world of leverage and the partner track, the everyday existence of Big Four employees is defined and oriented in relation to partners.

Competition among staff for entry to the partner track has long been an explicit goal of the partnership. Edgar Jones has written of how, at Price Waterhouse in the late 1960s, around one in two professional staff in the US practice aspired to become partner, but only nine in 100 graduate recruits could expect to progress to that level – a progression that would take twelve years to achieve. Along the journey, some staff relished the competition, while others found it merely tiring. The partnership, though, depended on a sufficiently high proportion of staff believing the partnership goal was attainable, and desirable.

The fine details of that goal were often mysterious for staff on the partner track. What starting salary could a new partner expect to earn? How did the points system work? What sales target would be set? How much would the new partner have to stump up for working capital and insurance? For the senior partners who orchestrate this game, all the uncertainties are tactical, just as the staff performance metrics are. The partner track is a rich ground for gamesmanship.

Dangling the prospect of imminent partnership in front of high-performing senior accountants is one more mainstay of the professional services model. Mark Stevens recorded an episode in which, for one accountant, the dangling went too far. The accountant was utterly absorbed in the partner track, at the expense of his marriage, his family life and his mental health. The prize of partnership was offered many times. On every occasion, though, it was snatched away. When that happened once too often, the accountant stopped hearing what his managers were saying, and 'just saw their mouths moving':

> I realized what they were doing. That it was all a sham, a scheme designed to make me work even harder. It wasn't enough that my personal life was near ruin and that I was on the brink of exhaustion. By dangling the carrot very close and then pulling it away, they hoped to wring a bit more out of me. In an instant, I saw through it all.

The following day, the accountant resigned. 'What frightens me,' he told Stevens, 'is that if I'd been made a partner, I'd have probably been sucked in for life.' Strategic dangling and snatching continues to be an everyday aspect of working in the Big Four.

# PART III

# The Difficulties of Adulthood

In this part we explore the deep-seated challenges that have confronted the Big Four in their maturity. We examine the litany of costly Big Four calamities, and identify some recurring causes: rule breaches; process failures; undetected frauds; apparent underinvestment in auditing effort; and fundamental conflicts between Big Four service lines – such as between audit and advisory – that have helped erode the brand value of auditing.

In this context, the 'audit expectation gap' has emerged as a battleground for the Big Four. Skirmishes on that battleground relate to whether auditors can be expected to detect fraud, and whether a clear audit opinion can be taken to mean that the audited business is likely to survive as a 'going concern'. We survey these skirmishes, along with efforts by auditors to protect themselves – such as by limiting their liability. The concept of 'audit quality' is an elusive one, and it seems that there are intrinsic problems that affect the reliability of audit opinions. In taxation services, too, there are problems that run just as deep, and consequences that are at least as severe. In Chapter 11 we consider Big Four tax disasters, and how a new ethic of disclosure is making old models of tax avoidance unviable.

We conclude by examining the rich suite of challenges facing the Big Four in China – challenges that highlight tensions in the Big Four businesses, and that point to a troublesome future.

# 9

# UNQUALIFIED

## Auditing as the foundation of the Big Four brands

### A point of distinction

All the Big Four provide audit and advisory services, and in all the firms there are significant differences across these two service lines with respect to: staff qualifications and experience, job sizes, charge rates, delivery timelines and contract types. Compared to advisory, auditing is a higher-cost, lower-margin business with different economics and a different culture. Audit and advisory practices occupy separate divisions within the Big Four firms, and are often physically separate too. A Big Four advisor can go a long time without even seeing a Big Four auditor, and vice versa. When young staff speak of Big Four work as 'indentured labour', they are more than likely speaking of audit work. The daily routine of a junior auditor is dull and repetitive – so much so that the Big Four seldom highlight audit in their corporate communications and marketing to graduates. Inside the firms, auditing is deprecated and its practitioners have low status. Most graduates view a stint in auditing as a stepping-stone towards something else. Anything else.

(The Big Four websites contain hundreds of pages of information, but visitors to those sites might be forgiven for wondering what line of business the firms are actually in. None of the pages sets out clearly and succinctly what the firms actually do. There is method in this. The firms would rather keep their powder dry and their options open. In principle, there are very few projects and very few fields in which the Big Four – as providers of 'strategic solutions' – would rule out any kind of involvement.)

Despite the rise of advisory, auditing remains a major source of revenue for the Big Four. And despite its low margins and low status, it is a profitable business line, thanks to the Big Four's de facto monopoly concession on public company auditing. It is also a business line that generates much more than revenue. Auditing is a large part of what distinguishes the Big Four from other advisory firms. Why has the American Academy of Motion Picture Arts and Sciences engaged PwC for so many years to tally the Oscars votes? Because the major accounting firms' reputations for probity and integrity largely survived their embrace of commercialism and diversification. To the extent that the Big Four brands still connote strong corporate values, those connotations depend for the most part on auditing.

## Imperilled

The Big Four have attempted to transfer their brand equity in audit and general accounting to other fields and services, such as strategy, IT consulting and real-estate advisory. This has certainly worked: clients looking for advice feel safe appointing auditors. Sprinkled all over with the magic dust of auditing, the firms have had no difficulty in winning advisory work. There are several ways, though, in which these service lines can conflict, and the expansion into advisory can heighten risk and weaken the firms' brands.

When, for example, non-auditors inside the Big Four provide audit-style services (such as evaluations, internal reviews, probity services and policy studies), clients can misperceive these products as providing audit-level assurance, and as having other attributes of traditional corporate audits. Methodologically, the boundaries between types of auditing (such as between financial auditing and performance auditing), and between auditing and evaluation, depend on hair-splitting distinctions that can easily become blurred or lost altogether. Moreover, service line distinctions that are stark within the firms are often invisible to outsiders, who just see the Big Four brand. Clients who treat non-audits as providing audit-style assurance, though, are on a slippery slope. Performing risky tricks above a false safety net is even worse than the 'moral hazard' problem of doing such tricks with a net. The danger is equally severe for the Big Four firms themselves. For this and other reasons, advisory work can dilute the firms' reputations for quality and probity at least as much as it can strengthen them.

The brand dilution is even stronger in the field of taxation advice. Several important types of tax services tend to destroy brand value. Helping high-wealth individuals and multinational corporations shift income or hide money abroad erodes rather than enhances the firms' reputations for probity.[12]

Beyond the dilutive effect of offering other services, the Big Four have done many things to weaken the auditing brand. Repeated scandals, for example, have chipped – and sometimes hacked – away at the brand's value. Over the past century or so, the firms have made proportionally smaller investments in sector-specific expertise. Audits have become more generic and standardised, and their quality has declined. Along with the rise of advisory, the imperilment of auditing is one of the accountancy megatrends of the past hundred years. How did we get here?

## The curious origins of modern auditing

Every year or so, scholars turn up earlier and more obscure episodes in the history of auditing. This has become something of an academic

12  Big Four taxation advice and services are the subject of Chapter 11.

game. Among the evidence so far unearthed, there is confirmation that public auditors operated in ancient Babylon, Mesopotamia, Egypt, Greece, Persia, Rome and – around 1000 BCE, during the Western Zhou Dynasty – China. The eleventh-century Domesday Book was founded on a system of auditing in which royal audits were seen to be on a par with 'the final reckoning of God', as no one could escape them. As we've already seen, communities in thirteenth-century England chose 'awdytours' to keep public bookkeepers honest. These early precedents were the basis for state audit institutions, which arose in western Europe at a surprisingly early date. The UK National Audit Office, for example, dates its first manifestation to 1314; the French Cour des Comptes to 1318; and the Dutch Algemene Rekenkamer to 1386.

The Medici Bank was built on a careful system of auditing. Each year, trusted staff checked and questioned every transaction, line by line. In 1467, for example, Angelo Tani was sent to review the books of the bank's London office, and specifically 'to pick out any dubious or past due accounts'. Isabella, Queen of Castile, sent an auditor with Christopher Columbus to ensure he accounted properly for the profits from his voyages to the West Indies. The principal shareholders of the Dutch East India Company were entitled to appoint auditors (*rekening-opnemers*) to scrutinise the company's annual accounts. Josiah Wedgwood's intricate systems of cost accounting enabled him to detect his head clerk's embezzlement. The upshot of all this history is an incontrovertible conclusion: auditing has been around for a long time, and encompasses a diverse set of practices, principles and intentions.

## Safety

In Luca Pacioli's very modern advice on auditing, he conceived of it as a process of checking financial records for errors. That conception was reflected in the first modern company legislation. The *Joint Stock Companies Act* of 1844 established a system whereby registered companies had to submit audited balance sheets; auditors, elected by shareholders, were required to scrutinise the accounts and report on them to the general meetings. The 1845 *Companies Clauses Act* codified the requirements for audits and auditors. The two acts shaped audit practices in Europe and America, and ultimately around the world.

In the United States, company audits were not compulsory before the 1930s. And yet by 1926 more than 90 per cent of industrial companies on the New York Stock Exchange were audited. The *Securities Act* of 1933 and the *Securities Exchange Act* of 1934 cemented that reality by requiring all new and continuing registrants to have their financial statements audited by an independent CPA. The new legislation was made urgent by a series of accounting scandals, most notably the 'Kreuger crash' of 1932.

The Bernie Madoff of his time, Ivan Kreuger made several fortunes through the manufacture and sale of safety matches. Though outwardly respectable, Kreuger perpetrated many of the old railway industry tricks: paying dividends from capital, abusing monopoly power, and relying on new investors to compensate old ones. Such practices were anything but safe. At bottom, Kreuger's business empire was a Ponzi scheme, and in due course it collapsed in spectacular fashion. The authors of the *Securities Act* and the *Securities Exchange Act* hoped this kind of scandal could never happen again. Instead, their legacy was a series of accounting and audit disasters, and a cycle of regulatory failure.

## A costly flood

In ancient Athens, slaves were regarded as the best auditors – because they could be tortured if they got it wrong. Now, failed auditors endure different modes of torture. Special inquiries. Court-appointed investigators. Congressional committees. Imprisonment with Bernie Madoff. (A television program co-produced by China's peak professional accounting body asked, 'Do you want to become a millionaire?

Please come to a partnership accounting firm, because it is heaven. Do you want to become bankrupt and sent to jail and ask your wife to bring you meals? Please come to a partnership accounting firm, because it is a hell.')

All the Big Four have approved financial statements that were later revealed to be materially incorrect. All four firms have endured audit calamities, just as their principal predecessors did. To take Price Waterhouse as an example, the Royal Mail Case of 1931 was a near disaster that attracted much public attention. Price Waterhouse partner H.J. Morland was charged under the *Larceny Act* for approving 'misleading' accounts at Britain's largest shipping business. Morland's defence lawyer remarked that his client was 'a devotedly religious man ... convinced that a divine interference would necessarily decide the issue'. After coolly enduring a vigorous cross-examination, Morland told Nicholas Waterhouse: 'Well, they treated Christ much worse for much less so why should I bother.'

In the Rolls Razor Case of 1965, Price Waterhouse was again alleged to have signed misleading accounts. The auditors had failed to detect stock falsification and other instances of accounting fraud. A claim by the liquidator against Price Waterhouse was settled out of court. The firm made a statement in the hope of minimising reputational damage: 'The auditors have at all times strenuously denied the allegations of liability and the settlement has been made simply to avoid the extremely lengthy and expensive enquiries which would have had to take place if the matter had gone to court.'

In subsequent years, as more and more large accounting firms found themselves in legal trouble, such statements would be issued again and again. With their deepish pockets and professional indemnity insurance, auditors were a favoured target for parties seeking damages. For many of the court cases, the causes of the trouble would be the same. Auditors failing to detect accounting errors or embezzlement or imminent insolvency. Auditors implicated in misaccounting or outright fraud. Investors, regulators and clients in hot pursuit. And a cycle of audit failings leading to new laws and new actions by regulators.

By the 1990s, as the legal settlements mounted, auditing was proving to be both risky and expensive. In 1992, for example, Coopers & Lybrand paid $92 million to settle a suit brought by investors in disk-drive maker MiniScribe. Later the same decade, Coopers made expensive payouts after settling claims regarding Robert Maxwell's failed media empire and the bankrupt Phar-Mor pharmacies. A drawn-out battle over Price Waterhouse's audit of the Bank of Credit and Commerce International ended in 1995 with a large payout. These and other lawsuits caused the firms' insurance costs to soar; 'many insurers refused to even cover the auditing practices of the Big 6 firms, forcing Coopers & Lybrand and Price Waterhouse to set aside money to cover themselves'.

## Enron, Sarbox and Peek-a-boo

The end of Enron was the defining corporate collapse of the early twenty-first century. The company was consumed by a fraud that ran so deep and so wide it was almost indistinguishable from Enron's ordinary activities. After famously shredding documents related to its audit work, Arthur Andersen was convicted in June 2002 of criminal complicity and felonious obstruction of justice. Under Securities and Exchange Commission rules, the firm could no longer conduct audits. It surrendered its CPA licenses and right to practise. Stripped of these tickets to trade, the firm had no future.[13] In the subsequent case of Arthur Andersen LLP v. United States, the Supreme Court would

13  Having split off in the nick of time, Andersen Consulting survived under the new brand name of Accenture.

reverse Andersen's conviction, finding that in the first trial there had been flaws in the jury instructions: the judge had failed to tell the jury it had to find proof that Andersen knew its actions had broken the law. This judgement, though, came too late for Arthur Andersen and its tens of thousands of employees.

The downfall of Enron – and of WorldCom and Waste Management and others – led to a regulatory response that largely focused on the role of the auditor. In the United States, the primary response came in the form of the *Sarbanes-Oxley Act* (known as 'Sarbox'), which was enacted in July 2002. Arthur Andersen had been Enron's adviser as well as auditor. Lawmakers believed the desire to win non-audit business had compromised Andersen's ability to assess Enron's financial statements independently. This belief led to a tightening of the range of non-audit services that the Big Four could sell their audit clients. Decisions about service line offerings would no longer be left largely to the audit firms' own judgement.

Sarbox also brought about major shifts in the practice of auditing. One controversial part was Section 404, which required the external auditor to report on the adequacy of the auditee's internal controls, a report that takes enormous effort to prepare. Another way Sarbox changed auditing practice was through the creation of the Public Company Accounting Oversight Board (PCAOB), a non-profit corporation charged with ensuring the relevance of audit standards and the quality of audits. Known among auditors as 'Peek-a-boo', the PCAOB superseded the Audit Standards Board of the AICPA.

Peek-a-boo's charter is a strong one. Empowered to 'oversee the audit of public companies ... in order to protect the interests of investors and further the public interest in the preparation of informative, accurate, and independent audit reports', it can inflict multi-million-dollar fines on auditors who don't follow the rules. Soon after its establishment, the agency was making trouble for the accounting firms. In August 2008, for example, it reported ten instances in which KPMG had not met the agency's expectations of audit conduct. The failures were diverse and included not confirming valuations and client assertions, and overlooking departures from the Generally Accepted Accounting Principles. Peek-a-boo's 2012 review of audit work by PwC found significant deficiencies in twenty-one of fifty-two audits; and in 2013 in nineteen of fifty-nine audits. KPMG's deficiency rate in that year was 46 per cent. There were repeated instances in which the firm 'had not obtained sufficient evidence to support its audit opinions or to demonstrate it had tested internal controls effectively'.

In 2015 Peek-a-boo inspected seventy-five firms, covering portions of 115 audits and 114 related attestation engagements. This was the first annual cycle in which all audits and related attestation engagements were required to be performed in accordance with PCAOB standards and amended *Exchange Act* Rule 17a-5. The agency continued to detect a high rate of deficiencies (77 per cent of the audits and 55 per cent of the attestation engagements). Peek-a-boo expressed its concern about 'the nature and consistently high number of deficiencies across the firms and the audits covered by the inspections':

> Many of these deficiencies continue to be similar in nature to those described in previous reports and relate to the fundamentals of auditing that are not necessarily dependent on whether the audit was performed under generally accepted auditing standards or PCAOB standards. Many of the inspected firms need to significantly improve their audit work to meet the requirements of the professional standards and SEC and PCAOB rules.

For the Big Four, who've long resisted being 'mere automata', and who've held tightly to their commercial independence, this heightened scrutiny is very annoying. The possibility of monetary consequences, though, has succeeded in catching the auditors' attention. Joe Ucuzoglu, chairman and CEO of Deloitte in the United States, told *The Economist* in 2014 that the PCAOB 'is what's on the mind of the everyday auditor today. Their work is going to have to stand up to inspection scrutiny. High-quality work is rewarded, but lapses can have severe consequences for their compensation.'

## Auditors and the 2008 financial crisis

The years since Enron's collapse saw a string of similar-sized calamities. During the 2008 financial crisis, for example, auditors were enmeshed in collapses of major banks and financial services corporations. All the Big Four had clients that collapsed or required bailing out or nationalisation. The firms' names were linked to some of the most spectacular failures. Deloitte had audited Bear Stearns and Fannie Mae. KPMG had audited Citigroup. PwC had audited American International Group and Goldman Sachs. EY had audited Lehman Brothers.

Lehman, Bear Sterns and Northern Rock all received unqualified audit opinions before their collapse. Thornburg Mortgage was America's second-largest independent mortgage provider; KPMG delivered an unqualified audit opinion on 27 February 2008, then quickly backpedalled. Less than a week after issuing the opinion, KPMG stated that its audit reports for the preceding three years 'should no longer be relied upon'. These and other reports couldn't reassure owners and investors. Failed audits were so conspicuous that they became a key theme of the financial crisis and its legal aftermath.

Formerly a KPMG partner, Paul Russell Moore became head of Group Regulatory Risk at Halifax Bank of Scotland (HBOS) at a time when the bank was growing fast and cultivating a rabidly commercial culture. Moore raised concerns with senior management about the bank's risk profile and sales strategies, including the awarding of loans to people with no capacity to service them. In 2005 the bank's auditors, KPMG, investigated Moore's concerns, but concluded that HBOS had appropriate risk controls in place. Three years later, during the financial crisis, HBOS got into very serious trouble, prompting a government rescue and a merger with Lloyds TSB to form the Lloyds Banking Group.

In another incident, this time involving KPMG in America, two of the firm's auditors were suspended for overlooking loan-loss reserves at failed Nebraska-based bank TierOne, which had collapsed in 2010. After an appeal, the Securities and Exchange Commission imposed even stronger penalties on the auditors. The commission concluded that their conduct was 'egregious, highly unreasonable and conclusively demonstrates that they lack competence to practice'. 'Respondents have failed to acknowledge the wrongful nature of their conduct or provide assurances against future violations,' it continued. 'Taken together, these facts lead us to conclude that there is a risk that respondents will commit future violations.'

## Auditors' role in the collapse of Lehman Brothers

Lehman Brothers was perhaps the most disturbing casualty of the crisis. EY audited Lehman for seven years to 2007. In the decade before its collapse, Lehman had paid EY US$185 million in fees. In the aftermath of the crisis, a New York bankruptcy court commissioned a report from Anton R. Valukas into the demise of Lehman. Valukas was chairman of law firm Jenner & Block. His report, completed in 2010, ran to some 2200 pages. To prepare the report, more than seventy attorneys searched and sampled from three petabytes of data – around 350 billion pages, or 150 Libraries of Congress.

Lehman had engaged in an aggressive form of financial window-dressing known as 'Repo 105'. The company 'sold' assets worth tens of billions of dollars off its balance sheet at the end of each quarter and then 'bought' them back again shortly thereafter. In the interim, it used the proceeds to reduce other debts, thereby concealing its extreme leverage. Like Bear Stearns, Lehman had a leverage ratio of more than thirty to one, which meant that a drop of only 3.3 per cent in the value of the company's assets would destroy the entire value of its equity and make it insolvent. This spectacular leverage was dramatised in the 2011 J.C. Chandor film *Margin Call*.

The term *repo* in Repo 105 refers to the repurchase agreement, which legally obliged Lehman to buy back the assets that had been 'sold' in the scheme. The number refers to the level of collateralisation – 105 per cent – that Lehman argued allowed it to account for the transactions as though it had truly sold the assets. The applicable accounting standards were clear that collateralisation between 98 per cent and 102 per cent would not receive such accounting treatment. In a perversion of accounting principles, Lehman suggested that by going to 105 per cent, the repurchase obligation disappeared. This is analogous to assuming that you are less likely to pay off your mortgage when your house is worth more, which contradicts both economic and accounting logic.

Bob Herz, former chair of the FASB, said the text that Lehman relied upon was merely an example that described 'typical collateral arrangements in repurchase agreements' – an example that was not intended to create a 'bright-line' accounting rule, as Lehman claimed. Yet Valukas found EY had been aware of the Repo 105 practice and still gave Lehman a clean audit. Lehman's chairman and CEO, Richard Fuld, was also informed, via email, about the transactions. When the case reached court, his attorney claimed, lamely, that Fuld was unaware of the sleight of hand because he 'did not use a computer' except a BlackBerry, on which he couldn't open attachments.

Worse than being aware of Repo 105, EY was accused of directly facilitating it, and of thereby misleading investors and regulators. Due to its role in the collapse, the firm was dragged into court cases in New York, New Jersey and California. Andrew Cuomo, New York's attorney-general, brought a lawsuit accusing the firm of helping Lehman disguise its financial condition. Vowing to defend itself vigorously, EY said Lehman's financial statements were fairly presented in accordance with the Generally Accepted Accounting Principles, and that Lehman's bankruptcy 'was not caused by any accounting issues'. The court, though, heard damning evidence of audit failure.

The court transcripts make vivid reading. A Lehman whistleblower and a junior EY auditor had both red-flagged Repo 105, but their concerns were allegedly ignored. Lehman senior vice president Matthew Lee had told the auditors he believed the use of Repo 105 was improper. EY auditor Bharat K. Jain had emailed his manager, Jennifer Jackson, to query the reputational risk associated with the manoeuvre. But despite these concerns being raised with EY's 'engagement partner' on the Lehman account, EY allegedly failed to investigate the concerns adequately or to advise the audit committee. The court also heard evidence of a cosy relationship between EY and Lehman. During much of the period in which the questionable transactions occurred, two of Lehman's chief financial officers were former EY employees.

The outcomes of the cases proved costly for EY: a US$99-million settlement of a class action brought by Lehman investors, a US$10-million settlement in New York, various other fines and settlements, and untold reputational damage.

## After the crisis

A House of Lords committee looked at whether UK auditors had been sufficiently sceptical when auditing banks in the lead-up to the financial crisis. The Big Four were accused of turning a blind eye to the excesses and mismanagement of their clients. Even harsher accusations were made. When representatives of the Big Four appeared before the committee, Lord Lipsey was scathing:

> ... where your duty is to report to investors the true state of the company, you were giving a statement that was deliberately

designed to mislead markets and investors as to the true state of the banks. That seems to me to be a very strange thing for an auditor to do.

Detached, circular and otherworldly, the testimony of the Big Four gave Lord Lipsey an 'Alice in Wonderland feeling'. The Lords' final report concluded that: 'the complacency of bank auditors was a significant contributory factor [to the crisis]. Either they were culpably unaware of the mounting dangers, or, if they were aware of them, they equally culpably failed to alert the supervisory authority of their concerns'.

The 2008 collapse of Bernie Madoff's Ponzi scheme brought back memories of the Kreuger crash and added a dose of pure fraud to the financial crisis. EY, PwC and KPMG audited 'feeder' investment funds that had placed billions of dollars into the scheme. A class-action suit was filed, alleging that some of the auditors had breached their fiduciary duties. When the case reached court, the attempt to implicate the auditors was thrown out. After the crisis, though, the string of audit disasters continued.

India, 2009. Technology company Satyam admitted faking more than US$1 billion in cash on its balance sheet. China, 2010. Timber company Sino-Forest claimed to own forests that did not exist. After this fakery was exposed, the company lost over 95 per cent of its value. Spain, 2011. Bankia allegedly misstated its finances prior to its float. Ten months later, it was nationalised to prevent its collapse. Japan, 2011. Optical device maker Olympus revealed it had hidden billions of dollars in losses. United States, 2012. Hewlett-Packard had to write off most of its US$10.3-billion purchase of software company Autonomy, whose sales forecasts had allegedly been inflated. Britain, 2012. PwC was fined £1.4 million for wrongly reporting that JP Morgan Securities had complied with rules governing the segregation and protection of client funds. China and the United States, 2013. Deloitte was sued after the assets of ChinaCast, a Chinese education company, were transferred to another entity in a 'brazen looting' that Deloitte allegedly failed to detect. Britain, 2014. A disastrous investment in Tesco cost Warren Buffett US$750 million. The auditors mentioned 'suspect rebates' as warranting heightened scrutiny, 'but still gave a clean audit' of Tesco's 2013 financial statements. The United States, 2015. Singing River Health System sued KPMG over allegedly systemic audit errors and 'one of the largest reported adjustments in history'.

With respect to their scale and consequences, the audit failings during the financial crisis and subsequent years were at least as bad as those of 2002. Judged against this record, the post-Andersen reforms, and their centrepiece, the *Sarbanes-Oxley Act*, had failed.

# 10

# CLEAN

## The impairment of Big Four auditing

### Is it all too hard?

The complexity of modern corporations is often put forward as a principal cause of the rich tableau of audit failures. The Royal Mail case was an early example of auditors trying to come to grips with complexity. The enterprise in question consisted of a large and diverse group of international shipping and trading businesses. Multiple subsidiaries transacted with the parent company in multiple ways. The parent and its subsidiaries maintained a complex set of reserves. Complicated transfers between those reserves were ultimately what concealed Royal Mail's significant trading losses. Thanks to the company's structure of divisions and accounts, it was – in the words of Edgar Jones – 'virtually impossible' for an external assessor to judge the company's viability. In the legal aftermath of the scandal, the auditors' lawyers took Herculean steps to marshal the complexity; the seven volumes of colour-coded defence documents became famous in legal circles as the 'rainbow brief'.

In the twenty-first century, developments in derivatives, intellectual property, corporate structuring and corporate accounting have made businesses even more complex, and even more difficult to audit.

The Australian goldminer Sons of Gwalia is a case in point. In 2004 the company collapsed; the ensuing administration and court case painted a picture of auditors out of their depth. Ferrier Hodgson, the company's administrators, claimed that EY, as the auditor of Sons of Gwalia, had failed to get on top of the company's accounting for complex and specialised gold and dollar hedging contracts. In 2009 EY agreed to an A$125-million settlement relating to the company's collapse.

This was just one in a growing file of cases in which auditors seemed to have lost the battle against corporate convolution. Historian Jacob Soll in 2014 pictured auditors struggling to keep up with the 'ever-mutating, bacteria-like financial tools and tricks', such as options, futures and complex financing. 'By the sheer complexity and scale of their operations, banks, corporations, and government bodies have rendered themselves unauditable,' he wrote. 'How many accountants, really, would it take to truly audit Goldman Sachs, were this indeed a realistic task?'

Auditing standards, though, increasingly require auditors to master the complexity, as do the expectations of clients, investors and regulators. Arguably, these expectations are entirely reasonable. Other professions routinely handle stunning complexity. For doctors, lawyers, engineers and scientists, grappling with complex bodies, cases, machines and systems is an everyday responsibility, and an everyday occurrence. Accountants, too, have a long history of mastering complexity: recall the nineteenth-century railways, and especially the Railway Clearing House. The first modern auditors got on top of complexity by allocating senior staff to audits; by specialising in particular industries and enterprises; and by making large investments in understanding and sculpting how companies recorded and reported their activities. All this was congruent with the mission and status of accountants as protectors of the public interest.

Complexity alone, therefore, is not sufficient as an explanation of the accountants' recent troubles. Something else must be going on.

That something has a lot to do with how auditors work, the incentives and market forces they face, and the breadth and depth of their services. As shown by the 'rainbow brief', and by Anton Valukas's 2000-page Lehman report, understanding complexity is expensive in time, money and effort. Costly investments such as these are largely alien to today's leveraged, commercial approach to accountancy, in which firms minimise costs and maximise profits by sending out less experienced and less specialised juniors, and having them do as little as possible. The succession of audit failures can properly be traced to a clash of expectations.

## The expectation gap

Jim Peterson, a former lawyer for Arthur Andersen, argued that, under modern auditing standards, a clear audit opinion meant only that the financial information was 'more or less OK, in general, so far as we can tell, most of the time'. The accounting profession had so defined auditing that it was a job at which no one could ever fail. Over time, company audits had narrowed in scope and become more limited in their conclusions. Auditors increasingly sampled transactions and tested controls in limited ways. Findings and conclusions were heavily caveated.

What had not changed were the expectations of non-auditors about what audits involved and what they should achieve. Those non-auditors included customers, shareholders, regulators, legislators, financiers, insurers, stock exchanges and the courts. This expectation gap was wide, and widening. It persisted because not everyone believed auditors should be defining the nature and scope of auditing.

The idea of an expectation gap seems generic and universal. In principle, patients might expect doctors to cure all ills; clients might want lawyers to win every case. But a quick Google search of 'expectation gap' reveals that the idea is largely specific to auditing. In the main, other professions and industries do not suffer from the same kind of gap.[14] Furthermore, the Google search reveals that the expectation gap is something that mostly captivates auditors, not those troublesome non-auditors with their pesky expectations.

## Curb your enthusiasm

The expectation gap debate pivots on the definition of auditing. What constitutes an audit? What can it do? What is it *for*?

The word *audit* – from the Latin for 'to hear' – belongs in a fiduciary *Gestalt* alongside terms such as *facts, truth, trust, accountability* and *independence*. Many of these words have been used to define the scope and purpose of public company audits. Broadly, that purpose is to help owners, investors and managers improve corporate accountability and performance. Michael Power called auditing 'a trust engendering technology' that reassures investors and the public that companies and their managers are accountable and not corrupt. According to Francine McKenna, 'The public accounting firms and their hundreds of thousands of auditors should be an investor's first line of independent defence.' Frederick Whinney told the Birmingham Chartered Accountants Students Society in 1894 that the duty of an auditor was 'to ascertain whether figures were facts'. As commonly understood, a clean audit is a green light that a company's accounts have passed muster; the audited statements give a 'true and fair' account of the company's affairs.

For much of the modern era of auditing, public company auditors have sought to temper expectations regarding the level of assurance their auditing provides. Auditors have emphasised, for example, that they do not 'guarantee' that financial statements are correct; they

---

14  Professions such as medicine and law also lack the Big Four tendency to cultivate buzzwords.

merely provide an opinion about the statements' adherence to standards and whether or not they are materially misleading. In 'The Dozy Watchdogs', the editors of the *Economist* observed that modern American audits contained no opinion about accuracy, just a 'boilerplate one-page pass/fail report' that provided only 'reasonable assurance' that a company's statements presented fairly, in all material respects, its financial position in conformity with Generally Accepted Accounting Principles. According to Sir Michael Rake, who headed KPMG before becoming chairman of the UK telco BT Group, 'The auditor is the long stop on the cricket pitch, not the slip.' In the *Wall Street Journal*, Michael Rapoport gave his take on the role of auditors: 'Auditing isn't meant to stop companies from making dumb business moves – just to make sure those moves are properly disclosed.'

Yet the expectation gap persists. It is more glaring in two areas. First, should auditors warn investors about impending insolvency? Second, should auditors be expected to detect fraud against the auditee?

## A going concern

Auditors' duties regarding auditee viability are at the centre of an especially hot topic in accountancy and corporate governance. In the early 2000s the UK auditing standards attempted to make the position clear: '[The] auditor's procedures necessarily involve a consideration of the entity's ability to continue in operational existence for the foreseeable future. In turn that necessitates consideration of both the current and the possible future circumstances of the business and the environment in which it operates.' In May 2011, however, the Association of Chartered Certified Accountants put forward a much more limited definition of auditors' duty regarding 'going concern':

The auditors' responsibility as regards going concern does not, in fact, require them to give any guarantee that the company will survive for the foreseeable future. Auditors need only assess whether the going concern assumption is appropriate as a basis for preparing the current financial statements. They must consider whether any events or liabilities (contingent or otherwise) might threaten the company's solvency but the responsibility does not require them to make any assessment of the company's financial health beyond an assessment of the company's prospects in so far as they affect the chosen basis of reporting.

Reckless lending at the Bank of Ireland saw its share price fall by 99 per cent during the 2008 financial crisis. PwC was the bank's auditor. John McDonnell, who led PwC's audits of the bank in the years after the crisis, appeared before a committee of inquiry into the Irish banking crisis. 'An audit,' McDonnell told the committee, 'does not exist to provide general comment or opinion on a company's business model.'

> Financial statements portray the effects of past transactions or events. They're not intended to provide all the information that users need to make economic decisions. The aim of accounting standards is to faithfully represent past transactions or events in financial statements. Matters such as stability, capital adequacy and future prospects are outside the remit of accounting standards.

As a possible solution to this impasse, some participants have called for the expansion of audit reports. In 2014, for example, Bob Moritz, chair of PwC in the United States, conceded that such reports would be more useful if they encompassed a broader range of 'value drivers', meaning the assets and activities that determined whether a company would continue to operate profitably.

Yet this might be one area in which the auditors' lamentations regarding the expectation gap have some merit. Predicting bankruptcy requires skills and information well beyond those required to audit financial statements. The need for a going concern opinion derives from the reality that the accounting for various assets is obviously very different if a company is about to go under, taking the value of its brands and specialised assets with it. Some might have come to believe that failure to issue a going concern opinion can be viewed as a sign of corporate health. But any examination of the track record of going concern opinions should be enough to temper such views.

## A mixed record

Whether auditors have a responsibility to investigate and detect fraud is equally contentious, and has been for many years. In a famous judgement, Lord Justice Lopes remarked in 1896 that:

> An auditor is not bound to be a detective, or ... to approach his work with suspicion, or with a forgone conclusion that there is something wrong. He is a watchdog, not a bloodhound. He is justified in believing tried servants of the company in whom confidence is placed by the company. He is entitled to assume that they are honest and rely upon their representations, provided he takes reasonable care.

In light of the succession of corporate frauds and audit scandals, the Lord Justice's words seem remarkably naive. And yet they are part of a discourse that has remained highly influential in accountancy.

In the 1940s the drug wholesaler McKesson & Robbins was the victim of an elaborate embezzlement scheme perpetrated by a senior executive and his three brothers. The fraudsters had 'grossly inflated' the company's receivables and inventory. The auditor was Price Waterhouse; it did not detect the scheme, neither confirming the receivables nor verifying the inventory. The auditors could have rightly argued, though, that neither of these tests was required under contemporary audit standards.

Fraud detection sits naturally alongside probity and accountability in the audit *Gestalt*. And yet the Big Four actually have a poor record when it comes to detecting fraud inside their auditees. Why? Because the leveraged professional services model involves sending out junior and less experienced staff to do the work. Because auditors are typically not trained as investigators. Because financial auditing focuses on controls and systems, not transactions. Because auditors typically test controls and systems on a sampling basis. And because auditors are typically at an informational disadvantage: unlike insiders, they don't know where the bodies are buried.

For reasons such as these, the Big Four have overlooked some gigantic frauds. In 2007 KPMG Germany was investigated for ignoring 'questionable payments' in a bribery case involving Siemens. In 2009 EY agreed to pay US$109 million to shareholders and bondholders at HealthSouth Corp to settle an accounting scandal relating to fraudulently overstated earnings. An EY accountant testified that his firm had received by email a detailed warning of possible fraud at the company. But EY still failed to detect an alleged US$2.5 billion overstatement of HealthSouth's profits. Also in 2009, politicians and the shareholders of Anglo Irish Bank criticised EY for failing to detect large loans to Seán FitzPatrick, the bank's chairman. The Irish government subsequently took full ownership of the bank, at a cost of €28 billion. An investigator was appointed to examine EY's conduct. And then there was the 2013 ChinaCast case, in which, according to the complainant, Deloitte 'put its name and brand behind the certification of financial statements that were almost entirely false'.

The growing mound of missed frauds also includes Xerox's 'accounting shenanigans' and the massive TBW–Colonial fraud, which both Deloitte and PwC failed to discover. The Bill & Melinda Gates Foundation recently sued PwC and Petrobras in relation to investment losses caused by corruption at the Brazilian oil giant. These mounting failures betray another uncomfortable truth: most frauds are not found by auditors. Frauds typically do come to light – after someone else discovers them. Regulators, whistleblowers, corruption commissions, ombudsmen, investigative journalists, private eyes, bounty hunters, insurers, police, courts, independent investors, research firms, activists and even students – all these non-auditors have strong records of finding and outing corporate fraud and misconduct.

In 2010 the short seller Jon Carnes revealed that a biodiesel factory which China Integrated Energy had said was producing at 'full blast' had in fact been dormant for months. CIE was a KPMG client. Research firm Muddy Waters discovered misreporting by Sino-Forest, an EY audit client. The massive accounting fraud at American International Group was unearthed by the Securities and Exchange Commission, possibly after a whistleblower tip-off. The SEC also unearthed the scandal at Tyco, whose CEO had conspired with the CFO to inflate company income by US\$500 million, and to steal US\$150 million; at the height of the scandal, CEO Dennis Kozlowski threw a \$2-million birthday party for his wife, complete with a performance by Jimmy Buffett.

Some of the highest-profile anti-corruption whistleblowers were Big Four personnel. The former PwC staff behind LuxLeaks are one example. Another is the EY partner who quit and went public with claims the firm had helped a Dubai gold refiner to cover up the buying and selling of 'conflict gold'. Worryingly for the reputation of the Big Four as champions of accountability and integrity, these personnel judged they could better serve their principles by severing their relations with their Big Four employers.

## Fraud busters

Much of the first audit work undertaken by professional accountants had a strongly investigative character. Recall, for example, William

Deloitte's uncovering of the frauds within Britain's nineteenth-century railway companies. For investigative journalist Mark Stevens, the very name Price Waterhouse brought to mind a film noir detective agency. Alexander Clark Smith wrote a series of novels in which the accountant protagonist is a 'private-eye action hero' who uses his accounting skills to unearth corruption. A story that passed into Arthur Andersen legend involves young Mike Gagel working in blistering summer heat to count bricks stacked on pallets in a storage yard near Marion, Ohio. His job was to certify the inventory of a million bricks – but every time he did his count, he was 100,000 bricks short. After the third count, the yard's owner looked into the discrepancy and discovered that his deputy had been coming to the yard each night to steal truckloads of bricks.

Jonathan Webb, an anti-corruption expert and regular contributor to *Forbes* magazine, wrote in 2016: 'Investors, customers, employees and even suppliers have an interest in [Big Four] partners behaving with integrity. When an auditor's name is on the books, it is assumed by all parties that "true and fair" also means that the accounts are free of fraud.'

After the Anglo Irish Bank bailout, EY argued that a typical audit would not detect the kind of year-end window-dressing and irregular loans that were at the heart of the scandal. Echoing Lord Justice 'Watchdog' Lopes, other Big Four defenders have also attempted to argue that fraud detection is beyond the scope of typical corporate audits. In one of the TBW–Colonial cases, Beth Tanis, lead trial lawyer for PwC, told the *Financial Times*: 'As the professional audit standards make clear, even a properly designed and executed audit may not detect fraud, especially in instances when there is collusion, fabrication of documents, and the override of controls, as there was at Colonial Bank.'

But to suggest that because auditors cannot be expected to detect *all* fraud even when doing their jobs correctly, they shouldn't be expected to detect *any* fraud would be ludicrous. Clearly, fraud is one of most pernicious reasons why financial statements can fail to comply with financial reporting standards or to give a 'true and fair' view of the financial performance and condition of the firm; the list of audit failures shows this emphatically. In one sense, the expectation gap is really a gap between what users of financial statements expect auditors to do and what auditors would like to be held accountable for. Given that audit standards have largely been written by auditors, and by the Big Four in particular, it is hardly valid for the profession to invoke those standards as an independent benchmark, or even a very reliable one.

The Big Four sometimes argue they cannot be expected to find frauds that are well hidden – frauds, for example, where the CFO takes deliberate steps to cover up the malfeasance. Yet observers note – we think reasonably – that discovering *hidden* frauds is precisely what is meant by uncovering fraud. No one ever said discovering fraud meant only discovering easy, obvious or incompetent frauds.

Wes Kelly worked on PwC's Colonial Bank audits. In a taped deposition presented to the Miami jury in one of the TBW–Colonial trials, Kelly stated that PwC had conducted its audits in accordance with auditing standards. Those standards, he said, required the consideration of the risk of fraud, but not the finding or detecting of it. 'We considered fraud in the risk assessments. But we did not design audit procedures to detect fraud because it's not a requirement under the audit procedures.'

A study by the Center for Audit Quality, an affiliate of the AICPA, found that external auditors felt the job of fraud detection fell to the audit committee and the board. But if it is unreasonable to expect audit teams of dozens or hundreds to detect fraud, how can it be reasonable to expect a typical audit committee of three part-timers to do so? Given that PwC identifies the key role of the audit committee as providing 'effective oversight of the performance, independence and objectivity of the auditor and the quality of the audit', it only stands to reason that if the audit committee is responsible for detection of fraud, then this is a function that is necessarily delegated to the auditors.

Some in the Big Four take a more sensible position. PwC's global chairman, Dennis Nally, told the *Wall Street Journal* in 2007 that the 'audit profession has always had a responsibility for the detection of fraud'. Notwithstanding protests about the expectation gap and the undemanding strictures of audit standards, accountability institutions such as regulators and courts have been prepared to hold the firms to account for overlooking white-collar crime. In 2008, for example, the UK Joint Disciplinary Scheme (JDS) forced KPMG to pay a £495,000 fine, plus costs of £1.15 million, for 'failing to complete a professional audit' of collapsed insurer Independent Insurance. The JDS found that KPMG 'had failed to take steps to check suspicious information provided by Independent's management' during the year 2000 audit.

To some extent, the fraud debate has reflected tensions within the Big Four firms: between, on the one hand, partners who are looking to sell forensic services and to grow sales in general, and, on the other hand, partners who are at the audit coalface and therefore know how hard and expensive fraud detection can be for traditional audit teams. The question of audit scope is another battleground between the firms' past and future.

## Limited liability

When it comes to reducing the scope of audits, the incentives of the Big Four are as strong as they are obvious. The same can be said of auditors' incentive to reduce their liability when things go wrong. States and countries around the world have passed laws to limit auditor liability. In New South Wales, for example, auditor liability is capped at ten times the audit fee. The public-policy rationale for such laws is questionable, especially as the courts are well equipped to determine and allocate liability. It is hard to see who benefits from liability caps apart from the auditors themselves. Is this another example of the cosy relationship between the Big Four and government?

The UK Economic Affairs Committee noted in 2011 that auditor liability caps may have merit as an encouragement for smaller firms to enter the audit market, and as a protection for auditors to report more fulsomely: 'A statutory cap on auditor liability would make it more attractive both for non-Big Four firms to bid for large company audits and also for auditors to extend their audit assurance beyond the financial statements.' Nevertheless, the Big Four are likely to be the main beneficiaries of the caps, which can give rise to a 'moral hazard' problem: the more protected they are, the more accountants are inclined to take risks.

## Independence, conflicts and 'self-audit'

Compromised independence is a third potential cause of audit failure. Even with the limited range of services provided by Price Waterhouse's MCS group in the 1960s (advice on management structures, management accounts, administrative systems, office procedures and mechanisation), there was a danger that the integrity of the firm's audits could be undermined – that the firm would be guilty of 'self-audit' by reviewing systems it had designed and helped to establish. Such conduct violates sacrosanct principles of accounting and corporate governance. It creates a conflict of interest: an auditor is more likely to be soft on his or her own work, and, regardless, the auditor cannot look at that work independently.

As the breadth of advisory services has grown – and as the firms have struggled to say no to advisory engagements – the risk of self-audit has multiplied. This has been a live issue for half a century. The collapse of Westec (in 1965), National Student Marketing (1969), Penn Central (1970) and Four Seasons Nursing Centers (also 1970) elevated concerns about auditor independence and whether the quality of audits could be impaired when accountants sold consulting services to their audit clients. The US Senate's 1976 Metcalf Report reached a blunt conclusion: the consulting practices of audit firms were 'incompatible with the responsibility of independent auditors and should be prohibited by federal standards of conduct'.

Prem Sikka, Emeritus Professor of Accounting at the University of Essex, agrees: '[Y]ou have one floor of big accountancy firms doing an audit and another floor giving advice on how to bypass rules and regulations and how to flatter their financial statements. And they make money whichever way things go.'

As we've already seen, lawmakers and regulators have sought to address the problem of audit–advisory conflict by inserting independence rules into audit standards and legislation. And the firms have repeatedly breached those rules. In 2004, for example, the SEC suspended EY from accepting new public-company audit engagements for six months because of independence violations relating to its audits of software firm PeopleSoft Inc. (EY had audited the company at the same time that its consulting arm was recommending PeopleSoft products to clients.) In 2014 the SEC charged KPMG with independence violations relating to the provision, on different occasions between 2007 and 2011, of non-audit services – such as bookkeeping and consulting advice – to affiliates of audit clients. Another breach was also found: KPMG personnel owned stock in audit clients and their affiliates, thereby undermining their ability to audit independently. KPMG paid a settlement worth US$8.2 million.

With arguments that have sometimes sounded self-serving, the Big Four have defended their diversification into management consulting and other fields. Arguments have included staff development, staff motivation, client service and simple practicality. KPMG global chair Michael Andrew spoke of the benefits to clients of a soup-to-nuts offering: 'we can help you fix not only the finance and tax part, we can also help you fix people, processes, IT – all of it.' Defenders have pointed to specific synergies between service lines. Jonathan Hayward of Independent Audit Ltd gave evidence to the House of Lords inquiry into the role and market power of auditors. Hayward told the UK committee in 2010 that 'doing advisory work can improve the auditor's ability to do it, because he has a better understanding of the business and of the motivations and pressures of management'. Auditors who know the business are less confrontational and more likely to 'get it right first time'. In its 2011 review of post–financial crisis inquiries, the Association of Chartered Certified Accountants stated: '[W]e do not believe that tax advisory work should be included on any prohibited list. Most companies would be rightly aggrieved at having to take on another firm of advisers to do tax work, as this seems costly and unnecessary'.

After the nationalisation of Northern Rock in the United Kingdom, the House of Commons Treasury Committee examined the sale of advisory services to audit clients. Should such sales, the committee asked, be banned? This was a question to which the Big Four–dominated Auditing Practices Board was happy to answer no: 'After Enron we consulted on this question of auditor conflicts of interest and there was no appetite for a blanket ban on non-audit services.'

## Junior auditors under pressure

Young staff at the Big Four firms live a somewhat proletarian, even Dickensian existence. Taking into account all the unpaid overtime, it is not uncommon for juniors to earn a lower hourly wage than pizza delivery drivers. Yet it is these staff who are often in the hot seat when audits go wrong. Remember the diligent PwC junior who was the hero of the Centro case. And the hapless PwC junior who, in the TBW–Colonial fiasco, was responsible for duties 'above his pay grade'.

In an important respect, the training and careers of auditors are backwards. Much of the work of auditing is performed by graduates, often straight out of college or university and not yet qualified as a Chartered Accountant or Certified Practising Accountant. The work of *checking* is in large part conducted by young men and women who have minimal experience of *doing*. Contrast this with surgeons, say, or pilots.

In medicine and aviation, typically the most experienced and competent practitioners are entrusted with the monitoring and review of others.

The firms' new commercial focus has transformed how junior staff are expected to function. Alongside the normal pressures of conformity and compliance, the exhaustive performance systems can make life claustrophobic for those staff. And the commercial drivers add to the accident-prone nature of working in the Big Four. Taught to value flexibility and compromise, staff are 'inculcated to appease clients and neglect wider social interests'. In that environment, the long hours and short deadlines can cause staff to cut corners. Authors such as Bhanu Raghunathan, Caroline Willett and Michael Page have noticed audit staff adopting a variety of irregular practices when placed under intense time pressure. The practices included premature sign-off of audit reports and the falsification of working papers. Irregular shortcuts were seen as essential survival skills. They were part of the culture.

## Shaky foundations

Auditing is the core generator of the Big Four's reputation for probity and integrity. And yet the reputational value of auditing rests on unstable ground. As the succession of audit failures has shown, both the practice and the perception of auditing are fragile. Arthur Andersen's brand, which for a time was arguably the best of all the Big Five, seems to have been based in large part on a gossamer-thin thread of anecdotes and folklore. With such precarious footings, it is no surprise that the brand's value evaporated overnight (although it congealed somewhat in 2014, when some brave former Androids relaunched a firm named Andersen Tax)[15].

15  Andersen Tax was originally founded under the name 'WTAS' in 2002; it adopted the name 'Andersen Tax' in 2014. The firm's website says this about the renaming: 'Like WTAS, Andersen Tax is an independent global tax firm with no audit practice that could impair the credibility or integrity of the services it provides.'

What are the firms doing today to protect the integrity and the brand value of auditing? Not much, it seems. The Big Four share a blind spot when it comes to inward-looking strategy. They've made a string of questionable decisions about the services they provide and how they present those services to the market. They've sponsored start-ups that promise to further commoditise and devalue the services of Big Four auditors, and, perversely, to increase the competition they face. They've mispriced and underappreciated risks. And they've made fortunes advising conglomerates to divest business units and 'stick to their knitting', while at the same time embarking on an aggressive program of diversification.

It is natural that the Big Four firms would have such blind spots. They are not public corporations, and they're certainly not audited as public corporations. The rules and frameworks they apply to others are not applied to their own activities. (This helps explain why some audit standards promoted by the Big Four are disconnected from how business actually takes place.) The Big Four have unusual structures and cultures. They face unique challenges.

## Making a name in auditing

Regulatory initiatives such as Sarbox and Peek-a-boo may have sharpened processes to ensure audit quality. A concern raised at the time of the Enron and WorldCom scandals was that the auditors viewed management as their client. But Sarbox requires the audit committee to be 'directly responsible for the appointment, compensation, and oversight' of the outside auditor, and the auditors are to report directly to the audit committee. Audit committees are now required to be fully independent, to have the ability to engage independent counsel and other advisors, and to have established procedures for handling tips regarding accounting and auditing matters.

Yet a fundamental question is whether these reforms promote genuine interest in audit quality. It is difficult to fault an audit committee that selects a Big Four firm – in much the same way that 'nobody ever got fired for choosing IBM'. While some academic studies suggest directors suffer consequences when firms whose boards they sit on have to restate or reissue financial reports, it is not clear that these consequences are serious enough to warrant strenuous monitoring of the Big Four auditor attesting to financial statements.

Additionally, it is not clear that such consequences will always have the desired effect. If information comes to light suggesting that a restatement may be warranted, a director concerned about reputational consequences from restatements might have an incentive (much like the auditor) to avoid making such restatements. Another question concerns how well audit committees can be expected to do their jobs. If they are not trained auditors themselves, how do they evaluate the performance of the auditor? If they are trained auditors, can they effectively monitor their professional peers? Or do they invoke exculpatory notions such as the expectation gap?

That there are deficiencies – not only with the auditors themselves but also in the effectiveness of the audit committee in monitoring the auditors – is reflected in the performance of audit firms in regular inspections by Peek-a-boo. How can these deficiencies be overcome? One idea is to give shareholders more direct say over auditor selection and retention. Of course, in many jurisdictions a shareholder vote ratifying the audit committee's choice of auditor is already required. In the United States, shareholders typically give more than 98 per cent support to the firm's choice of auditor. This can be hardly taken as an endorsement of the current process.

For one thing, on what basis might shareholders reject auditors? They don't have access to the detailed information on auditor performance that they would need in order to do so. The only observable output of the audit process is the audit report. But audit reports are widely recognised as bland and uninformative, and so provide no basis for choosing one auditor over another. Perhaps shareholders could read the PCAOB inspection reports and use those as a basis for rejecting an audit firm. But what would happen if they did so? Wouldn't the board just suggest another Big Four firm with a similarly dismal record of performance?

Another possible basis is to look at restatement statistics. How has the auditor done? What proportion of clients have had to restate financials? But this measure would also be problematic: restatements could well be the result of a brave auditor standing up to management and forcing the correction of prior periods' financial statements, for example. Viewing restatements as a discredit to the auditor has the perverse effect of creating an incentive to acquiesce in the failure to correct misstatements. And matters are surely unsatisfactory, but in a different way, when prior years have been audited by a different firm.

In theory, auditors have incentives to establish reputations for probity and diligence. In practice, the incentives to do so are weak. Outsider shareholders – notionally the principal beneficiaries of the auditor's services – have little basis for forming opinions on the merits of one Big Four firm over another. And even with their increased power post-Sarbox, audit committees appear to have little ability or incentive to hold the auditors' feet to the fire. So establishing a reputation by doing better audits just isn't the path to profits that we'd all hope it to be. And this, alas, is reflected in the prosaic nature of many of the audit failures discussed above.

## The seven deadly sins

Critiques of conventional auditing have accumulated over recent decades. Public company audits, critics say, are often ineffective and occasionally counterproductive. Traditional auditing may, for example, impede corporate performance by discouraging risk-taking and innovation among auditees. Auditors operating at an information disadvantage might focus on less important matters, such as minor compliance breaches, instead of focusing on the big strategic picture, and on vital questions such as whether the audited enterprise is performing to its potential, or whether it is likely to remain solvent. Auditing may increase 'red tape' by causing auditees to adopt administrative systems and procedures that are unnecessary, or even harmful to efficiency.

Much criticism of auditing has focused on the expectation gap – the difference in opinion about what an audit can and should achieve. As we've already seen, auditors seek to limit the scope of their work – and the extent to which people can rely on it – in order to manage their own risks and reduce their own effort. At the same time, though, owners, investors and managers may overestimate the scope and reliability of audit findings, and therefore overestimate the level of assurance provided by the audit. In that case, audits can have perversely negative effects on corporate decision-making.

Another stream of audit criticism has focused on the possibility that auditors may conceal, soften, sugar-coat or under-report adverse findings, particularly when the auditors are not independent of the auditee. Auditors, in other words, may be lapdogs, not watchdogs. In most modern capitalist countries, the auditee decides who will be the auditor.[16] This can give rise to a commercial conflict: if an auditor is too strident in his or her views, he or she may not be engaged as an auditor again, or his or her firm may lose lucrative advisory work. In the extreme, auditors are reduced to compliant subordinates of their auditees. As Ned O'Keeffe, a former member of the Irish government, colourfully put it: '[Auditors are] a joke and a waste of time. They are lick-arses for the management of companies, because corporate governance doesn't work in our society. [Auditors] are not independent but they are bloody-well paid.'

The Big Four franchise model exacerbates this problem of auditor timidity. A particular audit engagement may represent a large share of local income, even if it is immaterial to the firm globally.

16   We discuss other modes of engagement in Chapter 14.

Much criticism of auditing has focused on the methods the large firms adopt: sending out junior staff, armed with generic skills and ill-fitting templates, testing small samples of transactions and controls, in an effort to minimise the auditor's own costs. What is striking about the litany of audit failures is that so many of them arose not so much from business-line conflicts or the desire to please management, but from simple lassitude. Failing to test valuations. Failing to verify assets. Failing to understand the auditee's business. A lackadaisical approach to auditing is understandable when auditors have monopoly power and an informational advantage such that few people – even among those who care – can tell if the auditors are working hard or not.

The most fundamental critique is that auditing, as defined and delimited by modern standards and legislation, has become merely a 'ritual of comfort' or a 'ritual of pacification': a hollow, cynical exercise that fends off calls for greater scrutiny or transparency, without any expectation that it can or will generate substantive benefits, except perhaps for the auditors themselves. For the Big Four, one aspect of the 2008 financial crisis was especially unnerving. The market, it seems, *knew* the pre-crisis audit findings were worthless. In the days and weeks in which investors and depositors ran for the exits, the recently issued unqualified audit opinions for entities such as Northern Rock, Bear Sterns and Lehman Brothers were inconsequential. They provided no reassurance. The positive report on Northern Rock's accounts, for example, did not prevent a run on the bank during August and September 2007.

Twenty years ago, the accounting professor Michael Power put forward the idea of the 'audit society' as a framework for understanding the observed growth of auditing, and its apparently ritualistic nature. At a time when auditing was under the most intense criticism, there was an explosive proliferation of regulators, watchdogs and audit-style services. The demand for auditors, inspectors, reviewers and evaluators boomed. In the audit society, every policy conundrum or business problem can be solved by an audit or an investigation or a review.

Every Mickey Mouse government agency or professional body or sporting club claims to have an investigative capability and an investigative mandate. Reviews beget reviews in a torturous cycle. These phenomena, Power argued, imposed a cost on corporate governance and strategy, and ultimately on capitalism: 'The audit society is a society that endangers itself because it invests too heavily in shallow rituals of verification at the expense of other forms of organizational intelligence.' The Big Four have been the main beneficiaries of the audit reflex, the 'audit explosion' and the emergence of the audit society.

Lapdog. Slacker. Innovation killer. Nitpicker. Red-tape tangler. Under-deliverer. Hollow ritualist. Together, these critiques constitute the seven deadly sins of traditional auditing. The sum of these critiques is sobering: the conclusion that auditing can do harm as well as good, and may impose a net cost on society. Looked at against new developments in computing and governance, auditing is an old technology, institutionally entrenched for now, but rapidly reaching its use-by date.

Good systems have innovation and self-correction built in. The recent experience of audit scandals and fiascos has highlighted the lack of an adequate self-correction mechanism in the audit system. The practice of auditing, we now know, will continue even if it does not create public value. Michael Power's oracular warnings about the dangers of vacuous auditing remain just as powerful today. If audits are a joke, then the joke is on us all.

# 11

# GET READY TO DANCE
## Conflicting interests in Big Four taxation services

### Optimisation

Secrecy underpinned the Medici Bank's success, especially in its ecclesiastical dealings. Through patronage and opportunism, most senior churchmen accumulated savings and investments, such as grand estates within and beyond Italy's borders. Cardinal Hermann Dwerg, a friend of Pope Martin V, lived in 'a spirit of evangelical poverty' – while simultaneously holding 4000 florins, at a time when, according to author and banker Chris Skinner, 'thirty-five florins would have paid a year's rent on a small townhouse'. With each change of pope, the clerics faced the danger that their investments would be arbitrarily taxed or even confiscated by a new and unsympathetic man. The solution was a system of secret accounts, held by the Medici and accessible wherever the papal court resided. Cardinal Dwerg kept his 4000 florins in a Medici deposit account. In the twentieth century, secrecy was equally important to the success of the major accounting firms.

For the most part, Big Four taxation services originated in the Edwardian era, when income tax became more complex and burdensome, and advice on tax compliance – and tax minimisation – became indispensable. The simple days of the Domesday Book were long gone.

Companies engaged accountants to present their affairs in the best possible light for taxation purposes. Large dividends were reaped.

At the turn of the twentieth century there were thousands of national businesses, numerous international and transnational ones, but few true multinationals. As multinational corporations emerged, a new and highly profitable business line presented itself: helping companies comply with their international tax obligations, but also helping them minimise their overall tax liability. The key was knowledge of tax rates in different jurisdictions, and of how (and on what) taxes were levied.

## Stellar

Thus we entered the world of corporate tax shelters and 'transfer pricing'. Tax specialists helped multinationals move income to low-tax locations. They set beneficial prices for inter-office movements of inputs, outputs and cash. They generated paper losses, exploited favourable tax treatment of debt and depreciation, and otherwise engaged in practices whose rubbery, tricksy, self-serving character recalled the bad old days of the British railways.

Transfer pricing is not inherently sinister. Multinationals need to set prices to properly account for profits on internal transactions. Nor is it especially new. Varieties of the practice first appeared hundreds of years ago. The Medici Bank and the Dutch East India Company, for example, used versions of transfer pricing to move money between countries and business units. But the scope for abuse in transfer pricing is wide, and the practice has taken on a troubling shape. Troubling or not, though, transfer pricing is now one of the most profitable business lines of the Big Four.

The four firms have built that business through a series of small steps and large wins. Stephen Zeff wrote about the 1965 milestone at which, 'after thirty years of controversy and a protracted battle with the legal profession', Certified Practicing Accountants secured US Congressional approval to represent tax clients before the Treasury Department. As late as 1975, Price Waterhouse's UK tax team was still small, with only ten partners. The team's work was mostly routine, such as helping companies calculate and comply with their tax obligations. From that base, the growth was stellar. In 2015, of PwC's total UK revenue of £2.81 billion, £714 million came from its tax advisory practice. The firms now dominate the global tax avoidance industry, which enables multinationals such as Google and Ikea to pay very little tax on very considerable income.

## Taking advantage

In 2013 the House of Commons Committee of Public Accounts inquired into the role of large accounting firms in tax avoidance in the United Kingdom. The committee heard evidence directly from the Big Four, who conceded that international tax rules were overly complex, out of date and in need of change to reflect the reality of modern business. The committee's report, when it appeared, was damning. Several multinationals had paid hardly any corporate tax, despite doing a great deal of UK business. Revenue authorities were fighting an unwinnable battle.

> Companies can devote considerable resources to ensure that they minimise their tax liability. There is a large market for advising companies on how to take advantage of international tax law, and on the tax implications of different global structures. The four firms employ nearly 9,000 people and earn £2 billion from their tax work in the UK, and earn around US$25 billion from this work globally. [Her Majesty's Revenue & Customs] has far fewer resources. In the area of transfer pricing alone there are four times as many staff working for the four firms than for HMRC.

To earn their money, the firms employed all sorts of circumlocutory tactics – such as dragging out cases and making dubious gambles on favourable rulings. Stung by the loss of revenue, HMRC considered banning tax-avoiding companies from being awarded government contracts. When the Big Four insisted they no longer sold the aggressive tax-avoidance schemes they'd marketed a decade earlier, the committee responded with scepticism:

> While this may be the case, we believe they have simply moved to advising on other forms of tax avoidance which are profitable for their clients; such as the complex operating models they offer to major corporate clients to minimise tax by exploiting the lowest international tax rates. The four firms have developed internal guidelines on where the line between tax planning and aggressive avoidance lies, but these principles do not stop them selling schemes with as little as a 50% chance of succeeding if challenged in court. Clearly HMRC has to consider the risk to the taxpayer of a protracted legal battle. It would appear that firms and tax avoiders are taking advantage of the constraints under which HMRC is obliged to operate.

Of the thousands of people employed in the Big Four's UK tax practices, around 250 were transfer-pricing specialists. In contrast, HMRC employed just sixty-five such specialists.

## The revolving door

The parliamentary committee was especially critical of the firms' cosy relationship with government, a relationship that created the perception that the firms wielded 'undue influence on the tax system which they use to their advantage'. The Big Four confirmed they had seconded expert consultants to the revenue authorities – 'to provide technical advice on changes to tax laws'. Afterward, those staff advised multinationals on how best to arrange their affairs under those laws. For the committee, this was a matter of grave concern: a case of 'poacher, turned gamekeeper, turned poacher again, whereby individuals who advise government go back to their firms and advise their clients on how they can use those laws to reduce the amount of tax they pay'. The secondments created an unmistakable conflict of interest.

KPMG, for example, had provided staff to advise government on 'controlled foreign company' and 'patent box' rules. The firm then used its involvement as a selling point for tax services. According to the firm's marketing puff, KPMG could reduce companies' tax and help prepare a 'defendable expense allocation' – under the new legislation that the firm had helped draft.

The same revolving door has also been called out in the United States and continental Europe. During a stint at the US Treasury, former PwC tax specialist George Manousos helped design Section 199 of the *American Jobs Creation Act* (2004), 'an obscure corporate tax break' utilised by lingerie brand Victoria's Secret, among others. On Manousos's return to PwC, he made partner – and advised clients on how best to use Section 199. (Another example of the firms' close relationship with government: in the late 1990s, after a career in the bureaucracy and before his career in politics, Australia's future prime minister Kevin Rudd worked at KPMG as a China consultant.)

European critics have claimed that this kind of shuffling back and forth between accounting and government undermines authorities' efforts to police corporate conduct and protect the tax base. These critics, and the UK committee's findings, paint a picture of the Big Four that is far removed from the image of pro-social professionals, helpfully integrated into systems of good corporate governance. Rather, the picture is one of corporate pathology – of enemies inside the gates. Where in this picture is the 'foe of deceit and the champion of honesty'?

## A sham

Big Four tax specialists get into trouble almost as often as Big Four auditors do.

Singers Kenny Loggins and Willie Nelson were two of the more than 4000 high-wealth Price Waterhouse clients who, in the late 1970s and early 1980s, put money into a tax shelter operated by First Western Securities of San Francisco. Built upon government-backed securities, the shelter was designed to generate plentiful deductions that were several multiples larger than the amounts invested in the scheme. When the IRS disallowed the hoped-for deductions, several clients sued Price Waterhouse, accusing the firm of breaching its duties. In one of the cases, the court read the notes of Thomas Walsh, the Price Waterhouse tax specialist who in 1979 had performed due diligence on First Western. His notes were incriminatory. At one point, for example, he wrote: 'The biggest problem I see with the transactions is whether they are simply paper shuffling.' In another note he recorded the view of First Western computer programmer Robert Kramer that the shelter was 'a sham'.

In the 1990s and 2000s, Caterpillar Inc. paid PwC US$55 million to establish a tax arrangement that shifted profits from the United States to Switzerland, allegedly enabling an American tax saving of more than US$2.4 billion over a decade. PwC partner Thomas F. Quinn helped design it. Before the details came to light, Quinn wrote to a colleague with instructions on how to buttress the arrangement: they had to 'create a story' and 'put some distance' between Caterpillar's US managers and the company's Swiss spare-parts business. 'Get ready to do some dancing,' Quinn wrote. The colleague famously replied, with gallows irony, 'What the heck. We'll all be retired when this ... comes up on audit ... Baby boomers have their fun, and leave it to the kids to pay for it.'

In 2005 the US Department of Justice accused KPMG of marketing tax shelters that were 'abusive' and 'fraudulent'. KPMG admitted it had broken the law to help the rich avoid US$2.5 billion in taxes. To wealthy clients it sold a semi-Shakespearean 'alphabet soup' of tax shelters: FLIP, BLIPS, TEMPEST and OTHELLO. The firm agreed to pay US$456 million in penalties and settlements, in exchange for a deferred prosecution agreement with Justice and the IRS. That is the historic agreement which stopped the Big Four from shrinking to a Big Three. Attorney-General Alberto Gonzales acknowledged explicitly the costs of losing KPMG – costs that just had to be avoided. They included systemic costs as well as Andersen-style impacts on blameless staff in other KPMG divisions and offices. The agreement, Gonzales said, required the firm 'to accept responsibility and make amends for its criminal conduct while protecting innocent workers and others from the consequences of a conviction'.

KPMG would not face criminal prosecution if it complied with the terms of the agreement. The firm had to abide by permanent restrictions on its tax practice, and cooperate in the pursuit of individuals implicated in the sale of the offensive shelters. Several partners accused of unlawful conduct were let go. KPMG agreed to help authorities pursue the tax shelters' architects and salesmen; six former partners and the firm's former deputy chair were criminally prosecuted. The firm also tightened up its internal governance and risk management. The flow of cases, nevertheless, continued.

In November 2013 the development charity ActionAid accused Deloitte of advising large businesses on the use of Mauritius to avoid potentially hundreds of millions of dollars in tax. In 2015 the Canada Revenue Agency accused KPMG of selling tax-evasion schemes: 'The CRA alleges that the KPMG tax structure was in reality a "sham" that intended to deceive the taxman'. Documents tabled in courts and parliaments show the Big Four are fully alert to the risk of their tax-minimisation arrangements being illegal. A US Senate investigation's report described how a senior KPMG tax practitioner 'urged the firm to ignore IRS rules on registering tax shelters'. He calculated that the legal penalties 'would be no greater than $14,000 per $100,000 in fees that KPMG would collect'. An average deal, for example, 'would result in KPMG fees of $360,000 with a maximum penalty exposure of only $31,000'. The reputational costs were not so easily expressed in dollar terms.

## Different understandings

In his 1966 history of the ICAEW, Sir Harold Howitt recalled a turn-of-the-century incident that involved a particularly damning audit report. The chairman of the company in question was a disreputable fellow who would later serve time in prison. At the company's annual meeting, the audit report was to be read aloud for the benefit of shareholders. When the time came for the reading of the report, 'several queer characters' took that as their cue to ask 'in loud voices ... all manner of irrelevant questions. The audit report was duly read and no one heard a word of it.'

Over time, such tactics have become less and less viable. In the twenty-first century, companies operate in an environment of fishbowl transparency. Audit reports, annual reports, prospectuses and other financial and commercial documents are published online. Analyses of the performance of companies are issued and picked over in the business press and the popular press. Every skerrick of information is shared and rated and debated. And, with increasing frequency, information is leaked.

A new wave of transparency is washing through all the dark and secret places of the world. Orphanages, navy ships, abattoirs, locker rooms, casting couches – and the offices of tax advisers. In this new environment of transparency, unauthorised disclosures are not marginal or aberrant phenomena that can be overcome by tightening systems and contracts. They are at the core of a new reality: companies are see-through, and bad behaviour can no longer be hidden.

Staff, owners and stakeholders have a thousand new and easy ways to disclose corporate shortcomings, or activities with which they disagree, and there is a new ethic of disclosure. After the 2017 CIA leaks, for example, former CIA director Michael Hayden complained about the younger generation of specialists and their attitudes to secrecy: 'In order to do [surveillance work] we have to recruit from a certain demographic. And I don't mean to judge them at all, but this group of millennials and related groups simply have different understandings of the words loyalty, secrecy and transparency than certainly my generation did.' In the era of Wikileaks and Anonymous, transparency has become a social phenomenon.

Like the power of the Medici, the power of Big Four tax practices depends on discretion and mystery. The new transparency, though, is undermining that power. There are multiple points at which secret advice on tax avoidance and minimisation can come unstuck. Leaks from within the firm providing the advice. Leaks from within the organisation receiving the advice. Leaks from implementers, regulators or independent hackers. And official investigations launched by tax authorities or other arms of government. Each one of these channels has already led to the discovery of dubious Big Four dealings in tax.

Old-fashioned transfer pricing and tax shelters cannot survive in a world of greater scrutiny and visibility of what companies do, and what their advisers tell them. Never before have tax havens been so easy to set up. And never before have they been so dangerous for those who set them up. As the LuxLeaks episode demonstrates, secrecy is no longer viable as the basis for any kind of arms-length commercial service.

## Breached

Edward Snowden's 2013 leak of thousands of classified National Security Agency (NSA) documents was a near miss for the Big Four. Snowden accessed the documents while working for NSA contractor Booz Allen Hamilton, the former owner of Booz & Co., now Strategy&. When the leak came to light, Booz suffered shrinkage in its share price and its reputation. The overwhelming reaction inside the Big Four was

'Thank God he doesn't work here.' In 2017 contractors were again blamed when Wikileaks released a slew of CIA documents. Details are still to come about the identity of the leaker and his or her employer. But, with legions of Big Four staff and contractors actively advising armies and security agencies around the world, it is only a matter of time before one of the firms suffers a Snowden-style disclosure.

Like the 2017 Paradise Papers and the 2015 Panama Papers, the 2014 Luxembourg leaks, or LuxLeaks, reveal a lot about the viability of tax advice in the newly transparent world. In the first wave of LuxLeaks, 548 tax arrangements relating to multinational corporations became public. PwC had negotiated the arrangements, and bore the brunt of the ensuing scandal. A subsequent set of Luxembourg documents, though, showed that the other three major accounting firms had also brokered rulings there.

The Big Four have large tax practices in Luxembourg, a small country of approximately 600,000 people. Together, the firms have employed as many as 6000 personnel there – equivalent to one for every 100 Luxembourgers. PwC Luxembourg alone had turnover of €276 million for the year to June 2013.

The LuxLeaks scandal began when PwC employees Antoine Deltour and Raphael Halet provided more than 30,000 pages of documents to journalists. Prior to the publication of the Panama Papers, LuxLeaks was the biggest exposé of corporate tax deals the world had ever seen. The documents revealed generous tax arrangements utilised in Luxembourg by companies such as Accenture, Burberry, FedEx, Heinz, Ikea, Pepsi and Shire Pharmaceuticals. A total of 343 large companies had used the rulings to minimise, or annihilate, their tax payments. Luxembourg's accommodating tax office rubber-stamped the deals. Many of the companies – such as Procter & Gamble and J.P. Morgan – were longstanding Big Four clients.

The BBC's *Panorama* program, France 2 and *Private Eye* magazine received the documents and broke the story. The International

Consortium of Investigative Journalists then arranged an investigation, which was published two years after the story first appeared. PwC was accused of arranging the tax deals for its clients, and of looking the other way when those clients misbehaved. In a Luxembourg court the whistleblowers were accused of breaching their employment contracts, and Luxembourg's secrecy laws.

In June 2016 the court found Deltour and Halet guilty. They received twelve-month and nine-month prison sentences, respectively, although these were wholly suspended. PwC and the prosecutors had sought longer jail terms, insisting that their now former staff were thieves rather than whistleblowers. On appeal, the sentences were reduced but the convictions confirmed. Public accounting is supposed to be about transparency. In the LuxLeaks case, PwC found itself on wrong side of that principle.

## Tax transparency

Even without leaks, governments are increasingly working together to address the abuse of transfer pricing. Under the aegis of the Organisation for Economic Co-operation and Development (OECD), a push is underway for firms to provide 'country-by-country reporting' (CbCR) data to tax authorities in their home jurisdictions. Such data would include information on revenue, employees, income and taxes paid by jurisdiction. The belief is that (relatively) simple reporting such as this will highlight the disparities between where firms employ people, own plants and generate sales, and where they purport to generate income, which is often guided by tax minimisation more than by any commercial facts. But as CbCR has become a reality in many jurisdictions, there are calls for firms to also make CbCR data available to the general public.

In the short run, CbCR is likely to be a boon for the Big Four, as firms grapple with the new reporting requirements on short timelines.

But the long-term effects of increased transparency may be less favourable. Tax avoidance through aggressive income-shifting may struggle to withstand the concerted efforts of multiple jurisdictions, especially when the magnitude of taxes avoided is easy to see. And the pivotal role of the Big Four in facilitating this is unlikely to do much for what is left of their reputation for putting probity ahead of commercialism.

## The public interest

As architects of tax-avoidance schemes that cost governments and taxpayers more than US$1 trillion a year, the Big Four have been accused of predatory behaviour. With gusto, the firms are still 'Pulling Money from Government'. In a *Guardian* op-ed, Professor Prem Sikka wrote that the big firms 'create sham transactions, phoney losses and phantom assets to enable their clients to dodge taxes'.

The firms have taken this criticism in their stride. Far from retreating, they are expanding their tax service offerings. In 2014, for example, PwC launched Nifty R&D, an online tax-rebate tool for small businesses. Before this innovation, PwC had largely avoided selling tax services to the small-business sector; it simply wasn't lucrative enough.

The modern history of the big accounting firms is a transition from professional values to commercial ones. In no service line is this transition starker than in taxation advisory. The peak of tax shelter sales coincided with peak of commercialism in accountancy. In their tax services, the Big Four have done something Edwin Waterhouse would never have dreamed of doing: directly trading off reputation for cash. In one case, Deloitte was accused of failing adequately to consider the public interest in its advice on the accounting treatment of its client's tax losses. Deloitte's QC, however, argued that tax advisers must focus on the interests of their clients, not those of the public. It is in tax, more than in any other area, that the Big Four have sold their souls.

# 12

# ONE FOUR TEN
## The Big Four in China

### They came, they saw, they conquered

In China, the Big Four have attained a dominant position in the accounting services market. Each of the firms is generating billions in revenue there. In a sign of just how much the world has changed, some of China's largest state-owned enterprises have become Big Four clients. This surprising victory, though, is likely to be short-lived. At every step of their China foray, the firms have faced opposition from powerful forces. That opposition has now reached a crescendo. And it has reached the courts.

Disputes about something as seemingly incidental as audit working papers have become the centre of a transnational legal and regulatory battleground. In Shanghai, Deloitte recently found itself in a wicked dilemma. Deloitte had been the auditor of Longtop Financial Technologies. Longtop, a Chinese financial software company, had failed after accounting fraud was revealed. Longtop's chairman admitted to Deloitte that 'fake cash recorded on the books' was the result of 'fake revenue in the past', a reminder that the strictures of double-entry accounting extend even to fraud. The American SEC demanded that Deloitte hand over working papers related to the audit. But Deloitte argued that handing over the papers would place it and its personnel at 'substantial risk of prosecution' under Chinese law. Facing enforcement action from the SEC, Deloitte worked frantically to resolve the dispute.

In 2014, after two years of legal skirmishing, the SEC and Deloitte filed a joint motion to dismiss the lawsuit in the US District Court for the District of Columbia. The deadlock was broken when China's Securities Regulatory Commission (CSRC) handed over many of the documents the SEC had sought – reportedly amounting to more than 200,000 pages. Prudently, and perhaps strategically, the SEC backed off. It issued the following statement:

> In light of the substantial volume of documents produced, the cooperation that the CSRC recently has provided to the SEC with respect to Longtop, and [Deloitte's] statement that it will continue to cooperate with respect to CSRC requests for Longtop-related documents the SEC, at present, does not believe that there is a need for judicial relief with respect to the subpoena.

At the same time, though, the SEC left the door open for future legal action, should the tendered documents prove inadequate. And the SEC kept fighting on another front. In a separate case, an SEC administrative law judge ruled that the Chinese offices of the Big Four should be suspended from practising in the United States for six months – on the grounds that they hadn't complied with SEC document requests relating to nine Chinese companies. All four firms vowed to appeal.

The working papers battle has been waged among regulators as much as between regulators and the regulated. In Hong Kong, another regulator entered the fray. Hong Kong's market and securities watchdog took EY to court to force it to produce working papers from its audit of the China-based utility Standard Water. The Securities and Futures Commission (SFC) needed to see the papers to determine whether the audit had been properly conducted. EY, though, pushed back, arguing it did not have the papers as they were held by Ernst & Young Hua Ming (EYHM), its affiliate in mainland China.

During the trial, EY argued that Chinese law prevented it from producing audit working papers held by EYHM. But the court agreed with the SFC that the law did not prohibit the production of the documents. EY appealed, contending that the court erred in respect of the documents held by EYHM. After handing over a raft of working papers to the SFC, EY discontinued its appeal in 2015. The SFC, for its part, was satisfied that all requested documents had been produced and that EY had complied with the relevant orders. The SFC took this opportunity to remind Hong Kong audit firms of their obligation to provide working papers to the SFC in response to requests made under the Securities and Futures Ordinance:

> This will be the case even if the requested documents/records are held on behalf of Hong Kong auditors by their Mainland affiliates or agents, subject to clearance by the Mainland authorities. As well, the obligation to identify records held in the Mainland and to seek their clearance lies with the auditor.

According to Mark Steward, the SFC's Executive Director of Enforcement, 'EY could have avoided litigation by conducting proper searches of its own offices here in Hong Kong and, where necessary, cooperating with the Mainland authorities to seek clearance of records created by its affiliate firms on the Mainland.' Regulators are right to be worried about audit conduct and working papers, as the following case shows.

## The Akai case

*The company:* Akai Holdings, a Hong Kong–listed electronics conglomerate founded in 1982 by James Ting. At its peak, the company had annual sales of more than US$4 billion, over 100,000 staff and a raft of leading brands, such as Akai Electric and Singer Sewing Machines. Early in 1999 the company told shareholders it held assets worth US$2.3 billion. Ernst & Young was Akai's auditor.

*The theft:* In July 2000 Akai reported a full-year loss of US$1.72 billion, the largest in Hong Kong's history. For the *South China Morning Post*, Naomi Rovnick wrote a detailed account of the scandal that sat behind that figure. According to Rovnick, Ting was accused of plundering more than US$800 million from the company, and of using bogus bank accounts and investments to cover his trail.

*The banks:* Akai's lenders – including HSBC and Standard Chartered – were owed US$1.1 billion and had obtained legal permission to wind up the company.

*The liquidators:* In September 2001, when liquidators Borrelli Walsh arrived on the scene, 'Akai had just US$167,000 worth of cash and assets, no staff, no properties, no trademarks and only a few boxes of books and records'. The remaining documents were 'useless', consisting primarily of 'historic shipping records and import and export receipts'.

*The real documents:* The liquidator asked EY for its working papers relating to the Akai audits. EY refused to hand them over until, in 2003, the liquidator secured a court order forcing the firm to do so. Even then, not all the papers were delivered. So the liquidator returned to court. Judge Kwan was highly critical of EY: the firm had 'greatly exaggerated the time and effort that would be required to locate the missing documents in its own files'. EY 'should have greater knowledge of its own files than anyone else. It is quite inconceivable that an established organisation like the first respondent would not have maintained a proper filing system that would facilitate the retrieval of documents.'

*The court case:* The liquidator launched a US$1-billion audit negligence lawsuit against EY relating to the Akai audits and the company's collapse.

*The audits:* Through their lawyers, the liquidator claimed EY had done very little actual work in the course of auditing Akai. David Sun

Tak-kei, independent review partner on the audit from 1991 to 1999, had reportedly booked only seven hours of Akai time in the three years leading up to the collapse. Rovnick recounted how EY was accused of not using proper audit procedures: the liquidators claimed the auditors 'did not have most of the files and records that would usually be expected of a company auditor, such as audit planning documents or a detailed audit plan, and no documented procedures for examining Akai's cash balances or reviewing its general ledger'. EY had allegedly failed to seek independent evidence that Akai's bank accounts and investments were real. Even worse, the liquidators accused EY of fabricating and tampering with documents relating to the audits, and then of using the resulting 'evidence' in the negligence trial.

*The arrest*: Hong Kong's Commercial Crime Bureau raided EY's offices and arrested partner Edmund Dang, who had worked on the Akai audits. Dang was freed on bail without being charged.

*The settlement*: Having played hardball in court, EY settled in 2009 – without admitting liability. In Rovnick's words, EY's global network had to 'dig deep into its insurance coffers' to pay the settlement, thought to be around US$200 million.

## Inflated

The Akai case had a curious epilogue. Soon after the settlement was paid, EY moved to settle another negligence case involving a Hong Kong client. Moulin Global Eyecare had been wound up in 2006 with debts of HK$2.7 billion. Moulin's liquidators, Ferrier Hodgson, sought between HK$250 million and HK$300 million from EY.

For brands such as Benetton and Nikon, Moulin claimed to be producing more than 15 million glasses frames a year. The company, though, had allegedly inflated its revenues, and the size of its business. Rovnick reported that Ferrier Hodgson told creditors 'one of

Moulin's four biggest customers was really a Chinese restaurant in McCook, a town of 8,000 in Nebraska'. Hong Kong's Commercial Crime Bureau raided Moulin's offices in July 2005. This was just one of several parallels between the Moulin and Akai cases. The earlier case had had a demonstrable impact on EY. 'After Akai,' Rovnick concluded, 'Ernst & Young did not want another public fight over alleged audit negligence involving an allegedly fraudulent former client.' In a separate civil action, Moulin's creditors sued KPMG for HK$471 million over its role as the company's auditor prior to EY taking over in 2002.

## Chinese histories

Beneath these recent battles over working papers lies a fundamental question about the Big Four in China. Within a system of centralised state capitalism, how viable is a model of external, decentralised, professional scrutiny? Can the old professional services model survive in a world with different governance and very different boundaries between business and state? If it cannot, the risks for the Big Four are plain to see.

The firms have got themselves into a regulatory mess in China. Under several plausible scenarios, the China foray is a looming disaster, one in which they may lose control over their staff, their services, their standards and – perhaps most critically – their brands. To understand this predicament, it is necessary to look at the firms' Chinese histories, which fall into several distinct phases. In doing so, we draw upon our own analysis and experience, as well as the work of the London School of Economics' Emeritus Professor of Accounting, Richard Macve; Peter J. Williamson of Judge Business School, Cambridge; and Paul Gillis, who, after twenty-eight years at PwC, much of it in China, took early retirement to research the Chinese histories of the Big Four.

## Accounting master

Chinese merchants and accountants encountered double-entry book-keeping as early as the Renaissance, but largely maintained a receipt and payment system until the turn of the nineteenth century. Xi Yong Kai's 1905 *Interlocking Bookkeeping* and Xie Lin and Meng Sen's 1907 *Bank Bookkeeping* were important attempts to reconcile double-entry concepts with traditional Chinese bookkeeping. In 1916 the Bank of China officially adopted double-entry accounting.

The early history of the Big Four in China resembles their early history in America. Predominantly British firms established offices in China so they could service British companies operating there. At the start of the twentieth century, commercial Hong Kong and Shanghai were the main incubators of the accounting profession in China. Lowe & Bingham began in Hong Kong in 1902 and in Shanghai in 1906, and would ultimately become the PricewaterhouseCoopers member firm in China. Haskins & Sells arrived in Shanghai in 1917.

Licensed Chinese public accountants referred to themselves as *kuaijishi*, or 'accounting master', a term that was translated as 'chartered accountant' – and caused no end of trouble. Paul Gillis described how, in April 1925, the British Embassy wrote to the Chinese Ministry of Foreign Affairs 'complaining that the use of the term chartered accountant was confusing and inappropriate because British accountants were called chartered accountants and strict standards applied to the designation'.

The Chinese retorted that British accountants called themselves *kuaijishi* in Chinese, a term whose use required equally strict standards to be met. 'Besides,' the Chinese argued, 'if they were to use the term "certified public accountant" they would likely receive the same complaint from the Americans.'

## The essence of China

The Communist revolution of 1949 was an enormous setback for the Western accounting firms. By 1962 the Chinese economy had been fully nationalised, and for the next eighteen years the profession of public accountancy simply did not exist in China.

But as China began to open up its economy in the 1980s, foreign firms were lured by the scale of the opportunity China appeared to offer. While the then Big Eight were prohibited from auditing in China, they set up representative offices to advise the foreign-owned firms doing business in the newly opening economy. Much of the work was conducted in cramped rooms of the Beijing Hotel or the Jianguo Hotel. The Big Eight couldn't even employ staff directly. Chinese government agencies such as the Foreign Enterprise Human Resource Services Company provided and administered local staff for them.

Things were a little different in Hong Kong, which remained a British colony until 1997. Reflecting their British roots, the big firms, especially Price Waterhouse and KPMG, were dominant among auditing companies: in 1988 in Hong Kong, the era of the Big Eight elsewhere, the four largest firms had a market share of nearly 87 per cent.

By 1992 the firms had won the right to audit in mainland China. While they were compelled to operate in joint ventures with state institutions, the 'bigs' rapidly secured a dominant position in the market for foreign investment and initial public offerings. Local accountants referred to the incursion of the international firms as a 'civilised invasion by gentlemen'. Engaging with the firms was 'a dance with the wolves'.

For many years the firms' Chinese operations depended on well-connected 'fixers' and clever strategies to get around regulation. While foreign partners who were not licensed as Chinese CPAs escaped Chinese oversight, they could not sign audit reports there. Having a Chinese partner sign for work done by an unlicensed partner was expedient, but obviously less than ideal.

Having again established strong footholds in mainland China, the firms had to select Chinese names for themselves. PwC chose the Chinese characters *pu* and *hua*: according to Paul Gillis, these were considered 'the best phonetic representation of PW'. *Pu Hua* also has an appealing connotation: it can be translated as 'the essence of China'. Similarly, Ernst & Young became *Anyong* and Peat Marwick *Bimawei*.

After China acceded to the World Trade Organization, the Big Four were permitted to break up with their state-owned joint-venture partners. Gillis has described how that decision opened up new opportunities and ambitions for the firms. Quickly they grew into substantial enterprises with more than 4000 professional staff each, 'and the firms began to talk of the not-too-far-off days when the China firms would rival their American firms as the largest in the Big 4 networks'. Having initially focused on assisting foreign-owned companies in China, the firms were soon earning the majority of their Chinese income from Chinese companies.

China acknowledged that Western-style accounting practices were necessary for a market economy. In the 1990s the Chinese Ministry of Finance and the World Bank engaged Deloitte and PwC to assist China to develop accounting standards, continuing education and regulatory frameworks in harmony with international standards. By 2006 China had largely adopted the International Financial Reporting Standards.

China's rapid industrialisation and commercialisation created a shortage of accountants. In 2008 a representative of Deloitte said mainland China needed 350,000 qualified accountants – fewer than the more than 600,000 CPAs in the United States at the time, but many more than the 130,000 members of the Chinese Institute of Certified Public Accountants (CICPA). In China there were more state-owned enterprises than qualified accountants.

Flagrant poaching of staff was one consequence of the shortage. Anthony Wu, chairman of EY in China, conceded, 'We have no choice but to pay higher salaries to recruit experienced accountants from other Chinese accounting firms.' Economics and demography made the staffing situation more dire. In the midst of the China boom, staff with financial training were scarce; their opportunities in industry and elsewhere were plentiful, and retention rates were low.

## Stigmata

Today, each of the Big Four firms runs its mainland China and Hong Kong operations as a single business. But the legacy of their separate histories remains. For many years, professional relationships between mainlanders and people from Hong Kong, and between ethnic Chinese and people of British descent, were shot through with cultural prejudices. British-born partners in Hong Kong were known pejoratively as 'FILTH' – 'Failed in London, Try Hong Kong'. Paul Gillis characterised China as a bolthole for Big Four desperadoes: 'For many lower performing people who accepted the opportunity, China was possibly their last chance with the firm. One partner observed that their China firm was built by rejects and discards.'

The prejudices ran in all directions:

> Some Western partners referred to overseas Chinese staff as Hong Kong mercenaries, who came to China solely to collect the higher salaries available with no commitment to the development of a local practice. Local staff often complained of overseas Chinese, particularly those from Hong Kong, as coming to steal their birthright.

Some non-Chinese Big Four partners in China were caricatures of Britishness, in the mould of Colonel Tom 'Thangliena' Lewin. When the merger between Price Waterhouse and Coopers & Lybrand was announced, Sir John Stuttard, the English chairman of Coopers in China, was travelling through Tibet in the Beijing to Paris Rally – driving his pink 1934 Rolls-Royce.

## Equals

In cases like that of Longtop, China had made crystal-clear its position on the jurisdiction of non-Chinese regulators. According to China's Securities Regulatory Commission, 'the presence of foreign regulators acting on Chinese soil' was 'a breach of China's sovereignty'. The prohibition on foreign regulators has included a ban on Peek-a-boo coming to China to inspect China-based auditors registered with the US regulator.

In a 2009 comment letter on proposed inspection rules, the CSRC informed the SEC of China's position:

> Our position remains unchanged, i.e. cross-border inspection must abide by the principles of respecting mutual sovereignty and cooperating as equals ... To address the challenges of cross-border inspection which are brought up by listing of public companies in host jurisdictions, the SEC and the CSRC should work together as equals under the existing framework for regulatory cooperation. Therefore, the oversight of Chinese accounting firms should fully rely on the work of the CSRC ... We are strongly opposed to PCAOB's inspection on any Chinese accounting firm before any consensus has been reached between China and the United States.

## A fist

Some branches of the Chinese state were openly hostile to the Big Four. One way to push back against the incursion of the foreign firms was to meet them head-on in the marketplace. The idea of creating a Chinese Big Four – or a Big One, or a Big Ten – has captivated Chinese accounting regulators. In the 1990s the CICPA was the principal regulator of the accounting profession in China. Ding Pingzhun, head of the CICPA, came to believe that China needed to cultivate an indigenous firm large enough to compete with the foreign 'bigs'. Ding called the hypothetical firm the 'Big One'. The merger of Coopers & Lybrand and

Price Waterhouse offered Ding the opportunity to realise his plan. Gillis described the plan as follows:

> The firm would be established by merging four firms: Zhang & Chen CPAs; the Coopers & Lybrand CIEC joint venture with CITIC that was managed by Zhang Ke; Yangcheng CPAs, a local firm in Guangzhou that had a loose affiliation with Coopers & Lybrand; and PW Da Hua, PW's joint venture with SUFE in Shanghai. Ding thought that the merger would result in a firm controlled by the Chinese personnel. 'We hope that this "big" could not be handled by the foreigners at will.'

Thus, Ding foresaw, the local firms could 'unite together to form a fist' and take the fight to the foreign 'bigs'. There were several precedents for this proposal. The Chinese government had sponsored the emergence of locally owned competitors in sectors such as car manufacturing, electronics and heavy engineering. Ding's plan, though, faced strong resistance at home and abroad. He was outmanoeuvred, a fact he recorded with much regret in his memoir: 'In this way, the famous accounting firms in China at that time were eaten by PricewaterhouseCoopers. Our dream was broken by their civilized invasion.'

Ding and his colleagues then switched to a modified strategy that was even more ambitious. Not one but ten Chinese firms would take on the Big Four. In 2007 the CICPA released the new strategy in a document entitled *Opinions on Promoting More Competitive and Bigger Chinese Accounting Firms*: 'The strategy established a five to ten year goal for China to develop ten internationalised accounting firms capable of serving Chinese companies globally.' If large, Chinese-owned accounting firms could serve China's large, overseas-listed, state-owned enterprises, 'the safety of the national economic information' would likely be better protected. These 'Chinese Big 10' recommendations were ultimately accepted by the State Council, China's highest executive body.

In a victory for the CICPA – and a major setback for the Big Four – the recommendations became official government policy.

Data provided by Paul Gillis, who has tracked the revenues of the big accounting firms in China for several years, suggest that the new policy is having an impact. While the latest numbers (covering 2015) have PwC at number one, Gillis suggests PwC is likely to fall to second place behind Ruihua. Already, Deloitte, EY and KPMG are in spots four, five and six (BDO is at number three) and their market shares have been sliding for several years.[17]

Thus, escalating tensions between the United States and China in the trade and military spheres appear to have parallels in the 'dull' sphere of audit regulation. With this hostility, alongside policies like the 'Chinese Big Ten', the risks for the Big Four are clear. Despite the legacy stronghold in Hong Kong and the hard-earned status from scrappy roots in the 1980s, mainland China – the soon-to-be-largest economy in the world, the one that seems such an opportunity for so many businesses – might be the first place where the Big Four fall from their pedestal.

17  Interestingly, the imminent market leader, Ruihua, is a member firm of Crowe Horwath, whose Hong Kong affiliate was banned in July 2017 by the PCAOB from auditing US-traded companies for three years.

# PART IV

# The Twilight Years

Much can be learned from the history of Big Four challenges and calamities. In this part, we use those lessons to explore the future of the Big Four, and how a combination of old and new pressures is likely to force the firms into a radical transformation. The pressures include technological change, regulatory action and disruptive competition. It is likely these will affect the firms' people, ownership, structure, networks, services and methods. The methodological impacts are already playing out at a fundamental level, recasting the basic technology of advisory, audit and tax services.

The final chapter in this part returns to Renaissance Florence and the history of the Medici Bank, which provides an informative example of how an international, diversified, networked organisation can come crashing down.

# 13

# DISRUPTED

## The obsolescence of Big Four technology

### Mugged by reality

Since the reopening of China's economy, the country's government agencies and state-owned enterprises have gobbled up patents and other intellectual property in areas as diverse as microwave ovens, rare earth elements, telecommunications and solar power. The fields of accounting and auditing, too, were identified as potential areas of focus for the gathering of IP. According to Paul Gillis, Chinese officials initially saw joint ventures with the Big Four as a means of transferring technologies from the firms to China. That was the plan until the officials spent some time with the foreign firms and came to a surprising realisation: public accountancy depended on very few proprietary technologies, and most were available over the counter. The core innovations upon which accountancy depended had long been available in the public domain; there was very little technology for the Big Four to transfer.

This is not to say that accounting and audit are technology-free, or that there is no innovation taking place. In fact, accountancy today is a hotspot of innovation, and the impact on the Big Four of that innovation is profound. And complex – the industrial landscape of accounting is rapidly changing in multiple ways.

The Big Four's predecessor firms were eyewitnesses to economic disruption on a massive scale. They were present when railways replaced canals and horses for freight transport. And when cars replaced horses and carriages for personal transport. And when electric cars promised to replace petrol ones. Today, many of the Big Four's priority sectors and clients are undergoing intense digital disruption; consider the impacts of Uber and Airbnb on their respective sectors, for example. The firms have profited directly from the disruptions that saw the emergence of budget airlines and online retailers; new ways to buy travel, accommodation, financial services and real estate; and new ways to deliver utilities, education and health services. Now, though, the tables have turned. Accountancy and the Big Four are themselves subject to disruption.

Accodex is a new accounting firm that exploits several new trends in the profession – including business model innovation and the use of new developments in IT – to 'democratize business intelligence services'. Thanks to its cloud technology and Manila back office, the firm was recognised at the 2015 Australian Accounting Awards as 'the most innovative firm in Australia'. Hundreds if not thousands of similar accounting start-ups are appearing around the world, many of them populated with former Big Four partners and staff. There are as many new accounting firms today as there were in Samuel Price's heyday.

## The gig economy

For KPMG in Australia, Shomalin Naidoo came up with 'KPMG Marketplace', an online portal that matches bench-sitting staff with clients in need of short-term help. The aim is to improve KPMG's staff utilisation and help smooth those troublesome peaks and troughs in workflow. Clients pay a discounted rate for Marketplace staff. While the Marketplace was preparing for launch, Naidoo moved to PwC to start Task Central, whose stated mission is:

to disrupt the professional services industry by challenging the way consulting firms market their services, engage with their clients and win work.

Our solution is an [sic] simple platform for companies to compare services and prices from some of the world's largest, as well as local professional services firms.

Companies can post short term projects and secondments and will receive quotes/pitches from a range of professional services firms within 24 hours.

In part, Task Central took its inspiration from 'gig economy', transactional labour-hire enterprises such as Freelancer.com, Work Market, DesignCrowd and Task Rabbit. Work Market claims its clients achieve a 30 to 50 per cent reduction in labour costs while improving their quality and profitability. By making service offerings more transparent, and by making switching between service providers much easier, portals such as these pose a fundamental threat to the Big Four business model.

These new entrants focus on the allocation of labour and service providers. In essence, they create and improve 'matching markets'. Other entrants are disrupting at a deeper level, changing how accounting services are delivered, and indeed the very nature of those services.

## Big data

Technology-driven auditing involves applying advances such as artificial intelligence, machine learning and 'big data' to the task of auditing. 'Audit bots' can crawl over company data. Algorithms can search for anomalies, like an executive's unusual credit card use, or patterns in breaches of delegations, or inflated overheads, or accounting entries made at odd times. Less labour-intensive than traditional auditing, digital analytic programs can be built into business systems – such as those for purchasing, HR, compliance and reporting – and can analyse and report on financial information in real time. Compared with traditional auditing, such programs can be far more effective at identifying fraud.

In the era of technology-driven auditing, nearly every computational task is suddenly practical. Big data, for example, enables exhaustive analysis of company transactions, with no inherent need for sampling. It used to be true that auditors could not hope to verify more than a fraction of the millions of transactions made by their clients in the course of business. Sampling, a core feature of modern auditing, was about practicality. Now, though, the impossible is becoming possible. Instead of sending out ever more auditors, the new approaches solve the problem of scrutinising complex businesses by deploying systems and products that 'follow the money' and build a complete picture of corporate performance and integrity. Technologies of this kind are fundamentally disrupting auditing.

The tools of technology-based auditing, though, are not necessarily well suited to the Big Four model. Other types of organisation are prominent in the field. Software companies are developing analytics programs. Systems integrators and small specialist providers are delivering analytics services. The economics of accountancy have shifted in favour of more agile and less labour-intensive enterprises.

## Self-delusion

In advisory, too, the Big Four are experiencing technological disruption and new competition. At a time when the Big Four face intense competition for staff, clients and capital, they face unprecedented competition in the market for ideas. That market is increasingly crowded. Entry costs are low and falling. The Big Four face competition from above and below – from universities, colleges, non-profit think tanks, government bureaus (such as public service commissions and audit offices) and top-tier strategy firms such as the 'Elite Three', and from smaller players with low overheads and high agility. The latter include bloggers, freelancers, online brokers, crowdsourcers and sole traders, many of them ex–Big Four. As David Maister and his co-authors noted, 'One of the worst forms of self-delusion [in a professional services provider] is to assume that one is selling specialised knowledge and that there is a limited amount of it to go around.'

Kaggle exemplifies the new entrants. Founded in 2010 by Australian economist Anthony Goldbloom (and purchased by Google in 2017), Kaggle is a data science platform on which companies and researchers post their data, and statisticians and analysts around the world compete to produce the best algorithms and models. The platform makes explicit use of innovations in crowd sourcing, machine learning, cloud computing and big data. As many as 800,000 'Kagglers' compete for prize money offered by companies such as Facebook, General Electric and Merck.

Similar platforms include SIGKDD (which hosts the 'KDDCup' predictive modelling competition); CrowdANALYTIX; HackerRank; Clopinet; DrivenData; TunedIT; TopCoder; Analytics Vidhya; and Chinese website Tianchi. Wikistrat crowdsources analysis through a network of small- and medium-sized businesses. These and other entrants are transforming the provision of analysis and solutions. The internet is creating new markets in ideas, and is decentralising the provision of advice. In an irrevocable way, advice is becoming a commodity.

## The digital future

Digital disruption is a feature of all the likely future scenarios involving the Big Four. So are offshoring, crowdsourcing and remote delivery. Competition from boutiques, micro firms and one-man bands. Standardisation, commoditisation, automation, depersonalisation, disintermediation, routinisation, cannibalisation, stupidification.

The commoditisation of accounting services is a terrifying prospect for the Big Four, yet many of their services face some form of commoditisation in the future. Survey design, data collection, data recovery, stakeholder identification, knowledge management, project management, corporate services systems (such as for invoicing, accounts payable and general ledgers), investment logic mapping, asset valuation services, cost-of-capital calculation, program evaluation, business planning – all these are vulnerable to some form of bulk, cheap or remote delivery.

It is easy to see how many core Big Four products might be replaced by a computer program, a set of equations, a book, a website or a subscription service – or simply by someone far away who is not paid much. The first audits were designed to solve problems of distance and visibility; the auditor was a separate set of eyes and ears for the master or owner or funder. In a newly transparent and connected world, there are new ways to achieve visibility and to overcome distance. That is why audit, like advisory, is highly vulnerable to disruption.

## Open

If auditing is about accountability, how can organisations be held more fully and efficiently to account for their decisions and performance? One family of innovations answers that question in a novel way. New technology has merged with the new ethics of disclosure and transparency in the form of open systems and decentralised accountability mechanisms.

Public sector bodies and not-for-profit organisations have adopted open systems and open accounts, which make information about decisions and performance universally available – and scrutiny universally feasible. Community organisations and activists have undertaken citizen audits – in which outsiders analyse company performance by relying on a mixture of published and leaked information. (There is already a long tradition of citizen audits in India.) The internet and mobile communications are making such audits much simpler. Other non-audit accountability mechanisms include qui tam laws, which change the balance of incentives by strengthening rewards for whistle-blowers and independent investigators. As we've seen, whistleblowers and private agents have strong track records in uncovering fraud and misconduct.

Compared with audit bots, this emerging set of alternatives to traditional audit has a more social and democratic character – more analogue than digital. For the Big Four, stronger whistleblower protections and stronger incentives for bounty hunters are nothing less than kryptonite. These protections and incentives disrupt auditing in a different way to digital analysis, but in a way that is equally devastating for traditional models of scrutiny.

These open, decentralised systems seem less susceptible to auditing's 'seven deadly sins'. Information is less vulnerable to ex-post sugar-coating.[18] Putting scrutiny in the hands of people who care – such as customers and investors – can help overcome the hollow, ritualistic character of contemporary auditing, and keep the focus on the issues that matter.

## Enemy of innovation

World Firm. Global Firm. Global Head Office. International Headquarters. The Big Four adopt different titles for the same thing: an international entity, owned and funded by the national practices and whose ostensible purpose is to spur and foster common standards and practices, encourage service excellence, and, to some extent, sponsor a

---

18   Open systems can, however, cause perverse behaviours. People might avoid putting adverse information in writing, for example – a kind of ex-ante sugar-coating.

network-wide strategy. In reality, other purposes loom large. A stint of service in the world firm is a fitting reward for ambitious juniors – and an appropriate destination for aged seniors, especially those from the powerful US and UK firms. The global offices are also valuable as marketing baubles. For smaller practices bidding for work, the ability to call upon global resources and international 'centres of excellence' adds another touch of magic dust, another layer of glamour with which to dazzle current or prospective clients.

Strong forces, though, keep the global offices small and weak. The offices have a peculiar power relationship with the national practices. Each national firm allocates profits on a national basis, and decides independently on promotion to partnership. Each one maintains separate reserves of capital and retained profits. The 'head offices' are not actually head offices at all, but jointly owned subsidiaries of the national practices. Those practices strive to keep their overhead costs low, and to minimise curbs on their activities. Because of how clients are charged, how performance is measured and how profits are allocated, partners tend to favour their own business units over others. For the same reasons, national practices have few incentives to use foreign staff and resources when local ones are available. The distribution of power within the networks is strongly weighted towards the larger national hubs.

Together, these forces mean the world firms are underfunded, toothless and partly virtual. Permanently walking on thin ice, the head office personnel do their best not to annoy anyone inside or outside the network. The reports that emanate from the 'global centres of excellence' are commonsensical and inoffensive to the point of absurdity: they avoid taking controversial positions on innovation, taxation, privatisation, banking, manufacturing, outsourcing, pension schemes, population ageing – pretty well everything. On a case-by-case basis the most powerful national firms decide whether or not to cooperate with the 'centre'. Edgar Jones wrote of Price

Waterhouse in 1995: 'While the senior partners of the various national firms were enthusiastic about the role to be taken by the World Firm, in practice they were often unwilling to follow its lead.' When conflict breaks out between the national firms, 'head office' has little capacity to set things right.

(Conflict between national offices within the Big Four networks seldom makes it into the public domain, but certainly does happen. The networks aren't always happy families. Perennial sources of conflict include the funding of global projects – such as for branding and professional development; the opening of new offices; and the distribution of fee revenue from transnational engagements. A former Price Waterhouse partner called the Hong Kong office the 'pariah' of the network, 'because of the difficulty of negotiating fee arrangements on shared clients and the Hong Kong firm's unwillingness to contribute to global initiatives'. Michael Barrett, David J. Cooper and Karim Jamal studied the relationship between Big Four offices in smaller cities and those in large metropolitan centres such as New York and London. The smaller offices, often highly profitable and innovative, resented the status of the larger ones. And they resented the cost of belonging to a franchise network, including the payments they made to support the corporate headquarters. The smalls called such contributions 'throw-up'.)

This model – a network of separately owned franchises with a weak head office – is unusual and inherently unstable. The decentralisation of the firms' governance and risk management is one cause of the observed diversity of conduct among Big Four personnel, which in turn is one cause of the recurring scandals. Apart from the fact that it impairs the firms' risk management, the franchise structure is ill-suited to funding and supporting major IP development and IT commercialisation projects. The head offices, for example, cannot raise capital for the geographical partnerships in the way a corporate owner might. Yet those are the kinds of projects that are needed for the firms to embrace and get ahead of disruption.

## Innovation blockers

The Big Four do not participate directly in equity capital markets. They are hard to take over, and just as hard to sell. Combining accounting firms typically involves adding partners and delicately normalising their obligations and entitlements. As such, unlike standard corporate tie-ups, professional services mergers are highly personal exercises, much like the merging of gentlemen's clubs, with the same scope for scuppering and blackballing.

Several mooted mergers between accounting firms were abandoned due to challenges of the partnership structure. Difficulties of getting agreement across multiple jurisdictions and offices, and working out how losses and gains should be shared, can be prohibitive. These same difficulties are barriers to adequate Big Four investment in innovation.

Dependent on leverage and the partner track, and on collective decision-making, the firms cannot rapidly retool or reorient themselves. Within the partnership structure there is less latitude, compared with many corporates and most start-ups, to make rapid promotions, leap remuneration categories, pay one-off bonuses or share substantial equity. Or take big risks.

Every entrepreneur will agree that start-ups need the right amount of capital at the right time and on the right terms. Relying on partners' retained earnings and capital contributions is unlikely to produce the right quantum of capital with the right risk appetite at the right price. The 8th Audit Directive of the European Commission limits external ownership to 49 per cent and requires the majority of the management board of an audit firm to be approved EU auditors. In 2011 the UK's Economic Affairs Committee contemplated new ownership rules for the Big Four, to 'make it easier for firms to raise capital to expand into the market for the audits of the largest companies'. The committee noted that the cost of capital in professional services partnerships was 'considerably higher than in an external investment ownership model'.

Apart from appropriate capital, a well-nourished subsidiary needs internal permission and sufficient freedom to operate. The Big Four model tends to result in conservatism and slow decision-making: major strategic decisions must sometimes be made amid warring national firms, and always with regard to the impacts on diverse teams and clients. The firms' precious brands reinforce their high degree of risk aversion. To protect their reputations, the Big Four cannot afford too many failed experiments.

Over the past two decades, the Risk divisions of the Big Four have grown in scale and power. These divisions are naturally and intrinsically even more risk-averse than the other parts of the firms, yet entrepreneurship requires good doses of risk-seeking and risk-taking. Even if external regulators permit the Big Four to experiment with their fundamental business models, *internal* permission to do so will be highly circumscribed. Compared to a new, unfettered, well-capitalised 'Accounting Inc.', the Big Four are not in the game.

Professional services partnerships do not require much capital in ordinary times. Most of their value is in their people and client relationships, not in tangible assets. Partner capital, moreover, is illiquid, locked up in the firm and dependent on attracting and developing new partners. Partners at different stages of their career have conflicting incentives concerning investment in innovation. Older partners approaching retirement, for example, may oppose investments that have a long pay-off period. And yet it is those older partners who are most often in leadership positions within the firms. (In 2009, for instance, PwC China amended its partnership agreement to reduce the voting rights of recently admitted partners.) And innovation requires leadership.

If the unlikely happened and a Big Four firm succeeded in generating a major disruption of the old professional services model, there would be conflict between the national offices like never before. Faced with a new, internally generated product that promised to transform accounting services by making the firms' staff and infrastructure redundant, the firms' incentives would be even worse than those of a traditional car manufacturer that owned an electric car patent. Why worse? Because the typical car manufacturer is a corporation with one set of owners and one set of corporate imperatives. Within the Big Four networks, by contrast, the incentives of national practices are decidedly mixed. An individual national practice that came up with a way to transform accountancy globally may well be in breach of its licensing agreement, and would certainly create winners and losers within the franchise network.

The same problem plays out on a larger scale among the Big Four. If one of their number miraculously pulled off a transformative innovation, one or more of the other firms would be left behind. When it comes to radical change achieved through proprietary innovations, the firms cannot all succeed at the same time in the same way.

## The barrier of Big Four-ism

Apart from capital and organisational structure, there is another important barrier to innovation by the Big Four: culture. Peter Drucker noticed how every large organisation tended to discourage initiative and reward conformity. In the Big Four, these tendencies have always been especially strong. Large accounting firms have long celebrated the values of compliance, conformity, hard work and fitting in. The firms are populated for the most part by mid-ranking graduates from mid-ranking universities and colleges. They celebrate heroes who were noticeably modest in their achievements. As Mark Stevens observed, 'You don't have to be great to make it to partner. You have to be competent, dedicated and hard-driving. The rigid atmosphere of [the large firms] – the emphasis on conformity – actually screens out the brilliant, innovative and unorthodox minds.'

Yet these are the minds who are needed to meet the challenge of disruption. Despite efforts to import people from advertising and think tanks and circuses, the overwhelming culture of the Big Four is still one of conformity and averageness. And despite the diversification of the firms' workforces, the old prejudices against lateral hires persist, as do the old inflexibilities inherent in the professional services model and the partner track.

Transformative innovation in accountancy is inevitable, but, for all the reasons presented here, it is unlikely to be driven from within the Big Four. Confronted by deep-seated constraints on innovation, many key staff are doing the maths and leaving the firms to innovate and disrupt outside the strictures of the partner track and audit regulation and the professional services business model.

This brings us to another sobering conclusion: to the extent that the Big Four are feeding the transformation of accountancy, they are doing so mostly through the exit of staff and the defection of teams, who are setting up elsewhere with the intention of profiting from disruption. There is dynamism in the sector, but the big firms cannot control it, and it is largely not occurring for their benefit.

# 14

# CONCLUSION

## The endgame

Painful arthritic gout afflicted many of the Medici men. But Piero il Gottoso, 'frail, bedridden and bad-tempered', suffered at least as much as any of his brethren. A collector like his father, Piero accumulated gems, coins, tapestries, cameos, silverware, jewellery, tournament weapons, musical instruments and books. He was so crippled by his condition that he had to be carried into his barrel-vaulted study-cum-library, which Luca della Robbia had sumptuously decorated.[19]

Cosimo de Medici died in 1464. For the funeral, Piero bought mourning clothes for four female slaves: Catrina, Chateruccia, Cristina and Zita. Piero's library was a sanctuary, but his father's death plunged him into a crisis. Despite his illness, and his limited experience in

---

19 Piero's books were bound and shelved methodically in colour-coded categories: red for history, green for rhetoric and so on. Printing was still a novelty in Piero's day; Gutenberg's invention, which dated from the 1450s, spread only gradually over the rest of the century. Most of Piero's books were manuscripts that had been painstakingly (and expensively) copied by hand from other authoritative versions. Piero commissioned books with beautifully illuminated borders that set the standard for Florentine manuscript decoration for the rest of the century.

banking and business, Piero embraced his new role with a determination to live up to the legacies and the reputations of his father and grandfather. Florence was a dangerous, conspiratorial place. To navigate through its many pitfalls, Piero took advice from men such as the politician Diotisalvi Neroni, who'd also advised Cosimo. In the first months of Piero's new tenure, he chose a course of action that was the wrong one.

According to Niccolò Machiavelli's *History of Florence*, Neroni advised Piero to call in the bank's aged and sedentary debts. Piero seems to have done so without much regard for which loans were hard and which were soft – or which ones were commercial and which were political. Cosimo had used fungible loans liberally to accumulate friends and influence in Florence and abroad. The results of Piero's policy were entirely predictable. As soon as he demanded repayment, a chorus of complaint rang out. Borrowers called the Medici family's new head greedy and ungrateful. Several Florentine businesses collapsed. The aggrieved parties began plotting against Piero and his rule.

In the ensuing uproar, Diotisalvi Neroni changed sides, joining in a conspiracy that aimed, according to Machiavelli, 'to deprive Piero of his credit and authority'. Among the other conspirators were Luca Pitti, Agnolo Acciaiuoli, Niccolò Soderini, and Piero's own cousin Pierfrancesco de Medici. Tipped off about the coup plot by Giovanni II Bentivoglio, Piero was able to escape, and to retain his slim hold on power. In the face of a second coup, Piero again prevailed. But in 1469 he succumbed to his gout and his bad lungs. Having led the bank for only five years, he was laid to rest in the Church of San Lorenzo, alongside his brother Giovanni. Andrea del Verrocchio, the brilliant pupil of Donatello, made the tomb: a porphyry sarcophagus ornamented with acanthus leaves. The vast Medici fortune passed, more or less intact, but much more at risk, to Piero's eldest son, Lorenzo de Medici, later known as Il Magnifico.

Today, Piero il Gottoso is much less well known than his son and his father. But Piero is important because he is a bridge between the

Medici Bank's golden age and its endgame: he is the pivot point, the man who 'kept things going' but failed to position the network for the future. With Piero the Gouty, the rot set in.

Even uglier than his father and grandfather, Lorenzo was only twenty when he took over the family business. Niall Ferguson again used a Mafia metaphor to describe the rise of the Medici: the family started out as the Sopranos – a smallish-time crime syndicate – and became the Corleones, 'and more'. That was the case, until it all fell apart. A magnificent patron of the arts, Lorenzo was also, like his ancestors, an avid collector. He bought sacred relics and added to his father's collection of jewels, cameos, manuscripts and armour. The armour, though, was no help when trouble arrived.

The Florentine banks of the Peruzzi, the Bardi and the Acciaiuoli had collapsed after two extinction-level events: defaults by the profligate royal borrowers Edward III of England and Robert of Naples. Those collapses shaped the methods and structure of the Medici Bank. Its network model was intended to protect each office from the failures of the others. Instead of spreading to other branches and to the head office, the logic held, the contagion of bad decisions and bad debts could be contained. In reality, though, the network structure failed to prevent the bank's insolvency, and may in fact have hastened it.

Theoretically, the bank's branches were not liable for one another's debts. In the face of large losses, though, this protection buckled. During the War of the Roses, the bank made large loans to Edward IV of England. When Edward defaulted, just as his namesake had done, the bank's London branch collapsed. The English debts were taken on by the Bruges branch, which now laboured under a deficit of more than 70,000 gold florins. Soon that branch, too, was insolvent. Lorenzo de Medici instructed Rinieri da Ricasoli to dissolve Bruges and audit its books. Lorenzo remarked acidly, 'These are the great profits which are accruing to us through the management of Tommaso Portinari.'

The insurance inherent in the Medici Bank structure was adequate for small claims and small losses, such as those arising from badly packed wool. But the firewalls between the Medici branches could not contain very large losses; nor could they contain the reputational damage that is so dangerous for banks. The contagion spread all the way back to Florence. Faced with financial disaster, Lorenzo looked around for hollow logs to raid. The family vault, the state treasuries, a charitable fund for paying dowries – all were plundered in the rush to the Medici endgame.

Focus had been at the heart of the Medicis' success. Gradually, though, they had forgotten their core business. Diversification exposed the bank to different competitive pressures and different macro-economic risks. No longer mainly the financier to the church, the bank had become a commodity trader, an importer, a manufacturer, a miner and an underwriter. Each one of these activities brought new risks, a new appetite for capital and the need to develop new capabilities among the bank's personnel. Operating in multiple fields made it harder to find the right managers, and to monitor and reward those managers once found. The bank, too, had to be rewarded – for all those new risks it was taking on. But pricing the risks was difficult. Inevitably, the bank accumulated obligations for which it was not adequately compensated.

The diversified Medici Bank's articles of association stated its purpose of dealing in foreign exchange and merchandise, 'with the help of God and of good fortune'. But God and fortune had deserted the bank. One by one, the Medici businesses came under pressure. The alum business was not as profitable as the partners had hoped, and the monopoly not as effective. Rival suppliers broke the cartel by secretly importing alum from the Middle East. On the banking side, new means of lending and currency exchange emerged, disrupting the bank's business model. At the same time, an international recession and regional wars caused a falling-off in transnational trade. Fine English wool was an essential input for Italian textiles production, and the decline in trade helped starve the Medici mills of fibre.

Lorenzo's own conduct accelerated the bank's decline. As a businessman, an administrator and a commercial strategist, Lorenzo was far from magnificent. Going against Giovanni's deathbed imprecations, Lorenzo devoted much more of his time to politics than to business. Yet business was the basis for the Medici's political power, as well as for their wealth. Lorenzo also pursued a patrician, aristocratic way of life, in which he wrote poetry and maintained a 'portly mistress'.

Under Lorenzo, there were also more mundane and insidious slippages. He allowed the bank's internal administration and controls to atrophy. This opened the door to a series of frauds and scandals that were hard to detect and, once exposed, difficult to contain. Francesco Sassetti, for example, failed to discover a major fraud at the Lyons branch – 'until it was too late'. The branch's manager, Lionetto de Rossi, had incompetently underestimated the branch's bad loans. In an attempt to cover up his mistakes, he borrowed funds from other banks and misaccounted for them as hefty profits. In reality, the Lyons branch was unprofitable, and insolvent.

Having put the stewardship of the bank in the hands of inept men, Lorenzo gave them scant supervision. He knew too little about the business to guide the success of his managers, or to hold them to account for their mistakes. Angelo Tani tried to prevent the failure of the Bruges branch, and appealed to Lorenzo to overrule Sassetti and restrict the lending of the London branch. Lorenzo replied that he 'did not understand such matters'. Tommaso Portinari – the longstanding but incompetent manager of the Bruges branch – engaged in business dealings on the side, and ran the branch into the ground. Lorenzo admitted that his own lack of knowledge and understanding explained why he had approved Portinari's 'disastrous schemes'.

In 1492, so debilitated by gout that he could no longer visit his mistress, Lorenzo il Magnifico died at the age of forty-three. With the bank on the verge of bankruptcy and beset by multiple court cases, its leadership passed to Lorenzo's eldest son, Piero di Lorenzo – who soon came to be known as Piero the Fatuous.

This Piero had neither the experience nor the talent required to run the bank. He put his secretary and his great-uncle in charge, and they proceeded to mismanage the bank such that it slid further towards bankruptcy. That slide was only halted when it was overtaken by geopolitical events. In 1494, the year in which Pacioli's *Summa de Arithmetica* was published, Charles VIII of France invaded Italy. The Medici were no longer rich enough or strong enough to hold Florence. The bank's records were seized, and its assets distributed to creditors and others. All the subsidiary partnerships were dissolved.

## Dramatic loss of franchise value

Multiple factors came together in the Medici endgame. In seeking to be a manufacturer, insurer, slaver, toll collector and commodities trader, the enterprise lost sight of its core business: banking. Having long depended on meticulous bookkeeping, it allowed its systems of accounting and control to deteriorate. Critical risks were mispriced and mismanaged. Critical relationships were neglected. The bank faced disruptive competition from all sides.

Today, the diversified Big Four firms face a similar confluence of existential dangers. Every one of their major business lines is facing new competitive, regulatory and technological pressures. Every one of them is exposed to the risk of a calamitous failure. In 2011 Professor Michael Power told the UK Economic Affairs Committee to beware of 'shock events' affecting one or more of the four. 'I don't think we can rule out dramatic loss of franchise value,' he cautioned. Regulators in Britain and elsewhere are already preparing for the exit of a Big Four firm.

The firms' franchise model closely resembles the original Medici network of legally separate geographical partnerships. For the Big Four, this structure helps limit liability and contain the fallout from lawsuits and other misadventures. Just as the Medici did, the Big Four have used their franchise structure as an all-weather tool. It enables them to say, when it suits, that all the national practices are parts of a single international entity, and at other times to disavow togetherness, just as Deloitte has recently done in Shanghai, and EY in Hong Kong. But, again like the Medici, the protection is imperfect. Being sued after a high-profile corporate collapse or a failed audit or tax scandal wreaks real damage on the Big Four brands. A large share of the damage transcends geographies and service lines. The collapse of Arthur Andersen showed how hard it is for a multinational accounting firm to contain reputational damage and – just as important – the impact of regulatory reactions. The distributed partnership model is no protection from extinction-level events, like another TBW or Akai, or an IRS indictment.

Understanding the nature of the Big Four brands is important to understanding how a contagion might play out. Each of the four firms wears a hierarchy of brands. There is the service line brand, such as PwC Tax. There is the national practice brand, such as PwC LLP in the United States. There is the global brand. And then there is the meta-brand, 'Big Four'. That brand, while not directly or explicitly owned by any single firm, is just as important in the accounting marketplace as the firms' individual brands. In the hierarchy of accounting, there is the Big Four and then there is everyone else. This joint brand is pivotal to how a disaster might propagate among the firms. In the ecosystem of modern capitalism, the Big Four are parts of a single organism. They will live or die together.

What might a post–Big Four world look like, and how might we get there? Across the multiple dimensions of structure, ownership, governance, services, skills and regulation, there are multiple feasible scenarios and multiple pathways to the Big Four endgame. Those dimensions encompass how the accounting market is structured, including how many big accounting firms remain; how the firms are owned and organised – as partnerships, corporations or something else; how the firms work and are governed; what services they provide; how they are appointed to conduct audits; who works in the firms; the extent to which their current clients look to other sources for accounting and audit services; and precisely how the future is reached (via regulatory action, client defection, catastrophic collapse or another route). Some plausible futures are unrecognisably different from the status quo.

## Antitrust

Regulators, scholars and activists around the world have long been interested in the end of the Big Four monopoly and the future structure of a more competitive market for accounting services. Several authors have argued that lawmakers and regulators should have blocked the merger of Price Waterhouse and Coopers & Lybrand. Others have gone further, advocating the breaking up of the Big Four.

The 2010 European Commission Green Paper on *Audit Policy: Lessons from the Crisis* entertained the idea of downsizing or restructuring the firms on the grounds that their present size posed a systemic risk for the capitalist economies. The UK's Economic Affairs Committee appealed to the firms directly, 'as professional entities', to 'put the public interest first' and voluntarily break themselves up into a new Big Six, or perhaps even a Big Eight: 'The quid pro quo for society ceding monopoly rights to practice and other privileges, is that professionals place the ideal of public service above other considerations. A clear ultimatum, time-defined, might be set for the Big 4.'

In his career as a tax specialist, George Rozvany worked stints at EY, PwC and Arthur Andersen. In 2016 he argued that the Big Four, by becoming so powerful and pervasive, had 'sown the seeds of their own destruction': governments had no option but to pursue a Big Four breakup, just as antitrust regulators had broken up monopolies in other sectors such as telecommunications, energy and financial services.

Under the franchise model, each Big Four practice is already fractured along service lines; each one is a collection of smaller businesses with different cultures providing different services and charging different fees. In principle, therefore, breaking up the firms is a possibility. But such a breakup – into six or eight or some other number – would have far-reaching effects. The most profound would be the destruction of the firms' biggest assets: their brands.

The Chinese government is pursuing a pro-competition strategy by building indigenous accounting firms to take on the Big Four in China and abroad. In the West, too, calls have intensified for government to intervene and make accountancy – and especially auditing – more competitive. The House of Lords Economic Affairs committee, for example, considered creating new major audit firms based on the publicly owned UK Audit Commission and the UK National Audit Office. When this style of privatisation of public-sector audit was attempted in the late 1990s in Victoria, however, it was highly controversial and hastened the electoral defeat of the state government.

## Corporate form

Major change in how the firms are owned and structured is a likely feature of their future. Instead of a network of partnerships, the firms could become large corporations. Or they could adopt some other corporate form, such as a loose network of smaller, affiliated enterprises like those in the international Cordence family of advisory firms.

Corporatisation would require a difficult transition from partner ownership to shareholder ownership. The 'demutualisation' of member-based insurers provides an example of how such a transition might be accomplished. In the new corporate entity, partners could become equity-owning executives, and outside investors would also be able to participate in ownership of the Big Four. The change would necessarily involve a difficult process of international, inter-practice negotiation – as well as difficult decisions about the location, size and role of the new head office, and difficult conversations with regulators and clients about departing from the firms' origins and historical undertakings. But the prize could be large: observers have speculated that, in an initial public offering, the firms could be worth upwards of US$150 billion – each.

Investors from China and elsewhere have reportedly contemplated merging with or taking over one or more of the Big Four. Transactions of this kind could help solve the capital constraints on Big Four innovation; they might allow the firms to raise money on better terms and at a better cost. On its own, however, a change in corporate structure (or ownership) would not solve the Big Four's monopoly issue. Nor would it address problems and pressures within and between service lines, such as the potential conflicts between audit and advisory. Another set of possible endgames specifically aims to address such conflicts. These involve a 'retreat to audit': the creation of audit-only firms, with all other functions hived off to one or more demerged entities.

## Retreat to audit

The creation of audit-only firms involves using structure to solve the independence issue once and for all. The potential benefits of pure audit firms go far beyond regulatory support and improved independence. Though the audit monopoly gives the Big Four an enormous competitive advantage in other markets, such as strategic advisory, the need to comply with audit standards and regulations imposes a heavy red-tape burden on the firms' strategic advisory divisions. The need to adhere to audit standards and legislation is an everyday drag on those divisions. It restricts the types of contract they can sign and how engagements can be undertaken, and even whether they can be undertaken at all. There may be as many negative synergies between audit and advisory as there are positive ones.

Other breakups along functional lines have also been suggested, such as splitting tax from auditing, on the grounds of improved integrity and probity. George Rozvany, speaking to financial journalist Michael West, imagined splitting each of the four firms into separate tax and audit businesses, and then splitting each of the resulting firms again to enhance competition. 'International commerce will then have eight international audit firms and eight international tax firms from which to choose,' he said. Though this cut and re-cut option is as neat and fascinating as a Japanese chef slicing up sashimi, it would never be as simple as it sounds.

Of the many terrors that confront the Big Four, one is that legislators and regulators will solve the independence question by mandating audit-only firms. To repel this 'drastic' option, the Big Four have marshalled the flipsides of all the arguments they used to justify diversification in the first place. A compulsory move to audit-only firms, they say, would increase costs for clients, reduce innovation and discourage talent from entering accountancy, leading ultimately to less effective auditing and weaker corporate governance.

While a retreat to audit is a plausible outcome, it would leave many issues unresolved, such as the firms' professional values and monopoly power. It is an outcome, too, that has already been tried by three of the four firms. After seeking to create purer audit and pure advisory businesses (through the carving-out of BearingPoint, Capgemini and Monday in the early 2000s), the firms abandoned that endeavour and swung back enthusiastically – and possibly irreversibly – towards diversification.

## Lying awake

The current audit appointment model is based on several related ideas. First, that auditors seek to do thorough audits to maintain and enhance their reputations for probity and competence. Second, that audit committees are motivated to choose the auditor that will deliver a high-quality audit. While American auditors have been chosen by a subcommittee of the board of directors since Sarbox in 2002, we've highlighted the deficiencies in this model, as well as one in which shareholders appoint the auditor directly.

Various approaches have been suggested to address the shortcomings of the auditor appointment process. One idea is to force rotation of auditors. While the Big Four have managed to fend off this idea in much of the world, new EU rules require listed companies and other public-interest entities to put their audits out for tender every ten years, and to change auditor at least every twenty years. Deloitte audit managing partner Stephen Griggs summarised the new reality and its impact among auditors: 'Audit firms know they are going to lose all their existing clients. That's something to think about when you're lying awake at night.'

Compulsory tendering changes market dynamics in several decisive ways. It creates opportunities for smaller entrants; it encourages accounting practices to differentiate their service offerings; and it forces them to be more careful about audit/advisory conflicts – because advisory work can be both a barrier to winning a tender and an alternative to bidding at all. Gilly Lord, PwC's head of regulatory affairs, remarked: 'We have had to get much more agile at changing the nature of our relationships between audit and non-audit.'

## Covered

The UK Economic Affairs Committee considered 'a radical, innovative measure' to enhance audit competition, proposed by Professor Joshua Ronen of New York University. This was the introduction of a financial statements insurance market that would compete with the conventional audit market. The idea is that, as an alternative to buying a conventional audit, the audit committee (or whoever is responsible for auditor appointment) would purchase financial statement insurance (FSI) to cover the reliability of the financial statements.

> As with other forms of insurance, the insurer would be likely to review the company and set conditions before providing the cover ... The insurance premium and the limit of the cover would be published. Then the insurer would appoint an auditor, also from the approved list, whose scope of work would be determined by the degree of risk that the insurer was willing to bear. If the company failed this audit, it would have two options for the following year: first, to revert to a conventional audit; or to renegotiate the [FSI] cover. When a claim was made against an FSI policy – for example, after investors sought compensation for losses allegedly caused by relying on misleading financial statements – it would be assessed by an arbitration process.

Even more radical alternatives to audit are being considered by regulators and clients. In the near future, will companies look to the big accounting firms for services, or seek them elsewhere? Will the Big Four be disrupted into oblivion?

## Nationalisation

Another scenario goes much further in displacing the current model of audit committees appointing auditors from an ever-shrinking list of major firms. Nationalisation of the entire corporate audit function has been talked about since the beginning of modern corporate governance. Such a step would have ultimately the same effect as nationalisation of the Big Four audit businesses.

In the 1930s, during hearings on the proposed *Securities Act*, the US Senate Committee on Banking and Currency considered assigning to a government agency – perhaps the new Securities and Exchange

Commission – the role of auditing private corporations. The agency itself would employ and deploy the auditors. A senior partner at Haskins & Sells and the president of the New York State Society of Certified Public Accountants, Arthur H. Carter, was the man who voiced those famous words about auditors being audited by their consciences. Carter persuaded the committee to allow professional services firms to perform the audit function. In the words of Stephen A. Zeff, 'A government takeover of the auditing of publicly traded companies was averted.'

The idea, though, never really went away. In 2014, Professor Prem Sikka asked: 'Do people panic when the IRS descends on them, or when your friendly neighbourhood auditor that you pay does?' Audits of banks, in particular, were better suited to government provision, Sikka argued. If such audits were conducted by statutory regulators, the regulators would know much more about the regulated firms, and could regulate more effectively.

To a degree, nationalisation is already happening. Peek-a-boo's detailed inspections reflect an increased government role in corporate auditing. Given the continued failure of the historical model, the US government has effectively stepped in to set the quality standards that auditors need to deliver, perhaps paving the way for taking over the job of auditing itself.

## Halved

Technological substitution is disrupting auditing. In the rapidly emerging future, the functions and objectives previously performed and pursued by audit teams are instead being acquitted by digital analytics and 'audit bots', by more open systems and organisations, and by stronger incentives for good performance, and disclosure of bad performance. These trends are already affecting the workforces of the Big Four. Some national practices are adjusting radically their hiring plans.

EY, for example, predicted in 2016 a possible *halving* of its junior auditor intake by 2020.

Accounting partnerships were built on a high degree of employee loyalty and commitment. The modern workforce, however, is notable for the waning of commitment both from employee and employer. Amid high scepticism about traditional modes of work, new ways of working and new types of employment relationship are emerging. Up to one in three workers in the United States, for example, has an unconventional employment relationship, such as working freelance, or as a casual or temp. Careers are taking different shapes and playing out over different timeframes.

The probability that some types of accounting, auditing and tax jobs will be automated in the next decade is 100 per cent. The repetitive work of auditing is well suited to robots. Large swathes of audit and advisory work can be replaced by smart algorithms and cognitive artificial intelligence. If the firms survive the impending digital disruption, their human workforces are likely to have a much higher proportion of computer scientists and other IT people than they do today. Will accountancy become just a sub-branch of IT? The relative importance of accounting expertise will decline as the value of other skills increases. Why limit the set of potential auditors to accountants?

Both in the field and in universities, the boundaries between accountancy and IT are already breaking down. Brigham Young University, for example, now teaches technology systems developed by Oracle and SAP – alongside traditional accounting. The current breed of Big Four audit partners is arguably ill-suited to supervising data science teams and other IT practitioners. In 2015–16 the Australian offices of the Big Four promoted 274 new partners; only fifty-nine were in traditional audit and assurance services; digital and cyber skills were a strong focus of non-audit recruitment. And there is an even more fundamental problem. The leveraged, labour-intensive, partner-track model doesn't fit the digital future.

The professional services business model was developed to reward labour. But analytics are intensive in capital, not labour. Once the innovations are produced, they can be deployed with fewer staff. Robots don't need to be recruited or incentivised or promoted. And the partnership model will collapse without the flow of juniors into the mafia-like hierarchy, or without the continuation of bubble-like growth.

## Step change

The history of industrial transformation in capitalist countries contains a host of sobering lessons for the Big Four. In their respective industries – whether automotive, energy, communications, media, services or elsewhere – major industrial players have struggled to lead major industrial disruption. Indeed, many such players have failed even to *survive* disruption. Instead, disruption has tended to come from outside established industries. Grab and Lyft disrupted the taxi market from outside, for example, while Kodak and Nokia failed to grasp the opportunities of disruption within the photography and telephony markets. Right now, fundamental disruption in the car and energy industries is being driven by outsiders such as Tesla, Nest, SolarCity and Google.

There is mounting evidence that accountancy, too, is an industry in which disruption will come largely from outside – and it may well leave the insiders behind. That evidence includes the history of gradual and often superficial changes to Big Four standards and methods. With respect to standards, the profession has responded to previous emergencies by revising auditing standards and codes of ethics in incremental ways. As Prem Sikka argued in 'Financial Crisis and the Silence of Auditors', such incremental changes will not be enough to meet the present challenges. Auditing, for example, cannot be reinvigorated unless audit standards reflect the reality of modern auditing, including 'the processes associated with the production of audits, changes in capitalism, [and the] limits of auditing'.

With regard to the outputs and internal methods of the Big Four, the firms have regularly reinvented themselves by entering new markets and adopting new languages; examples from advisory include the terminologies of 'corporate social responsibility', 'social capital', 'commissioning', 'public value' – even 'corporate mindfulness'. The firms have refined procedures and adopted new modes of internal organisation. In large part, though, all these changes are wafer-thin. The ownership, business model, technology and activities of the Big Four have not changed in fundamental ways for decades. It now seems clear that step-changes in accountancy will likely come from outside the Big Four, and even from outside the profession.

## At risk

The rapid expansion of the Big Four was made possible by the firms taking on more and more risk, such as by going deeper into the perilous fields of insolvency, advocacy and tax, and by cutting corners in auditing. The firms have been accused of short-termism in trading off integrity and quality against profitability. Sooner or later, though, the short term ends. The drive for cash at the expense of standards cannot be sustainable. Under a plausible 'music stops' scenario, the firms' spectacular growth is indeed a bubble, and risks will accelerate as the burst approaches. Ralph Walters' prescient words are worth repeating: 'The major firms are on a growth treadmill that inevitably will stop.'

Advisory services, once seen as the cycle-smoothing saviour of accountancy, have brought unexpected risks that could hasten the end of the Big Four. It is in audit and tax, however, where the dangers of an extinction-level event are especially daunting. The flow of tax- and audit-related lawsuits has not abated. PwC, for example, is currently the target of a class-action claim relating to a failed education provider, Vocation. Some of the lawsuits are terrifyingly large, such as the US$1-billion MF

Global malpractice case, and the long-running, multi-billion-dollar Akai and TBW–Colonial sagas.

Regulators have said they will not allow the Big Four to become the Big Three. This injunction has a clear impact on the firms' incentives. It creates a situation of moral hazard on a colossal scale. Organisations that are insured against failure take bigger risks; recall every banking disaster over the past century or more. Insurance against failure has the perverse effect of making failure more likely.

There are many examples from other industries of seemingly stable oligopolies rapidly going out of business thanks to the actions of competitors or disruptors. Manufacturing, media, energy and financial services industries have each experienced what Niall Ferguson termed a 'great dying' – an event he likened to the end-Permian calamity in which nine-tenths of Earth's species were killed off. Matthew Crawford offered one such example: 'In 1900 there were 7632 wagon and carriage manufacturers in the United States. Adopting [Henry] Ford's methods, the industry would soon be reduced to the Big Three.' In the face of the same industry-reshaping risk in accountancy, it is timely for the Big Four to update their living wills.

## Pathways to the future

This, then, is what we are confronting. How will the firms reach their imminent destinations? Aside from a chaotic, Andersen-style meltdown caused by a major dispute or internal breach, there are several potential routes to the future that involve external causes such as client defection and regulatory action.

Imagine that a major corporate client decides it has had enough of the current 'necessary evil' model of corporate audit. The client chooses to defect to a different mode of scrutiny and accountability, and a different source of advice. If other corporations followed, the defection could change the corporate terrain fundamentally.

Is this scenario plausible? A major client could only submit to a different mode of audit – such as fully open accounts or fully automated scrutiny – if it had regulatory permission to do so. Regulators are concerned about the Big Four's performance, and are equally ambitious to break out of the current bind. Permission, therefore, could be forthcoming. The defecting company would be required to adopt an approach that promised to deliver measurably equivalent or better impacts on accountability and performance. (This is why the Big Four are terrified by grey-letter law, and by outcomes-based regulation and standards. The firms are at least as wedded to the audit journey as they are to the destination.) The change could be adopted experimentally and incrementally at first, with one or more companies collaborating with one or more regulators, perhaps to augment the traditional audit approach in a particular jurisdiction, or for a particular type of enterprise or business activity.

The modern history of the Big Four is one of recurrent scandals, followed by efforts by regulators to establish remedial laws and institutions and standards. Many authors in the fields of accounting, regulation and governance have seen this regulatory dance as a mere ritual, designed to take the heat out of the scandals and thereby to preserve the status quo, modified only in modest and incremental ways. This dance, though, may yet come to an end – with a more fundamental regulatory shift. Regulators in the United States, Europe or China could pursue a 'regulatory reboot': a step-change that leads to an altogether different way of purchasing and providing accounting services.

## Mystery

Obsolete equipment. Out-evolved megafauna. Melting icebergs. Stolen cheese. Whichever metaphor you choose, the Big Four are in trouble. The exclusive patch of turf that made them rich is shrinking fast. In the new era of transparency and regulatory activism, for example, old forms of tax avoidance are no longer viable. So, too, many other advisory services. In auditing, new technologies are simultaneously eroding and encroaching upon the Big Four's monopoly concession.

The Big Four are not public companies, so their end will not resemble any of the stock-market busts of the last four centuries. (When PwC helped botch the 2017 Best Picture announcement at the Academy Awards, there was no subsequent slump in its share price – it doesn't have one.) The firms are not subject to scrutiny by market analysts, stock exchanges, outside shareholders, conventional corporate boards or the investing public. Nor, typically, do they scrutinise each other. Largely free of conventional debt finance, the firms are not probed by lenders to any significant extent. Accounting professionals, even those in academia, are reluctant to be too critical of firms that may well be their future employers or funders. All of us, after all, know where our bread is buttered.

The firms' franchise structures, moreover, make them less transparent. None of the firms publishes a full set of global accounts that reveals a detailed breakdown of income or the value of key assets such as brands or IP. Many of the Big Four's special ingredients are mysterious. Because of the firms' partnership structures, partners' individual tax returns are often more revealing than what the firms themselves report to tax authorities.

In the emerging, more transparent world, however, much that is mysterious about the Big Four will cease to be so. Clients will know much more about the firms' staff, costs, charging (including what competitors pay for like services), capabilities, production methods, internal gossip, intermittent fiascos and the value, if any, that is created by the firms' outputs. None of these forces will necessarily make clients more likely to buy Big Four services.

As Peek-a-boo calls out breaches and lifts overall audit quality, it will weaken auditing as a source of brand identity for the Big Four. To the extent that there is a difference in quality and methodology between the Big Four and other regulated auditors, that difference will disappear. More fundamentally, the traditional practice of auditing is under threat. Are Big Four staff correct in their suspicion that audits add no value? Was Michael Power right to characterise public company auditing as a hollow ritual? A disaster scenario for the Big Four is that clients will come to view audits as a generic commodity, a necessary evil that generates no benefit. That scenario has already arrived, and regulators are more and more ready to do something about it.

Both advisory and audit services are being disrupted, commoditised, digitised and offshored. The Big Four need to invest big to meet the disruption, but their franchise structure and partnership model are barriers to large-scale investment in the necessary innovations. Disruption is coming from other directions, too. China is a looming disaster on an unprecedented scale for the Big Four. Nowhere is there a more imminent risk to the firms' brands. Nowhere more than in China have the modern Big Four attributes of commerciality and compromise been on such vivid display.

The leverage model and the partner track depend on growth, but, given all these pressures, the current rate of Big Four growth is unsustainable. In the face of technological disruption, the firms are suffering an exodus of ideas and talent. They imagine they can control digital technologies and 'disrupt themselves'. They cannot.

## Mispriced

Faced with the growing riskiness of modern accountancy, and the growing litigiousness of investors and clients, the Big Four have invested massively in risk management. They've established large Risk departments, recruited armies of compliance officers and built systems upon systems. The firms are vulnerable, though, to a common problem in risk management: that managers will focus on the wrong scales and categories of risk. The biggest and most fundamental risks facing the industry – such as market disruption and service obsolescence – cannot be solved by compliance officers.

Another danger is that risks will be mispriced. The firms are vulnerable to their own version of the 2008 financial crisis. By conducting major company audits, for example, they take on risks that are often not adequately reflected in audit fees. Like Lorenzo the Magnificent and Piero the Fatuous, the Big Four are bad at pricing risk. The extinction-level events show that audit and tax services, in particular, have been fundamentally mispriced, which suggests that the structure of the accounting services market, and the nature of those services, may not be conducive of correct pricing. In this environment, the firms have taken a slew of miscalculated risks.

## Paradox

The value of the Big Four brands is anchored in the firms' history, but the firms' current incarnations are largely disconnected from that history. The Big Four as we know them today owe more to the 1980s and 1990s than to the 1850s and 1860s. The firms have come too far to return to their principles-based past. Yet they will only be able to meet their future, and will only be able to understand and grapple with disruption, if they understand where they've come from.

As David Maister has noted, the 'soup to nuts', 'supermarket' approach to business 'has been tried in numerous industries and professions, and has been discredited almost everywhere'. Yet it is a core pillar of Big Four strategy today. Looking at the size and the growth of the Big Four, there is an inherent tension between the rush for size and the need to maintain human-scale operations. Other paradoxes, too, loom large. Is the future of auditing about standardisation or differentiation? Should the Big Four serve the public interest, or only private ones? The firms have drawn from a set of cultural influences as diverse as austere Quakerism and high-octane investment banking. They have open doors for recruitment and diversity, but their internal pressures for conformity and averageness are strong.

At the start of the twentieth century, many accountants were freemasons, some were spiritualists and a few brushed up against even darker and more otherworldly spheres. Sir Gilbert Garnsey, an early London partner at Price Waterhouse, was so deft with numbers that he was accused of dabbling in the occult. Nicholas Waterhouse rubbed shoulders with real occultists. In the early centuries of accountancy and mathematics, those disciplines had an aura of magic about them. And the disciplines never fully lost that aura, which is helpful because the longstanding relationship between accountancy and science has broken down. The contradictions in accountancy today are so stark that only magic can reconcile them.

If the Big Four disappear, what will we have lost? And what would be their legacy? There is no doubt they've helped make the world's businesses more accountable and more efficient. But so have boards, banks, competition authorities, strategy firms, systems engineers, economic consultants, specialist corporate advisors, internal improvement units, front-line staff and technical advances in business systems and reporting. The Big Four's accountability and advisory functions are highly contestable and substitutable.

Perhaps the biggest loss would be anthropological. The partner track, the partner lounge, the partner car space – all these would become as strange and remote as the rites of a lost Amazonian tribe, or the dealings of a late medieval bank, or the intricate, circular deliberations of the Railway Clearing House.

# Epilogue

The Big Four audited several of the 'feeder funds' that invested in Bernie Madoff's Ponzi scheme. But, as Cindy Fornelli from the Center for Audit Quality told *Time* magazine in late 2008, 'it is not the responsibility of the accountant for a capital-management firm to audit the underlying investments of the firms [in which] it invests'. Madoff himself steered well clear of the Big Four, relying instead on an audit firm reportedly connected to his brother-in-law. Other reports link him to the tiny firm Friehling & Horowitz, whose entire staff occupied a thirteen-by-eighteen-foot office in a suburban complex thirty miles north of New York.

Friehling & Horowitz signed off on Madoff's 2006 financial statements, attesting that they were 'in conformity with accounting principles generally accepted in the United States'. When the Ponzi scheme collapsed, the five largest investor victims included Bank Medici of Austria. The bank was so wounded that, a year after the crisis, it lost its banking licence.

# Acknowledgements

In writing this book, our goal was not to produce a thudding academic tome. For source material, we cast a wide net: institutional histories, founder memoirs, early trade periodicals, historical journals, press articles, social media, Big Four staff blogs, archival material, and the direct experiences of current and former Big Four personnel, captured through interviews. Where we include the recollections of current or former Big Four partners and staff, we give real ranks but not real names. We express here our thanks to the Big Four people who assisted with this book and who otherwise supported and inspired its authors.

Details of specific textual sources are provided in the bibliography and the notes. We acknowledge in particular Mark Stevens, Julia Irvine, David Maister, Paul Gillis, Francine McKenna, Raymond Doherty and Stephen Zeff for their work on professional services; Christian Wolmar for his work on the history of Britain's railways; and Tim Parks, Niall Ferguson, Christopher Hibbert and Gene Brucker for their research on the Medici Bank. We also gratefully acknowledge the support and insights of colleagues at Harvard Business School and Monash University, and the team at Black Inc. – particularly Sophy Williams,

## ACKNOWLEDGEMENTS

Chris Feik, Julian Welch, Kirstie Innes-Will, Anna Lensky and Kim Ferguson. And we thank our families and friends for indulging our immersion in what at times was an all-consuming project.

# Endnotes

**p. 2:** 'supranational organisations': Paul Gillis, *The Big Four and the Development of the Accounting Profession in China* (Emerald Group Publishing, 2014), p. 262.

**p. 3:** 'the biggest, looniest deal ever': Carol J. Loomis, 'The Biggest Looniest Deal Ever', *Fortune Magazine*, 18 June 1990.

**p. 4:** 'like wooing a pretty young lady': Anthony Wu, chairman of EY in China, quoted in Gillis, *The Big Four in China*, p. 193.

**p. 4:** 'Four big firms are too few': 'Accountancy's Big Four Need More Competition' (editorial), *Financial Times*, 24 August 2016.

**p. 4:** 'reduce the choice for auditing services': Christopher Pearce, finance director of Rentokil, quoted in 'Accountancy Mergers: Double entries', *The Economist*, 11 December 1997.

**p. 4:** 'the Big 8 are so large and influential': *Report of the Senate Subcommittee on Reports, Accounting and Management* (the Metcalf Report), quoted in Mark Stevens, *The Big Eight* (Simon & Schuster, 2010), p. 9.

**p. 5:** 'potentially catastrophic litigation': Association of Chartered Certified Accountants, *Audit Under Fire: A review of the post-financial crisis inquiries* (ACCA, May 2011), p. 1.

**p. 6:** 'consummate fraudster': Federal prosecutors, quoted in Patrick Fitzgerald, 'PricewaterhouseCoopers Settles $5.5 Billion Crisis Era Lawsuit', *The Wall Street Journal*, 26 August 2016.

**p. 6:** 'burly college dropout': Brian O'Keefe, 'The Man Behind 2009's Biggest Bank Bust', *Fortune Magazine*, 12 October 2009.

**p. 6:** 'pathological liar': Alison Frankel, quoted in Francine McKenna, 'A Tale of Two Lawsuits – PricewaterhouseCoopers and Colonial Bank', *Forbes*, 10 November 2012.

**p. 6:** 'as generous as he was vicious': Matt Hennie, 'Former Blake's Owner a Mean, Garish Queen', *Project Q Atlanta* (online), 27 July 2012.

**p. 6:** 'Farkased': Jason Moore, in the CNBC documentary *American Greed: Lee Farkas' Mortgage Loan Scam*, 11 July 2012.

**p. 7:** 'a broad pattern of negligence and complicity': Liz Rappaport & Michael Rapoport, 'Ernst Accused of Lehman Whitewash', *The Wall Street Journal*, 21 December 2010.

**p. 8:** 'everything would be OK': Joe Berardino, Arthur Andersen's global CEO, quoted in Gillis, *The Big Four in China*, p. 193.

**p. 8:** 'The good news is': George W. Bush, quoted in Barbara Ley Toffler, *Final Accounting: Ambition, greed, and the fall of Arthur Andersen* (Broadway Books, 2003), p. 217.

**p. 8:** 'had nothing to do with Enron', 'Some senior partners': Robert Reich, 'Dear Mr. Corporation', *The American Interest* (online), 1 July 2010.

**p. 9:** 'Does this mean': Jonathan D. Glater & Alexei Barrionuevo, 'Decision Rekindles Debate Over Andersen Indictment', *The New York Times*, 1 June 2005.

**p. 9:** 'whiggish in their perspectives': Paul L. Gillis, 'The Big Four in China: Hegemony and Counterhegemony in the Development of the Accounting Profession in China', PhD thesis, Macquarie Graduate School of Management, Macquarie University, 2011, p. 41.

**pp. 9–10:** 'tended to concentrate': M. Burrage, 'Introduction: The professions in sociology and history', in M. Burrage & R. Torstendahl (eds), *Professions in Theory and History: Rethinking the study of professions* (Sage, 1990), pp. 5–6.

**p. 10:** 'Today's professional economists': Robert Skidelsky, 'Is Economics Education Failing?', *World Economic Forum* (online), 4 January 2017.

**p. 12:** 'innocent of romance': Nicholas A.H. Stacey, 'The Accountant in Literature', *The Accounting Review*, Vol. 33, No. 1 (January 1958), pp. 102–5.

**p. 19:** 'ruined himself': Janet Ross (trans. & ed.), *Lives of the Early Medici as Told in Their Correspondence* (Chatto & Windus, 1910), p. 8.

**p. 25:** 'a sound virgin, free from disease': quoted in Tim Parks, *Medici Money: Banking, metaphysics and art in fifteenth-century Florence* (Profile Books, 2013), p. 63.

**p. 30:** 'awdytours', 'verify the honesty': Sean M. O'Connor, 'Be Careful What You Wish For: How accountants and Congress created the problem of auditor independence', *Boston College Law Review*, Vol. 45, No. 4, 2004, pp. 741–828.

**p. 31:** 'could give no proper account of themselves': Lord Brougham, quoted in Richard Brown, *A History of Accounting and Accountants* (Augustus M. Kelley, 1905), p. 234.

**p. 35:** 'The way big corporations around the world are run today': James Meek, *London Review of Books*, Vol. 38, No. 9, 5 May 2016.

**p. 35:** 'the greater portion of it', 'as it climbed on to and through the Mendips': Adrian Vaughan, *Railwaymen, Politics and Money* (John Murray, 1997), p. 116.

**p. 35:** 'to pay the bills': Christian Wolmar, *Fire & Steam* (Atlantic Books, 2007), p. 87.

p. 40: 'What methods assure': Sir Albert Wyon, 'The Organization of Large Accountants' Offices in Connection with the Accountant's Responsibility', *The Accountant*, Vol. 75, No. 2696, 7 August 1926.

p. 41: 'We stood waiting': Nicholas Waterhouse, quoted in Edgar Jones, *True and Fair: A history of Price Waterhouse* (Hamish Hamilton, 1995), p. 30.

p. 42: 'We are not for Names': Edward Burroughs, 'To the Present Distracted and Broken Nation of England, and to all her inhabitants', in *The Memorable Works of a Son of Thunder and Consolation: Namely, that True Prophet, and Faithful Servant of God, and Sufferer for the Testimony of Jesus, Edward Burroughs* (1672), p. 604.

pp. 42–3: 'to report any speeding or other misdemeanours': Wolmar, *Fire & Steam*, p. 17.

p. 43: 'senator barkley: Is there any relationship': Charles D. Niemeier, 'Independent Oversight of the Auditing Profession: Lessons from U.S. History', German Public Auditors Conference 2007, 8 November 2007.

p. 44: 'dull Victorian souls', 'served their time in India', 'So straitlaced', 'going native': Frank McLynn, 'A Bureaucrat Goes Native Among the Hill Folk: Thangliena: The life of T H Lewin' (book review), *The Independent*, 3 May 1993.

p. 45: 'the only complete autobiography': Michael J. Mepham, 'The Memoirs of Edwin Waterhouse: A Founder of Price Waterhouse' (book review), *The Accounting Historians Journal*, Vol. 17, No. 1, June 1990.

p. 46: 'being the discipline closest to accountancy': Jones, *True and Fair*, p. 84.

p. 46: 'My dear boy': Edwin Waterhouse, quoted in Jones, *True and Fair*, p. 86.

p. 46: 'blatant example': Nicholas Waterhouse, quoted in Jones, *True and Fair*, p. 85.

p. 47: 'a cloud of Turkish cigarettes and Chanel No. 5', 'for fear of losing her beautiful figure': Charlotte Breese, *Hutch* (Bloomsbury, 1999), p. 65.

p. 47: 'scenes of open debauch': Breese, *Hutch*, p. 64.

p. 47: 'stimulated by drink and cocaine': Breese, *Hutch*, p. 65.

p. 48: 'well-wishers established', 'WHERE'S THE FUCKING STIPEND?': David Trotter, 'A Most Modern Misanthrope: Wyndham Lewis and the pursuit of anti-pathos', *The Guardian*, 23 January 2001.

p. 49: 'I think you realise': Nicholas Waterhouse, letter to Mrs Robson, 30 July 1953, quoted in Jones, *True and Fair*, p. 218.

p. 53: 'They're not productive': Henry Ford, quoted in David Halberstam, *The Reckoning* (William Morrow, 1986), p. 99.

p. 55: 'The work our firm did': Walter E. Hanson, quoted in Stevens, *The Big Eight*, p. 4.

p. 56: 'government work introduced the firm': Jones, *True and Fair*, p. 110.

p. 57: 'unwelcome developments', 'the potential to dilute firm income': Prem Sikka, 'Audit Policy-Making in the UK: The case of "the auditor's considerations in respect of going concern"', *European Accounting Review*, Vol. 1, No. 2, 1992, pp. 349–92.

p. 57: 'to block reforms': James Moore, 'PwC Links to Independent Anti-Reform Lobbyist Revealed', *The Independent*, 19 July 2013.

**pp. 57–8:** 'I think we should': 'The Institute of Chartered Accountants in England & Wales: The Autumnal Meeting', *The Accountant*, 27 October 1888, p. 692.

**p. 58:** 'Despite the fact': O'Connor, 'Be Careful What You Wish For'.

**p. 59:** 'the conjuror's patter', 'incomprehensible jargon': Lawrence James, *The Middle Class: A History* (Hachette, 2010), p. 62.

**p. 63:** 'periodic reviews of management organisation': Jones, *True and Fair*, p. 234.

**p. 63:** 'The curse of public accounting': Paul Grady, quoted in G.J. Previts, *The Scope of CPA Services: A study of the development of the concept of independence and the profession's role in society* (Wiley, 1985), p. 89.

**p. 64:** 'it was so quiet': Jones, *True and Fair*, p. 69.

**p. 73:** 'the subliminal marketing value of "price"': Alison Leigh Cowan, 'Price Waterhouse-Andersen Merger Blues', *The New York Times*, 7 August 1989.

**p. 73:** 'caused such a stink': 'A Cutting Sense of History at PwC', *The Evening Standard*, 30 December 2008.

**p. 76:** 'an obscure ... membership structure': Andrew Clark, 'Deloitte Touche Tohmatsu Quits Swiss System to Make UK Its New Legal Home', *The Guardian*, 21 September 2010.

**p. 76:** 'It was a gentleman's profession': Rick Connor, quoted in Ianthe Jeanne Dugan, 'Before Enron, Greed Helped Sink the Respectability of Accounting', *The Wall Street Journal*, 14 March 2002.

**p. 77:** 'the conscience of capitalism': Dugan, 'Before Enron'.

**p. 78:** 'In 1972, the Institute gave in': Stephen A. Zeff, 'How the U.S. Accounting Profession Got Where it is Today: Part 1', *Accounting Horizons*, Vol. 17, No. 3, September 2003, p. 202.

**p. 78:** 'prepare an effective and persuasive response', 'would assist your company': Touche Ross & Co., *Employers' Accounting for Pensions* (Touche Ross & Co., 1983), p. 3.

**p. 78:** 'willing to become a blind advocate': Zeff, 'How the U.S. Accounting Profession Got Where it is Today: Part 1', p. 201.

**p. 79:** 'potentially misleading', 'reliability and accuracy': Australian Customs & Border Protection, response to a *Media Watch* (ABC) query, 10 June 2011.

**p. 79:** 'baseless', 'deceptive' and 'bogus': Brendan O'Connor, quoted in Joe Hildebrand, 'Report Shows Climb in Black Market Cigarettes Is Costing $2 Billion a Year', *The Daily Telegraph*, 12 July 2011.

**p. 79:** 'Sticking Points and other Problems', 'Get Even', 'Beanie Baby': Minority Staff of the Permanent Subcommittee on Investigations of the Committee on Governmental Affairs, United States Senate, *U.S. Tax Shelter Industry: The Role of Accountants, Lawyers, and Financial Professionals. Four KPMG Case Studies: Flip, Opis, Blips, and Sc2* (U.S. Government Printing Office, 2003), pp. 54–5.

**p. 79:** 'multi-line professional service firms': American Institute of Certified Public Accountants, *Strengthening the Professionalism of the Independent Auditor: Report to the Public Oversight Board of the SEC Practice Section, AICPA from the Advisory Panel on Auditor Independence* (Public Oversight Board, 1994), p. 6.

**p. 81:** 'This made me laugh': WoodShedd: Web Hosting Master, in *Thread: Price Waterhouse – Donkeys*, 8 December 2002 (www.webhostingtalk.com/showthread.php?t=66696).

**p. 83:** 'a full review of the accounts': Sarah Danckert, 'Centro Auditor Banned by ASIC', *The Australian Business Review*, 20 November 2012.

**p. 86:** 'locked in a library ever since puberty', 'the old image of the accountant': Stevens, *The Big Eight*, p. 19.

**p. 89:** 'femininely': Nancy Levit, *The Gender Line: Men, Women, and the Law* (NYU Press, 1998), p. 212.

**p. 90:** 'In my day, lunchtime': Stevens, *The Big Eight*, p. 22.

**p. 90:** 'inclusiveness commitment', 'a work environment': EY, 'Life at EY: EY recognised for LGBTI inclusion' (www.ey.com/au/en/careers/experienced/life-at-ey#fragment-1-na).

**pp. 90–1:** 'GLOBE's vision': Deloitte, 'About Us: GLOBE: Deloitte's LGBTI Network' (www2.deloitte.com/au/en/pages/about-deloitte/articles/globe.html).

**p. 91:** 'getting our unfair share of female talent': Deloitte, 'About Us: Inspiring Women' (www2.deloitte.com/au/en/pages/about-deloitte/articles/inspiring-women.html).

**p. 91:** 'diversity hire': Comment posted in response to Adrienne Gonzalez, 'Failed PwC Auditor Finds Success in Burning Bridges with This Ridiculous Farewell Email', *Going Concern* (online), 7 November 2013.

**p. 92:** 'an atmosphere of insularity', 'too wrapped up in its own affairs', 'the be-all and end-all of existence': Sir W.E. (Ted) Parker, quoted in Jones, *True and Fair*, pp. 198–9.

**pp. 92–3:** 'There are unwritten laws': Stevens, *The Big Eight*, p. 24.

**p. 94:** 'Word has it he leaves his shirt on': Stevens, *The Big Eight*, p. 25.

**p. 94:** 'conformity for conformity's sake': Stevens, *The Big Eight*, p. 24.

**p. 94:** 'cloaked behind a veil of blandness', 'you have to convincingly act': Andrea Whittle, Frank Mueller & Chris Carter, 'The "Big Four" in the Spotlight: Accountability and professional legitimacy in the UK audit market', *Journal of Professions and Organization*, Vol. 3, No. 2, 1 September 2016, pp. 119–41.

**p. 95:** 'a place of moral education': Matthew Crawford, *The Case for Working with Your Hands: Or why office work is bad for us and fixing things feels good* (Penguin, 2010), p. 126.

**p. 97:** 'except in rare instances', 'If a partner secured', 'with its full resources', 'the pinnacle of one's career': Zeff, 'How the U.S. Accounting Profession Got Where It Is Today: Part I', p. 195.

**p. 98:** 'effectively functioning': David Maister, *True Professionalism: The courage to care about your clients & career* (Simon & Schuster, 2012), p. 94.

**p. 98:** 'puffed up with pride', 'speak not as though': Giovanni di Bicci de' Medici, quoted in Ross (trans. & ed.), *Lives of the Early Medici*, p. 6.

**p. 98:** 'customized, one-off, situational', 'gut-feel and instinct': David H. Maister, Robert Galford & Charles Green, *The Trusted Advisor* (Simon & Schuster, 2012), p. 160.

pp. 99–100: 'It seems that the effects of the phenomenal growth': William Gregory, quoted in Stephen A. Zeff, 'How the U.S. Accounting Profession Got Where it is Today: Part II': *Accounting Horizons*, Vol. 17, No. 4, December 2003, p. 267.

p. 100: 'Five years ago': L. Berton, 'Total War: CPA firms diversify, cut fees, steal clients in battle for business', *The Wall Street Journal*, 20 September 1985.

p. 100: 'cut-throat competition': Eli Mason, quoted in Zeff, 'How the U.S. Accounting Profession Got Where it is Today: Part II', p. 202.

p. 100: 'perhaps restructuring a major vehicle': Zeff, 'How the U.S. Accounting Profession Got Where it is Today: Part II', p. 203.

p. 101: 'The major firms are on a growth treadmill': Ralph Walters, quoted in Zeff, 'How the U.S. Accounting Profession Got Where it is Today: Part II', p. 272.

pp. 101–2: 'project management and technical tasks': Paul Bloom, 'Effective Marketing for Professional Services', *Harvard Business Review*, September 1984.

p. 102: 'Simply because it is deemed unprofessional': Stevens, *The Big Eight*, p. 18.

p. 102: 'anything under the sun', 'Are you my auditor or a salesperson?': C. Anthony Rider, quoted in Dugan, 'Before Enron'.

p. 103: 'well paid … but not wealthy': Mark Stevens, *The Big Six* (Simon & Schuster, 1991), p. 251.

p. 105: 'good second-class BA degree': Jones, *True and Fair*, p. 33.

p. 105: 'growing their own', 'promotion from within', 'unlike most of our competitors': Ian Brindle, 'Foreword', in Jones, *True and Fair*, p. xvii.

p. 105: 'By the 1990s': Zeff, 'How the U.S. Accounting Profession Got Where it is Today: Part II', p. 270.

p. 106: 'flexibility, creative work': PwC, 'Work Like a Start-Up' (www.pwc.com.au/careers/be-entrepreneurial-like-a-start-up.html).

p. 106: 'a place where professional rigour': PwC, 'Thrive in a Great Team' (www.pwc.com.au/careers/thrive-in-a-great-team.html).

p. 107: 'They are average Joes', 'filling out useless workpapers', 'for people who truly don't': Lacey Donohue, 'This Is the Best "I Quit" Email You'll Read All Week', *Gawker* (online), 18 November 2013.

pp. 109–110: 'just saw their mouths moving', 'I realized what they were doing', 'What frightens me': Stevens, *The Big Eight*, pp. 29–30.

p. 116: 'the final reckoning of God': Jacob Soll, *The Reckoning: Financial accountability and the making and breaking of nations* (Penguin, 2015), p. 7.

p. 116: 'to pick out any dubious or past due accounts': Raymond de Roover, *The Rise and Decline of the Medici Bank: 1397–1494* (Beard Books, 1999), p. 100.

p. 118: 'a devotedly religious man': Sir Patrick Hastings, *Cases in Court* (William Heinemann, 1949), p. 217.

p. 118: 'Well, they treated Christ much worse': Harold John Morland, quoted in Jones, *True and Fair*, p. 155.

# ENDNOTES

p. 118: 'The auditors have at all times': quoted in Jones, *True and Fair*, p. 277.

p. 119: 'many insurers refused': 'PricewaterhouseCoopers History', in *International Directory of Company Histories*, Vol. 29, St James Press, 1999.

p. 121: 'had not obtained sufficient evidence': Pat Sweet, 'US Regulator Attacks KPMG Response to Audit Quality Criticism', *CCH Daily Accountancy Live* (online), 27 October 2014.

p. 121: 'the nature and consistently high number', 'Many of these deficiencies': PCAOB, *Annual Report on the Interim Inspection Program Related to Audits of Brokers and Dealers*, PCAOB Release No. 2016-004. 18 August 2016.

p. 122: 'is what's on the mind': Joe Ucuzoglu, quoted in 'Accounting Scandals: The dozy watchdogs', *The Economist*, 11 December 2014.

p. 123: 'egregious, highly unreasonable': Securities and Exchange Commission, Washington, DC, *Securities Exchange Act of 1934. Release No. 78490 / August 5, 2016. Admin. Proc. File No. 3-15168. In the Matter of John J. Aesoph, CPA and Darren M. Bennett, CPA. Corrected Opinion of the Commission. Rule 102(e) Proceeding. Grounds for Remedial Action. Improper Professional Conduct*, pp. 22–3 (www.sec.gov/litigation/opinions/2016/34-78490.pdf).

p. 124: 'typical collateral arrangements', 'bright-line': Robert H. Herz, Submission, 'Re: Discussion of Selected Accounting Guidance Relevant to Lehman Accounting Practices', 19 April 2020, p. 4.

p. 124: 'did not use a computer': Francesco Guerrera, 'Evidence Suggests Former Chief Knew Of "Accounting Gimmick"', *Financial Times*, 13 March 2010.

p. 125: 'was not caused by any accounting issues': 'Ernst & Young's Letter About Lehman Accounting', Reuters, 23 March 2010.

pp. 125–6: 'where your duty is': Select Committee on Economic Affairs (UK Parliament, House of Lords), *Auditors: Market Concentration and Their Role, Second Report of Session 2010–11, Vol. 2: Evidence* (The Stationery Office, 2011), pp. 227–8.

p. 126: 'Alice in Wonderland feeling': Select Committee on Economic Affairs (UK), *Auditors*, p. 227.

p. 126: 'the complacency of bank auditors': Select Committee on Economic Affairs (UK), *Auditors*, p. 51.

p. 126–7: 'brazen looting': 'Deloitte Sued Over Audits of Chinacast Education', *Reuters*, 20 February 2013.

p. 127: 'suspect rebates', 'but still gave a clean audit': 'The dozy watchdogs', *The Economist*, 11 December 2014.

p. 127: 'one of the largest reported adjustments in history': 'Singing River Health System Sues KPMG: "Colossal" error': *The Washington Times*, 18 January 2015.

p. 128: 'virtually impossible': Jones, *True and Fair*, p. 147.

p. 128: 'rainbow brief': Jones, *True and Fair*, p. 155.

p. 129: 'ever-mutating, bacteria-like financial tools and tricks', 'By the sheer complexity': Soll, *The Reckoning*, p. 204.

p. 130: 'more or less OK': 'The dozy watchdogs', *The Economist*, 11 December 2014.

p. 131: 'a trust engendering technology': Prem Sikka, Steven Filling & Pik Liew, *The Audit Crunch: Reforming Auditing*, Working Paper No. WP 09/01, Essex Business School, January 2009.

p. 131: 'The public accounting firms': Francine McKenna, 'Will Auditors Be Held Accountable? The PCAOB Has a Plan', *re: TheAuditors* (online), 21 March 2011.

p. 131: 'to ascertain whether figures were facts': Roy A. Chandler & John Richard Edwards (eds), *Recurring Issues in Auditing: Professional Debate 1875–1900* (Routledge, 2014), p. 202.

p. 132: 'boilerplate': 'The dozy watchdogs', *The Economist*, 11 December 2014. In 2017, PCAOB imposed a controversial requirement for US auditors to report on 'critical audit matters', defined as matters: that have been communicated to the audit committee, are related to accounts or disclosures material to the financial statements, and involve especially challenging, subjective or complex auditor judgement.

p. 132: 'The auditor is the long stop': Jeremy Warner, 'Dereliction of the Big Four Blamed for Financial Crisis', *The Telegraph*, 31 March 2011.

p. 132: 'Auditing isn't meant to stop': Michael Rapoport, 'Role of Auditors in Crisis Gets Look', *The Wall Street Journal*, 23 December 2010.

pp. 132–3: 'The auditors' responsibility': ACCA, *Audit Under Fire*, p. 13.

p. 133: 'An audit does not exist', 'Financial statements portray': John McDonnell, *Opening Submission to the Banking Inquiry*, pp. 6 & 3 (https://inquiries.oireachtas.ie/banking/wp-content/uploads/2015/05/John-McDonnell-Opening-Statement.pdf).

p. 133: 'value drivers': Bob Moritz, quoted in 'The dozy watchdogs', *The Economist*, 11 December 2014.

p. 134: 'An auditor is not bound': *re Kingston Cotton Mill Company (No. 2) [1896] 2 Ch. 279*, (U.K. Court of Appeal), per Lopes LJ at pp. 288–9.

p. 134: 'grossly inflated': Zeff, 'How the U.S. Accounting Profession Got Where it is Today: Part I', p. 192.

p. 135: 'questionable payments': Mike Esterl, David Crawford & David Reilly, 'KPMG Germany's Failure to Spot Siemens Problems Raises Questions', *The Wall Street Journal*, 24 February 2007.

p. 135: 'put its name and brand behind': 'Deloitte Sued over Audits of ChinaCast Education', *Reuters*, 20 February 2013.

p. 136: 'conflict gold': Simon Bowers, 'Billion Dollar Gold Market in Dubai Where Not All Was As It Seemed', *The Guardian*, 26 February 2014.

p. 137: 'private-eye action hero': L. Evans, 'The Accountant's Social Background and Stereotype in Popular Culture: The novels of Alexander Clark Smith', *Accounting, Auditing and Accountability Journal*, Vol. 25, No. 6, 2012, p. 964.

p. 137: 'Investors, customers, employees': Jonathan Webb, 'PwC Sued For Missing $2.9 Billion Scam: Do auditors have a public responsibility to prevent fraud?', *Forbes*, 25 August 2016.

p. 137: 'As the professional audit standards make clear': 'PwC sued for $5.5bn over mortgage underwriter TBW's collapse', *Financial Times*, 14 August 2016.

p. 138: 'We considered fraud': Wes Kelly, quoted in Carolina Bolado, 'PwC Auditor Says No Duty To Detect $5B Taylor Bean Fraud', *Law360* (online), 17 August 2016.

p. 138: 'effective oversight': PwC, *Effective Audit Committee Oversight of the External Auditor and Audit*, 19 July 2013.

p. 139: 'audit profession has always': Dennis Nally, quoted in David Reilly, 'Accounting's Crisis Killer: Tumult eases for PwC's Nally; does he do his own taxes?', *Wall Street Journal*, 23 March 2007.

p. 139: 'failing to complete a professional audit', 'had failed to take': Ian Fraser, 'Time to Audit the Auditors – and Especially KPMG?', *Ian Fraser* (online) 8 January 2009.

p. 140: 'A statutory cap': 'Appendix 3: List of Measures Raised in Evidence to Improve Choice, Competition and Quality in the Audit Market' in Select Committee on Economic Affairs (UK), *Auditors*.

pp. 140–1: 'incompatible with': United States Senate, Subcommittee on Reports, Accounting and Management of the Committee on Government Operations, *The Accounting Establishment. A Staff Study* (U.S. Government Printing Office, 1976), p. 22.

p. 141: '[Y]ou have one floor of big accountancy firms': Prem Sikka, quoted by Jane Gleeson-White in *Double Entry* (Allen & Unwin, 2011), p. 216.

p. 141: 'we can help you fix': Michael Andrew, quoted in Vinod Mahanta, 'Big Four Accounting Firms PwC, Deloitte, KPMG, E&Y Back in Consulting Business', *The Economic Times*, 30 April 2013.

p. 142: 'doing advisory work': Select Committee on Economic Affairs (UK), *Auditors*, p. 98.

p. 142: '[W]e do not believe': ACCA, *Audit Under Fire*, p. 7.

p. 142: 'After Enron': Prem Sikka, 'Called to Account', *The Guardian*, 14 December 2008.

p.143: 'inculcated to appease': Prem Sikka, 'Financial Crisis and the Silence of the Auditors', *Accounting, Organizations and Society*, Centre for Global Accountability, University of Essex, 2009, p. 5, drawing on G. Hanlon, *The Commercialisation of Accountancy: Flexible accumulation and the transformation of the service class* (Macmillan, 1994).

p. 143: 'Authors such as': Bhanu Raghunathan, 'Premature Signing-Off of Audit Procedures: An analysis', *Accounting Horizons*, Vol. 5, No. 2, 1991, p. 71; C. Willett & M. Page, 'A Survey of Time Budget Pressure and Irregular Auditing Practices Amongst Newly Qualified UK Chartered Accountants', *British Accounting Review*, Vol. 28, No. 2, 1996, pp. 1–120.

p. 144: 'directly responsible': Sarbanes Oxley Act Section 301: 2: Public Law 107–204, 107th Congress, www.sec.gov/about/laws/soa2002.pdf.

p. 147: 'a joke and a waste of time': Ned O'Keeffe, quoted in Marie O'Halloran, 'Firms "Have Case to Answer" on Banks Crisis', *The Irish Times*, 5 November 2017.

**p. 148:** 'The audit society': Michael Power, *The Audit Society: Rituals of Verification* (OUP, 1999), p. 123.

**p. 150:** 'thirty-five florins': Chris Skinner, 'What Did the Medici Bankers Ever Do for Us?', *Chris Skinner's Blog*.

**pp. 151–2:** 'after thirty years of controversy': Zeff, 'How the U.S. Accounting Profession Got Where it is Today: Part I', p. 194.

**p. 152:** 'Companies can devote': House of Commons, Committee of Public Accounts, *Tax Avoidance: The Role of Large Accountancy Firms, Forty-fourth Report of Session 2012-13, Report, Together with Formal Minutes, Oral and Written Evidence* (The Stationery Office, 2013), p. 3.

**p. 153:** 'While this may be the case': House of Commons, Committee of Public Accounts, *Tax Avoidance*, pp. 3–4.

**p. 153:** 'undue influence': House of Commons, Committee of Public Accounts, *Tax Avoidance*, p. 4.

**p. 154:** 'poacher, turned gamekeeper': House of Commons, Committee of Public Accounts, *Tax Avoidance*, p. 4.

**p. 154:** 'defendable expense allocation': House of Commons, Committee of Public Accounts, *Tax Avoidance*, p. 10.

**p. 154:** 'an obscure corporate tax break': Guy Rolnik, 'PwC and the Oscars: When Auditors Take Investors to La La Land', University of Oxford, Faculty of Law blog, 12 March 2017.

**p. 154:** 'foe of deceit and the champion of honesty': D.A. Keister, 'The Public Accountant', *The Book-keeper*, July 1896, pp. 21–2.

**p. 155:** 'The biggest problem I see', 'a sham': Thomas Walsh, quoted in David Cay Johnston, 'Tax Shelter of Rich and Famous Has Final Date in Court', *The New York Times*, 4 November 1995.

**p. 155:** 'create a story', 'put some distance', 'Get ready to do some dancing': Thomas Quinn, quoted in Gonzalez, 'This PwC Quote'.

**p. 155:** 'What the heck': Steven Williams, quoted in Gonzalez, 'This PwC Quote'.

**p. 155:** 'abusive', 'fraudulent': Department of Justice, 'Superseding Indictment of 19 Individuals Filed in KPMG Criminal Tax Fraud Case', Media release, 17 October 2005.

**p. 156:** 'alphabet soup': Michael Hudson, Sasha Chavkin & Bart Mos: 'Big Four Audit Firms Behind Global Profit Shifting', *The Sydney Morning Herald*, 6 November 2014.

**p. 156:** 'to accept responsibility': Attorney General Alberto R. Gonzales, quoted in IRS, 'KPMG to Pay $456 Million for Criminal Violations', Media Release, IR-2005-83, 29 August 2005.

**p. 156:** 'The CRA alleges': Harvey Cashore, Dave Seglins & Frederic Zalac, 'KPMG Offshore "Sham" Deceived Tax Authorities, CRA Alleges', *CBC News* (online), 9 September 2015.

**pp. 156–7:** 'urged the firm', 'would result in KPMG fees': Hudson, Chavkin & Mos, 'Big Four Audit Firms Behind Global Profit Shifting'.

p. 158: 'In order to do': quoted in Mark Berman, 'Ex-CIA director Hayden says millennials leak secrets because they are "culturally" different', *The Washington Post*, 10 March 2017.

p. 161: 'create sham transactions': Prem Sikka, 'The Predatory Practices of Major Accountancy Firms', *The Guardian*, 8 December 2012.

p. 162: 'fake cash recorded on the books', 'fake revenue in the past': Henry Blodget, 'China Stock Fraud Shocker: Banks Were Complicit in Longtop Fraud', *Business Insider Australia*, 26 May 2011.

p. 163: 'substantial risk of prosecution': Julia Irvine, 'Deloitte in Catch 22 over Former Chinese Client', *Economia* (online), 11 May 2012.

p. 163: 'In light of the substantial volume': U.S. Securities and Exchange Commission, *Litigation Release No. 22911 / January 27, 2014, Accounting and Auditing Enforcement Release No. 3531 / January 27, 2014, Securities and Exchange Commission v. Deloitte Touche Tohmatsu CPA Ltd., Civil Action No. 1:11-MC-00512*, D.D.C. filed 8 September 8 2011, (www.sec.gov/litigation/litreleases/2014/lr22911.htm).

p. 164: 'This will be the case': Securities and Futures Commission, 'EY's Appeal Over Audit Working Papers Discontinued' (online), 23 July 2015.

p. 164: 'EY could have avoided litigation': Mark Steward, quoted in Securities and Futures Commission, 'EY's Appeal'.

p. 165: 'Akai had just US$167,000 worth': Naomi Rovnick, 'Hard Work Pays Off for "Vicious" Akai Liquidator', *South China Morning Post*, 6 October 2009.

p. 165: 'greatly exaggerated', 'should have greater knowledge': Rovnick, 'Hard Work Pays Off'.

p. 166: 'did not have most of the files and records', 'dig deep into its insurance coffers': Rovnick, 'Hard Work Pays Off'.

pp. 166–7: 'one of Moulin's four biggest customers', 'After Akai, Ernst & Young': Naomi Rovnick, 'Ernst & Young Pays Up to Settle Negligence Claim', *South China Morning Post*, 27 January 2010.

p. 168: 'complaining that the use of the term', 'Besides, if they were to use the term': Gillis, *The Big Four in China*, p. 71.

p. 169: 'civilised invasion by gentlemen': Ding Pingzhun, quoted in Gillis, *The Big Four in China*, p. 113.

p. 169: 'a dance with the wolves': Ding Pingzhun, quoted in Gillis, *The Big Four in China*, p. 215.

p. 170: 'the best phonetic representation of PW', 'the essence of China': Gillis, *The Big Four in China*, p. 202.

p. 170: 'and the firms began': Gillis, *The Big Four in China*, p. 4.

pp. 170–1: 'We have no choice': Anthony Wu, quoted in Gillis, 'The Big Four in China', p. 164.

p. 171: 'FILTH' – 'Failed in London, Try Hong Kong', 'For many lower performing people': Gillis, 'The Big Four in China', pp. 108 & 111.

**p. 171:** 'Some Western partners': Gillis, 'The Big Four in China', p. 153.

**p. 172:** 'the presence of foreign regulators', 'a breach of China's sovereignty': Gillis, 'The Big Four in China', p. 254.

**p. 172:** 'Our position remains unchanged': China Securities Regulatory Commission, *REPublic Company Accounting Oversight Board; Notice of Filing of Proposed Amendment to Board Rules Relating to Inspection (File No. PCAOB-2008-06)*, 15 May 2009 (www.sec.gov/comments/pcaob-2008-06/pcaob200806-1.pdf).

**p. 173:** 'The firm would be established', 'We hope that this "big"', 'unite together to form a fist': Ding Pingzhun, quoted in Gillis, *The Big Four in China*, p. 184.

**p. 173:** 'In this way': Ding Pingzhun, quoted in Gillis, 'The Big Four in China', p. 171.

**p. 173:** 'The strategy established': Gillis, *The Big Four in China*, pp. 217 & 225.

**p. 178:** 'democratize business intelligence services', 'the most innovative firm in Australia': 'Accodex: Our Mission Re-Defined', *Accodex* (online), accessed 24 November 2017.

**p. 179:** 'to disrupt the professional services industry': Task Central, https://au.linkedin. com/company/task-central.

**p. 181:** 'One of the worst forms of self-delusion': Maister, Galford & Green, *The Trusted Advisor*, p. 168.

**p. 185:** 'While the senior': Jones, *True and Fair*, p. 7.

**p. 185:** 'pariah', 'because of the difficulty': Gillis, *The Big Four in China*, p. 94.

**p. 185:** 'throw-up': Michael Barrett, David J. Cooper & Karim Jamal, 'Globalization and the Coordinating of Work in Multinational Audits', *Accounting, Organizations and Society*, Vol. 30, 2005, p. 21.

**p. 186:** 'make it easier': Economic Affairs Committee, *Auditors: Market concentration and their role*, Vol. I, 2nd Report of Session 2010–11 (The Stationery Office, March 2011), p. 61.

**p. 188:** 'You don't have to be great': Stevens, *The Big Eight*, p. 22.

**p. 190:** 'frail, bedridden and bad-tempered': Parks, *Medici Money*, pp. 3–4.

**p. 192:** 'These are the great profits': Lorenzo de Medici, quoted in de Roover, *The Rise and Decline of the Medici Bank*, p. 349.

**p. 193:** 'with the help of God and of good fortune': de Roover, *The Rise and Decline of the Medici Bank*, p. 108.

**p. 194:** 'portly mistress': Parks, *Medici Money*, p. 4.

**p. 195:** 'shock events', 'I don't think': Michael Power, quoted in Select Committee on Economic Affairs (UK), *Auditors*, p. 10.

**p. 197:** 'as professional entities', 'put the public interest first', 'The quid pro quo': Select Committee on Economic Affairs (UK), *Auditors*, p. 65.

**p. 197:** 'sown the seeds': Michael West, '"Tax Avoidance" Masters Revealed: Exclusive', *The New Daily* (online), 11 July 2016.

p. 200: 'International commerce': George Rozvany, quoted in Michael West, 'Oligarchs of the Treasure Islands', 11 July 2016, www.michaelwest.com.au/oligarchs-of-the-treasure-islands.

p. 201: 'Audit firms know': Stephen Griggs, quoted in Caroline Biebuyck, 'How Mandatory Audit Rotation Is Impacting Firms', *Economia* (online), 20 July 2016.

p. 201: 'We have had to get much more agile': Gilly Lord, quoted in Biebuyck, 'How Mandatory Audit Rotation Is Impacting Firms'.

pp. 201–2: 'a radical, innovative measure', 'As with other forms of insurance': Select Committee on Economic Affairs (UK), *Auditors*, p. 62.

p. 203: 'A government takeover': Zeff, 'How the U.S. Accounting Profession Got Where it is Today: Part I', p. 192.

p. 203: 'Do people panic': Prem Sikka, quoted in 'The dozy watchdogs', *The Economist*, 11 December 2014.

pp. 205: 'the processes': Sikka, 'Financial Crisis and the Silence of the Auditors', p. 6.

p. 206: 'The major firms': Ralph Walters, quoted in Zeff, 'How the U.S. Accounting Profession Got Where it is Today: Part II', p. 272.

p. 207: 'great dying': Niall Ferguson, 'The Great Dying', *Financial Times*, 14 December 2007.

p. 207: 'In 1900': Crawford, *The Case for Working with Your Hands*, p. 42.

p. 213: 'it is not the responsibility': Cindy Fornelli, quoted in Stephen Gandel, 'The Madoff Fraud: How culpable were the auditors?', *Time*, 17 December 2008.

# Bibliography

Accodex. 'Accodex: Our mission re-defined' (www.accodex.com/blog/accodex-our-mission-re-defined).

'Accountable: Two controversies ensnare the Big Four', *The Economist*, 8 December 2012.

'Accountancy Mergers: Double entries', *The Economist*, 11 December 1997.

'Accountancy's Big Four Need More Competition' (editorial), *Financial Times*, 24 August 2016.

Aharoni, Yair & Lilach Nachum. *Globalization of Services: Some implications for theory and practice* (Routledge, 2002).

Allen, David Grayson & Kathleen McDermott. *Accounting for Success: A history of Price Waterhouse in America 1890–1990* (Harvard Business School Press, 1993).

Alles, Lakshman. 'Fair Value Accounting, Credit Ratings and Cyclicality: Implications for the stability of financial institutions', *JASSA, the Finsia Journal of Applied Finance*, No. 3, 2009, pp. 7–10.

Alston, Jon P. *The American Samurai: Blending American and Japanese managerial practices* (Walter de Gruyter, 1989).

Altintas, Nalan & Fatih Yilmaz. 'The Accounting Profession: A descriptive study of the Common and Code Law Countries', *Journal of Modern Accounting and Auditing*, Vol. 8, No. 7, July 2012, pp. 932–50.

Anderson, Donald. 'Moneyed Victorians', *Abinger & Coldharbour Parish News*, July 2000.

Armitstead, Louise & Philip Aldrick. 'Former HBOS chief executive Andy Hornby was specifically warned about risks, whistleblower Paul Moore tells MPs', *The Telegraph*, 27 February 2009.

Ascher, Bernard. *The Audit Industry: World's weakest oligopoly?* AAI Working Paper No. 08-03 (The American Antitrust Institute, August 2008).

Association of Chartered Certified Accountants, *Audit Under Fire: A review of the post-financial crisis inquiries* (ACCA, May 2011).

Aubin, Dena. 'Accountants to Face Malpractice Claims in Alabama's Colonial Bancorp Failure', *Insurance Journal*, 11 September 2014.

Aubin, Dena & Kevin Drawbaugh. 'PwC Gobbles Up Booz & Co As Big 4 Rebuild in Consulting', *Reuters*, 30 October 2013.

Australian Customs & Border Protection. Response to a *Media Watch* (ABC) query, 10 June 2011.

Baer, Justin & Henny Sender. 'Valukas Report Finds Few Heroes', *Financial Times*, 12 March 2010.

Barrett, Michael, David J. Cooper & Karim Jamal. 'Globalization and the coordinating of work in multinational audits', *Accounting, Organizations and Society*, Vol. 30, 2005.

Baskerville, R. & D. Hay. 'The Effect of Accounting Firm Mergers on the Market for Audit Services: New Zealand evidence', *Abacus*, Vol. 42, No. 1, 2006, pp. 87–104.

BBC News. 'Vatican Appoints PricewaterhouseCoopers to Audit Accounts', 5 December 2015.

'Beautiful Failures', *The Guardian*, 18 October 2013.

Bell, Simon & Gemma Bell. *Introduction and History of Sheep Farming in the UK: Research report for the UK* (Estonian University of Life Sciences, November 2011).

Berman, Mark. 'Ex-CIA Director Hayden Says Millennials Leak Secrets Because They Are "Culturally" Different', *The Washington Post*, 10 March 2017.

Berton, L. 'Total War: CPA firms diversify, cut fees, steal clients in battle for business', *The Wall Street Journal*, 20 September 1985.

Bhattacharjee, Rajarshi. 'Culture is What People Do When No One Is Looking: Gerard Seijts', *Business Standard*, 24 September 2012.

Biebuyck, Caroline. 'How Mandatory Audit Rotation Is Impacting Firms', *Economia*, 20 July 2016.

Bierman, Stanley M. 'The Sir Nicholas E. Waterhouse, Kbe, Sales', *Chronicle of the U.S. Classic Postal Issues*, Vol. 36, No. 1, February 1984, Whole No. 121.

'Bill Gates Sues Oil Giant Petrobras and Pwc Over Corruption Scandal', *The Telegraph*, 25 September 2015.

Blodget, Henry. 'China Stock Fraud Shocker: Banks were complicit in Longtop fraud', *Business Insider Australia*, 26 May 2011.

Bloom, Paul. 'Effective Marketing for Professional Services', *Harvard Business Review*, September 1984.

Bloom, Paul. 'Managing People: Effective marketing for professional services', *Effective Marketing for Professional Services*, September 1984.

Bodoni, Stephanie. 'Former PwC Employees Found Guilty in "Luxleaks" Tax Scandal', *The Independent*, 30 June 2016.

# BIBLIOGRAPHY

Bolado, Carolina. 'PwC Auditor Says No Duty to Detect $5B Taylor Bean Fraud', *Law360* (online), 17 August 2016.

Bowers, Simon. 'Billion Dollar Gold Market in Dubai Where Not All Was As It Seemed', *The Guardian*, 26 February 2014.

Bowers, Simon. 'Former PwC Employees Face Trial Over Role in Luxleaks Scandal', *The Guardian*, 25 April 2016.

Boyns, Trevor & John Richard Edwards. 'The Development of Accounting in Mid-Nineteenth Century Britain: A non-disciplinary view', *Accounting, Auditing & Accountability Journal*, Vol. 9, No. 3, 1996, pp. 40–60.

Boyns, Trevor, John R. Edwards & Marc Nikitin (eds). *The Birth of Industrial Accounting in France and Britain* (Routledge, 2013).

Boys, Peter. *Past Presidents of the Institute of Chartered Accountants in England and Wales, 1880–2005* (ICAEW, 2011).

Breese, Charlotte. *Hutch: A Biography* (Bloomsbury, 2000).

Brewster, Mike. *Unaccountable: How the accounting profession forfeited a public trust* (John Wiley & Sons, 2003).

Brinded, Lianna. 'KPMG's US Boss Gave Us 8 Pieces of Advice for Women Looking to Get Promoted at Work', *Business Insider Australia*, 23 January 2016.

Brock, David & Christopher Robin Hinings. *Restructuring the Professional Organization: Accounting, health care and law* (Psychology Press, 1999).

Brown, Richard. *A History of Accounting and Accountants* (Augustus M. Kelley, 1905).

Brucker, Gene A. 'The Medici in the Fourteenth Century', *Speculum*, Vol. 32, No. 1, January 1957, pp. 1–26.

Brucker, Gene A. *Florentine Politics and Society, 1343–1378* (Princeton University Press, 2015).

Buchan, James. 'Making Money the Medici Way – And Spending it the Modern Way', *The Observer*, 25 July 2005.

Bufithis, Gregory P. 'The Valukas Report on the Lehman Brothers Collapse: The e-discovery aspects', *The Posse List* (online), 20 March 2010.

Buiter, Willem H. 'Lessons from the Global Financial Crisis for Regulators and Supervisors', Discussion Paper No. 635. Paper presented at the 25th anniversary workshop 'The Global Financial Crisis: Lessons and Outlook' of the Advanced Studies Program of the IFW, Kiel, 8–9 May 2009.

'Burning Bridges: Young auditor quits job with ranting email filled with hashtags that attacks "fake coworkers"', *Daily Mail*, 20 November 2013.

Burrage, M. & R. Torstendahl (eds). *Professions in Theory and History: Rethinking the study of professions* (Sage, 1990).

Burroughs, Edward. 'To the Present Distracted and Broken Nation of England, and to all her inhabitants', in *The Memorable Works of a Son of Thunder and Consolation: Namely, that*

*True Prophet, and Faithful Servant of God, and Sufferer for the Testimony of Jesus, Edward Burroughs* (Printed and published for the good and benefit of generations to come, 1672).

Caramanis, C. 'International Accounting Firms Versus Indigenous Auditors: Intra-professional conflict in the Greek auditing profession, 1990–1993', *Critical Perspectives on Accounting*, Vol. 10, No. 2, 1999, pp. 153–96.

Cashore, Harvey, Dave Seglins & Frederic Zalac, 'KPMG Offshore "Sham" Deceived Tax Authorities, CRA Alleges', *CBC News*, 9 September 2015.

Cassell, Catherine & Bill Lee (eds). *Challenges and Controversies in Management Research* (Routledge, 2011).

Ceresney, Andrew. 'The SEC Enforcement Division's Focus on Auditors and Auditing', Keynote address: American Law Institute Conference on Accountants' Liability 2016: Confronting Enforcement and Litigation Risks. Washington, DC, 22 September 2016.

Chandler, Roy A. & J.R. Edwards (eds). *Recurring Issues in Auditing: Professional debate 1875–1900* (Routledge, 2014).

Channon, Geoffrey. 'The Business Morals of British Railway Companies in the Mid-nineteenth Century', *Business and Economic History*, Vol. 28, No. 2, Fall 1999, pp. 69–79.

Chapman, Lisa. 'Should Big Four Firms Enter the Credit Ratings Business?' *Big4* (online), www.big4.com/andersen/should-big-four-firms-enter-the-credit-ratings-business-522.

Chatfield, Michael & Richard Vangermeersch. *History of Accounting: An international encyclopedia* (Garland, 1996).

Chen, George. 'Satyam Scandal Rattles Confidence in Accounting Big Four', *Reuters*, 8 January 2009.

Chin, Eric. 'Limitless? Big Four strategic moves in consulting', *Beaton Capital* (online), 14 April 2014.

Chin, Eric. 'Big Four vs BigLaw: Clash of professions', *Beaton Capital* (online), 9 December 2014.

China Securities Regulatory Commission. 'RE: Public Company Accounting Oversight Board; Notice of Filing of Proposed Amendment to Board Rules Relating to Inspection (File No. PCAOB-2008-06)', 15 May 2009 (www.sec.gov/comments/pcaob-2008-06/pcaob200806-1.pdf).

Claessens, Stijn & Laura Kodres. 'The Regulatory Responses to the Global Financial Crisis: Some uncomfortable questions', IMF Working Paper WP/14/46, 2014.

Clark, Andrew. 'Deloitte Touche Tohmatsu Quits Swiss System To Make UK Its New Legal Home', *The Guardian*, 21 September 2010.

Clayton, Ellie. 'Hilary Lindsay Is New President of ICAEW', *Economia*, 8 June 2016.

Clikeman, Paul M. *Called to Account: Financial frauds that shaped the accounting profession* (Routledge, 2013).

CNBC. *American Greed: Lee Farkas' Mortgage Loan Scam*, television documentary, 11 July 2012.

# BIBLIOGRAPHY

Commentator, in Adrienne Gonzalez, 'Failed PwC Auditor Finds Success in Burning Bridges With This Ridiculous Farewell Email', *Going Concern*, 7 November 2013.

'Complacency of Auditors Contributed to Financial Crisis', 30 March 2011 (www.parliament.uk/business/committees/committees-a-z/lords-select/economic-affairs-committee/news/big-4-auditors-inquiry-report).

Cooper, D.J. & K. Robson. 'Practitioners, work and firms', in J.R. Edwards & S. Walker (eds), *The Routledge Companion to Accounting History Research* (Routledge, 2009), pp. 274–96.

Cooper, D.J., R. Greenwood, C. Hinings & J.L. Brown. 'Globalization and Nationalism in a Multinational Accounting Firm: The case of opening new markets in Eastern Europe', *Accounting, Organizations & Society*, Vol. 23, No. 5/6, 1998, pp. 531–48.

Cowan, Alison Leigh. 'Price Waterhouse-Andersen Merger Blues', *The New York Times*, 7 August 1989.

Craver, Richard. 'Federal Appeals Court Reopens FDIC Lawsuit in Colonial Bank Securities Case', *Winston-Salem Journal*, 20 May 2016.

Crawford, Matthew. *The Case for Working with Your Hands: Or why office work is bad for us and fixing things feels good* (Penguin, 2010).

Cummings, Chris. 'Why Brexit Risks Weakening All Our Financial Services', *The Telegraph*, 7 March 2016.

'A Cutting Sense Of History at PwC', *Evening Standard*, 30 December 2008.

Cypert, Samuel A. *Following the Money: The inside story of accounting's first mega-merger* (AMACOM, 1991).

Danckert, Sarah. 'Centro Auditor Banned by ASIC', *The Australian Business Review*, 20 November 2012.

Daniels, Melissa. 'SEC bars KPMG auditors after TierOne mortgage case roles', *Law360* (online), 5 August 2016.

Deloitte. 'About Us: GLOBE: Deloitte's LGBTI Network' (www2.deloitte.com/au/en/pages/about-deloitte/articles/globe.html).

Deloitte. 'About Us: Inspiring Women' (www2.deloitte.com/au/en/pages/about-deloitte/articles/inspiring-women.html).

Deloitte. *The Politics of Tax Reform in the 114th Congress* (Deloitte Development LLC, 15 April 2015).

'Deloitte sued over audits of ChinaCast Education', *Reuters*, 20 February 2013 (www.reuters.com/article/us-lawsuit-deloitte/deloitte-sued-over-audits-of-chinacast-education-idUSBRE91I16N20130219).

DeMond, C.W. *Price Waterhouse and Company in America: A history of a public accounting firm* (Comet Press, 1951).

Department of Justice, 'Superseding Indictment of 19 Individuals Filed in Kpmg Criminal Tax Fraud Case', media release, 17 October 2005.

Department of Justice/Office of Public Affairs. 'Former Chairman of Taylor, Bean & Whitaker Convicted for $2.9 Billion Fraud Scheme that Contributed to the Failure of Colonial Bank', 19 April 2011 (www.justice.gov/opa/pr/former-chairman-taylor-bean-whitaker-convicted-29-billion-fraud-scheme-contributed-failure).

de Roover, Raymond. *The Rise and Decline of the Medici Bank: 1397–1494* (Beard Books, 1999).

Dewing, Ian P. & Peter O. Russell. 'Whistleblowing on "Fraud" – Audit, Governance, Risk and Regulation at HBOS'. Draft paper. Norwich Business School, University of East Anglia.

Doherty, Raymond. 'HK Regulator to Take E&Y to Court', *Economia*, 29 August 2012.

Doherty, Raymond. 'Deloitte Sued by US funds', *Economia*, 21 February 2013.

Doherty, Raymond. 'Deloitte MG Tribunal Begins', *Economia*, 5 March 2013.

Doherty, Raymond. 'SEC Pursues Deloitte China', *Economia*, 5 March 2013.

Doherty, Raymond. 'Deloitte Compromised "Professional Judgement" over MG Rover', *Economia*, 6 March 2013.

Doherty, Raymond. 'FRC Hits Deloitte with Record Fine', *Economia*, 9 September 2013.

Doherty, Raymond. 'Unilever Drops PwC', *Economia*, 2 December 2013.

Doherty, Raymond. 'FRC Drops PwC Barclays Investigation', *Economia*, 6 December 2013.

Doherty, Raymond. 'M&S and Berkeley drop PwC', *Economia*, 6 December 2013.

Doherty, Raymond. 'British Land Drops Deloitte as Auditor', *Economia*, 29 January 2014.

Doherty, Raymond. 'Deloitte has Overtaken PwC as the World's Largest Firm by Income', *Economia*, 30 January 2014.

Donohue, Lacey. 'This Is the Best "I Quit" Email You'll Read All Week', *Gawker*, 18 November 2013.

'The dozy watchdogs. Some 13 years after Enron, auditors still can't stop managers cooking the books. Time for some serious reforms', *The Economist*, 13 December 2014.

Dugan, Ianthe Jeanne. 'Before Enron, Greed Helped Sink the Respectability of Accounting', *Wall Street Journal*, 14 March 2002.

Edwards, J.D. *History of Public Accounting in the United States* (Bureau of Business and Economic Research, Michigan State University, 1960).

Edwards, John Richard. 'Accounting Education in Britain During the Early Modern Period', *Accounting History Review*, Vol. 21, No. 1, 2011, pp. 37–67.

Edwards, John Richard & Stephen P. Walker. *The Routledge Companion to Accounting History* (Routledge, 2008).

Engwall, Lars, Matthias Kipping & Behlül Üsdiken. *Defining Management: Business Schools* (Routledge, 2016).

'Ernst & Young's letter about Lehman accounting', *Reuters*, 23 March 2010 (www.reuters.com/article/lehman-ernstyoung/text-ernst-youngs-letter-about-lehman-accounting-idUSN2221089720100322).

Ernst & Young. 'UK House of Lords Economic Affairs Committee issues its final report "Auditors: Market concentration and their role"' Overview series (Ernst & Young, April 2011).

Esterl, Mike, David Crawford & David Reilly, 'KPMG Germany's Failure to Spot Siemens Problems Raises Questions', *The Wall Street Journal*, 24 February 2007.

European Commission. *Audit Policy: Lessons from the Crisis*. Green Paper issued for comment by the European Commission. COM(2010) 561 final.

Evans, L. 'The Accountant's Social Background and Stereotype in Popular Culture: The novels of Alexander Clark Smith', *Accounting, Auditing and Accountability Journal*, Vol. 25, No. 6, 2012.

'Even Bush Mocks Andersen', *News24* (online), 17 March 2002.

EY, 'Life at EY: EY recognised for LGBTI inclusion' (www.ey.com/au/en/careers/experienced/life-at-ey#fragment-1-na).

Farrell, Elijah D. 'Accounting Firms and the Unauthorized Practice of Law: Who is the Bar really trying to protect?', *Indiana Law Review*, Vol. 33, 2000, pp. 599–629.

Faulkner, David, Satu Teerikangas & Richard J. Joseph. *The Handbook of Mergers and Acquisitions* (OUP, 2012).

Feil, Martin. *The Great Multinational Tax Rort: How we're all being robbed* (Scribe, 2016).

Ferguson, Niall. 'The Great Dying', *Financial Times*, 14 December 2007.

Fitzgerald, Patrick. 'PricewaterhouseCoopers Settles $5.5 Billion Crisis Era Lawsuit', *Wall Street Journal*, 26 August 2016.

Follain, John. 'Pope Orders Audit of Church's Wealth as Whistleblowers Pursued', *Bloomberg* (online), 1 December 2015.

Fraser, Ian. 'Time to Audit the Auditors – and especially KPMG?', *Ian Fraser* (online), 8 January 2009.

Fraser, Ian. 'Big Four Audit Firms Had Pivotal Role in Global Financial Crisis', *Ian Fraser* (online), 23 November 2009.

Gandel, Stephen. 'The Madoff Fraud: How culpable were the auditors?', *Time*, 17 December 2008.

Gilbert, Alorie. 'EY Punished over PeopleSoft Dealings', *CNET* (online), 16 April 2004.

Gillis, Paul L. 'The Big Four in China: Hegemony and Counter-hegemony in the Development of the Accounting Profession in China', PhD thesis, Macquarie Graduate School of Management, Macquarie University, June 2011.

Gillis, Paul. *The Big Four and the Development of the Accounting Profession in China* (Emerald Group Publishing, 2014).

Gipper, Brandon, Brett Lombardi & Douglas J. Skinner. 'The Politics of Accounting Standard-Setting: A review of empirical research', draft paper prepared for the Australian Journal of Management conference, University of Melbourne, July 2013.

Giroux, Gary. *Business Scandals, Corruption, and Reform: An encyclopedia* (ABC-CLIO, 2013).

# BIBLIOGRAPHY

Glater, Jonathan D. & Alexei Barrionuevo. 'Decision rekindles debate over Andersen indictment', *The New York Times*, 1 June 2005.

Gonzalez, Adrienne. 'This PwC Quote Regarding Caterpillar's Tax Dodging Will Make You Outraged', *Going Concern*, 1 April 2014.

Goodley, Simon. 'PriceWaterhouseCoopers Chief Kevin Nicholson Denies Lying Over Tax Deals', *The Guardian*, 9 December 2014.

Gow, Ian & Stuart Kells. 'Measuring the Performance of Australian Businesses', in Peter Dawkins et al. (eds), *How Big Business Performs* (Allen & Unwin, in association with the Melbourne Institute of Applied Economic and Social Research, 1999, pp. 12–26).

Grabosky, Peter. 'Professional Advisers and White-Collar Illegality: Towards explaining and excusing professional failure', *University of New South Wales Law Journal*, Vol. 13, No. 1, 1990.

Grant Thornton. *The Impact of 'Brexit' on the Financial Services Sector* (Grant Thornton UK LLP, April 2016).

Griffin, Oliver. 'HBoS Whistleblower Lambasts KPMG', *Economia*, 17 November 2015.

Grim, Ryan. 'PwC's Other Debacle: A tax boondoggle that has ballooned out of control', *Huffington Post*, 2 March 2017.

Guerrera, Francesco. 'Evidence Suggests Former Chief Knew of "Accounting Gimmick"', *Financial Times*, 13 March 2010.

Habgood, Wendy. *Chartered Accountants in England and Wales: A guide to historical records* (Manchester University Press, 1994).

Halberstam, David. *The Reckoning* (William Morrow, 1986).

Hancock, Ciarán. 'Banking Inquiry: PwC stands over past audits of Irish banks', *Irish Times*, 20 May 2015.

Hastings, Patrick. *Cases in Court* (William Heinemann, 1949).

Hayes, David A. & Marian Kamlish. *The King's Cross Fraudster: Leopold Redpath, his life and times* (Camden History Society, 2013).

'HBoS Whistleblower Statement. Memorandum from Paul Moore, Ex-head of Group Regulatory Risk, HBoS Plc'. *BBC News* (online), 10 February 2009.

'Health System Sues KPMG over "One of The Largest Reported Adjustments in History"', *HealthcareDIVE* (online), 21 January 2015.

Heier, Jan R. 'Review of *A History of Cooper Brothers & Co.: 1854 to 1954*'. *Accounting Information* (online).

Hennie, Matt. 'Former Blake's Owner a Mean, Garish Queen', *ProjectQ Atlanta* (online), 27 July 2012.

Herrera, Chabeli. 'Largest Lawsuit Against an Auditor Goes to Court for $5.5 Billion', *Miami Herald*, 29 July 2016.

Herz, Robert H. (Submission): 'Re: Discussion of Selected Accounting Guidance Relevant to Lehman Accounting Practices', 19 April 2020, p. 4 (http://archives. financialservices.house.gov/media/file/hearings/111/fsb_testimony_4.20.10.pdf).

Hibbert, Christopher. 'The Rise and Fall of the Medici Bank', *History Today*, Vol. 24, No. 8, August 1974.

Hibbert, C. *The Rise and Fall of the House of Medici* (Penguin, 2001).

History of KPMG: http://us-jobs.kpmg.com/why-kpmg/our-history; http://kpmgcampus.com/kpmg-family/kpmg-history.shtml; http://www.kpmgcampus. com/why-kpmg/history.

Hildebrand, Joe. 'Report Shows Climb in Black Market Cigarettes Is Costing $2 Billion a Year', *The Daily Telegraph*, 12 July 2011.

Holliday, Adrian. 'Great Wall of China Finance', *Economia*, 31 August 2012.

Hongo, Jun. 'CPAs in Kanebo Fraud Avoid Prison', *Japan Times*, 10 August 2006.

House of Commons Committee of Public Accounts. *Tax Avoidance: The role of large accountancy firms*, 44th Report of Session 2012–13. Report, together with formal minutes, oral and written evidence. Stationery Office, 26 April 2013.

House of Lords, Select Committee on Economic Affairs. *Auditors: Market concentration and their role, second report of session 2010–11, Vol. 1: Report* (The Stationery Office, 2011).

House of Lords, Economic Affairs Committee. 'Complacency of auditors contributed to financial crisis', 30 March 2011 (www.parliament.uk/business/committees/committees-a-z/lords-select/economic-affairs-committee/news/big-4-auditors-inquiry-report).

House of Lords, Select Committee on Economic Affairs. *Auditors: Market concentration and their role, Volume II: Evidence*. 2nd Report of Session 2010–11. Stationery Office, 2011.

Schreiber, Uschi. 'How professional services can disrupt its way out of automation', *Knowledge @ Wharton* (online), 5 November 2015.

Hudson, Michael, Sasha Chavkin & Bart Mos. 'Big 4 audit firms play big role in offshore murk', *ICIJ* (online), 5 November 2014.

Hudson, Michael, Sasha Chavkin & Bart Mos. 'Big four Audit Firms Behind Global Profit Shifting', *Sydney Morning Herald*, 6 November 2014.

Hurley, Lawrence. 'U.S. Top Court Rejects Banks Over FDIC Lawsuit', *Reuters*, 9 January 2017.

ICAEW. *The Development of the Accountancy Profession in the UK and ICAEW's Role* (ICAEW, 2012).

ICAEW. 'Female Firsts. *ICAEW* (online), (www.icaew.com/en/library/historical-resources/female-firsts).

ICAEW. 'Price Waterhouse: A simplified family tree for the firm of Price Waterhouse showing the development of the firm and how the firm's name has evolved', *ICAEW* (online), (www.icaew.com/en/library/historical-resources/guide-to-historical-resources/firm-histories/whats-in-a-name/price-waterhouse).

# BIBLIOGRAPHY

ICAEW. 'What's in a Name: Firms' simplified family trees on the web', *ICAEW (online)*, (www.icaew.com/en/library/subject-gateways/accounting-history/resources/whats-in-a-name).

Ingram, David & Dena Aubin. 'Big 4 auditors spend more than ever on U.S. lobbying', *Reuters*, 13 March 2012.

*Initial decision release No. 249/administrative proceeding/file No. 3-10933/United States of America/Before the Securities and Exchange Commission/In the Matter of Ernst & Young LLP.* Transcript of ruling (www.sec.gov/litigation/aljdec/id249bpm.htm).

'The Institute of Chartered Accountants in England & Wales: The Autumnal Meeting', *The Accountant*, 27 October 1888.

IRS. 'KPMG to Pay $456 Million for Criminal Violations', media release, IR-2005-83, 29 August 2005 (www.irs.gov/newsroom/kpmg-to-pay-456-million-for-criminal-violations).

Irvine, Julia. 'FRC Opts for "Comply or Explain" on Audit Tendering', *Economia*, 20 April 2012.

Irvine, Julia. 'Deloitte in Catch 22 Over Former Chinese Client', *Economia*, 11 May 2012.

Irvine, Julia. 'China orders Big Four to localise practices', *Economia*, 14 May 2012.

Irvine, Julia. 'Deloitte Fails to Get Case Struck Out', *Economia*, 30 July 2012.

Irvine, Julia. 'Deloitte Implicated in Standard Chartered Scandal', *Economia*, 7 August 2012.

Irvine, Julia. 'Big Four Dominance Won't Last in China', *Economia*, 20 November 2012.

Irvine, Julia. 'SEC Charges Big Four Over Chinese Audits', *Economia*, 4 December 2012.

Irvine, Julia. 'European Business Rejects Audit Rotation', *Economia*, 18 April 2013.

Irvine, Julia. 'US Blocks Mandatory Auditor Rotation', *Economia*, 9 July 2013.

Irvine, Julia. 'ICAEW "Disappointed" By CC's Tender Proposal', *Economia*, 14 August 2013.

Irvine, Julia. 'Mixed Feelings About CC Remedies', *Economia*, 2 September 2013.

Irvine, Julia. 'Mandatory Auditor Rotation Agreed', *Economia*, 7 October 2013.

James, Lawrence. *The Middle Class: A history* (Hachette, 2010).

Johnston, Bruce. 'Can Dynasty Detectives Unearth the Medici Secrets?', *The Telegraph*, 13 December 2003.

Johnston, David Cay. 'Tax Shelter of Rich And Famous Has Final Date in Court', *New York Times*, 4 November 1995.

Jones, Adam. 'Auditors Criticised for Role in Financial Crisis', *Financial Times*, 30 March 2011.

Jones, Edgar. *True and Fair: A history of Price Waterhouse* (Hamish Hamilton, 1995).

Jones, E. (ed.). *The Memoirs of Edwin Waterhouse: A founder of Price Waterhouse* (B.T. Batsford, 1988).

Kahle, John J. *American Accountants and Their Contributions to Accounting Thought: 1900–1930* (Routledge, 2014).

Kehoe, John. 'The Jobs We'll Lose to Machines – And the Ones We Won't', *Australian Financial Review*, 14 August 2016.

Kells, Stuart. 'A Look Inside the Performance Auditing Box: Victoria's new ticketing system tender', *Accounting, Accountability & Performance*, Vol. 16, No. 1 & 2, 2010, pp. 85–110.

Kells, Stuart. 'Thrusters, Scoopers, Scroungers and Squirrels: A taxonomy of public sector audit and accountability mechanisms', *Journal of Contemporary Issues in Business and Government*, Vol. 16, No. 1, 2010, pp. 1–25.

Kells, Stuart. 'Conflict Between Independent Scrutinisers of Transport Megaprojects: Evidence from Australia', *European Journal of Transport and Infrastructure Research*, Vol. 11, No. 1, January 2011, pp. 61–79.

Kells, Stuart. 'The Seven Deadly Sins of Performance Auditing: Implications for monitoring public audit institutions', *Australian Accounting Review*, No. 59, Vol. 21, Issue 4, 2011, pp. 383–396.

Kells, Stuart & Arie Freiberg. 'Economic Regulation', in A. Freiberg, *The Tools of Regulation* (Federation Press, 2011).

Kells, Stuart & Graeme Hodge. 'Performance Auditing in the Public Sector: Reconceptualising the task', *Journal of Contemporary Issues in Business and Government*, Vol. 15, No. 2, 2009, pp. 33–60.

Kells, Stuart & Graeme Hodge. 'Redefining the Performance Auditing Space', *Asia Pacific Journal of Public Administration*, Vol. 32, No. 1, June 2010, pp. 63–88.

Kells, Stuart & Graeme Hodge. 'Performance Auditing And Public Sector Innovation: Friends with benefits or strange bedfellows?', *Asia Pacific Journal of Public Administration*, Vol. 33, No. 2, December 2011, pp. 163–184.

Keister, D.A. 'The Public Accountant', *The Book-keeper*, July 1896.

Kennedy, Joseph V. 'Three Paths to Update Labor Law for the Gig Economy', *ITIF* (online), 18 April 2016.

Ketz, J. Edward. *Accounting Ethics: Critical perspectives on business and management. Volume IV: Crisis in accounting ethics* (Routledge, 2006).

King, Agnes. 'PwC Shakes Up Leadership Team and Increases Female Representation', *Australian Financial Review*, 17 May 2016.

King, Agnes & Ben Potter. 'How Big 4 Accounting Firms Embrace Internal Disrupters', *Australian Financial Review Weekend*, 15 July 2015.

King, Agnes & Katie Walsh. 'Big Four Accounting Firms Push into Legal Services', *Australian Financial Review*, 21 July 2015.

Kirchgaessner, Stephanie. 'Vatican's Suspension of Major PwC Audit Exposes Internal Rift', *The Guardian*, 22 April 2016.

Knapp, Jeffrey. 'Big Four Accounting Firms Avoid Scrutiny in Multinational Tax Avoidance', *The Conversation* (online), 25 February 2016.

'KPMG: A history of abetting fraud', *Cheating Culture* (online), 6 January 2011.

# BIBLIOGRAPHY

Lamb, Christopher. 'Blow for Financial Transparency as Vatican Cancels PWC Audit of Church's Finances', *The Tablet* (online), 10 June 2016.

Lee, T.A. *The Development of the American Public Accounting Profession: Scottish Chartered Accountants and the Early American Public Accountancy Profession* (Routledge, 2007).

Lee, Thomas A. 'Assimilation and Americanisation in the Progressive Era: Price, Waterhouse & Company in the US, 1890–1914', *Accounting History*, Vol. 19, No. 1, February 2014, pp. 13–30.

*Lehman Brothers Holdings Inc. Chapter 11. Case # 08-13555.* (http://dm.epiq11.com/#/case/LBH/info).

*Lehman Brothers Holdings Inc. Chapter 11 Proceedings Examiner's Report* (https://web.stanford.edu/~jbulow/Lehmandocs/origIndex.html).

Levit, Nancy. *The Gender Line: Men, women, and the law* (NYU Press, 1998).

Lewis, Michael. 'KPMG Has History of Public Sector Consulting Work', *The Star*, 20 July 2011.

Lewis, T. *In Partnership: KPMG's 60 years in Hong Kong and 20 years in China* (KPMG, 2005).

Library of Congress, Business Reference Services. *The History of Accounting* (www.loc.gov/rr/business/accounting/history/accthistory_main.html).

Loomis, Carol J. 'The biggest looniest deal ever', *Fortune Magazine*, 18 June 1990.

Lowe, Zach. 'Lehman to Judge: Make the Examiner's Report public', *The Am Law Daily* (online), 9 March 2010.

McDonnell, John. 'Opening Submission to the Banking Inquiry', pp. 6 & 3 (https://inquiries.oireachtas.ie/banking/wp-content/uploads/2015/05/John-McDonnell-Opening-Statement.pdf).

McDougald, Megan S. & Royston Greenwood. 'Cuckoo in the nest? The rise of management consulting in large accounting firms', in Matthias Kipping & Timothy Clark (eds), *The Oxford Handbook of Management Consulting* (OUP, 2012), pp. 93–116.

McHugh, Robert. 'Banking Inquiry to Hear from Auditors PWC and Ernst & Young', *Business World* (online), 19 May 2015.

McKenna, Francine. 'PwC Faces 3 Major Trials That Threaten Its Business', *Market Watch* (online), 18 August 2016.

McKenna, Francine. 'A Tale of Two Lawsuits – PricewaterhouseCoopers and Colonial Bank', *Forbes*, 10 November 2012.

McKenna Francine. 'Will Auditors Be Held Accountable? The PCAOB has a plan', *Re: TheAuditors*, 21 March 2011.

McLannahan, Ben. 'PwC Sued for $5.5bn Over Mortgage Underwriter TBW's Collapse', *Financial Times*, 15 August 2016.

McLannahan, B. 'PwC Settles $7.3b Fraud Detection Failure Lawsuit', *Australian Financial Review*, 29 August 2016.

McLynn, Frank. 'A Bureaucrat Goes Native Among the Hill Folk: Thangliena: The life of T H Lewin', *The Independent*, 3 May 1993.

McNulty, Lucy. 'HBoS Whistleblower And Senior Lawmaker Call for KPMG Investigation', *Financial News*, 20 November 2015.

McRoberts, Flynn et al. 'The Fall of Andersen: Part I', *Chicago Tribune*, 1 September 2002.

Macquarie. 'Disrupting Professional Services: The way forward', *Macquarie*, (www.macquarie.com/au/business-banking/business-strategy/expertise/digital-disruption-professional-services).

Mahanta, Vinod. 'Big Four Accounting Firms Pwc, Deloitte, KPMG, E&Y Back in Consulting Business', *Economic Times*, 28 April 2013.

Maister, David. *True Professionalism: The courage to care about your clients & career* (Simon & Schuster, 2012).

Maister, David H., Robert Galford & Charles Green, *The Trusted Advisor* (Simon & Schuster, 2012).

Malone, Scott & Martha Graybow. 'Pricewaterhouse to Pay $225 mln in Tyco Settlement', *Reuters*, 6 July 2007.

'The Management Consulting Industry: Growth of consulting services in India: Panel discussion', *IIMB Management Review*, Vol. 26, No. 4, December 2014, pp. 257–70.

Markham, Jerry W. *A Financial History of the United States: From Enron-era scandals to the Subprime Crisis (2004–2006); From the Subprime Crisis to the Great Recession (2006–2009)* (M.E. Sharpe, 2010).

Markham, J.W. *A Financial History of Modern U.S. Corporate Scandals: From Enron to Reform* (Routledge, 2015).

Markus, Hugh Brian. *The History of the German Public Accounting Profession* (Routledge, 1997).

Martin, Jessie E. 'Cosimo de' Medici: Patron, Banker, and *Pater Patriae*', *The Cupola*, Paper 261, Fall 2014.

Matthews, Derek, Malcolm Anderson & J.R. Edwards. *The Priesthood of Industry: The rise of the professional accountant in British management* (OUP, 1998).

Matthews, Derek & Jim Pirie. *The Auditors Talk: An oral history of a profession from the 1920s to the present day* (Garland, 2001).

Mathiason, Nick. 'Three Weeks That Changed the World', *The Guardian*, 28 December 2008.

'The Medici Family – The Leaders of Florence', *Italian Tribune*, 12 March 2014.

Mee Jr., Charles L. *Life in the Renaissance* (New Word City, 2016).

Meek, James. 'Trains in space', *London Review of Books*, Vol. 38, No. 9, 5 May 2016.

Mehta, Mihir N. & Wanli Zhao. 'Auditor-Relevant Congressional Committees and Audit Quality', 24 August 2014. Audit Symposium Session IV.

Mepham, Michael J. 'The Memoirs of Edwin Waterhouse: A founder of Price Waterhouse', *The Accounting Historians Journal*, Vol. 17, No. 1, June 1990.

Merz, Theo. 'Father wins sex discrimination case after request to work part-time rejected', *The Telegraph*, 4 November 2014.

Minority Staff of the Permanent Subcommittee on Investigations of the Committee on Governmental Affairs, United States Senate, *U.S. Tax Shelter Industry: The role of accountants, lawyers, and financial professionals. Four KPMG case studies: Flip, Opis, Blips, and Sc2* (U.S. Government Printing Office, 2003).

Moizer, Peter. 'Auditor Reputation: The international empirical evidence', *International Journal of Auditing*, Vol. 1, No. 1, 1997, pp. 61–74.

'Money: My illustration – Mr Frederick Whinney', *The Tatler*, No. 123, 4 November 1903, p. 199.

Moore, James. 'PwC Links to Independent Anti-Reform Lobbyist Revealed', *The Independent*, 19 July 2013.

Morrow, Ross. 'A Critical Analysis of the US Causes of the Global Financial Crisis of 2007–2008', *Australian Marxist Review*, Issue 53, October 2010.

Morton, Rick & Rachel Baxendale. 'PricewaterhouseCoopers can count on same-sex cause', *The Australian*, 15 March 2016.

Moshinsky, Ben. 'PwC Is Being Sued for $US5.5 Billion Over the 6th Largest Banking Collapse in US History', *Business Insider*, 16 August 2016.

Müller, Sigrid & Cornelia Schweiger. *Between Creativity and Norm-Making: Tensions in the early modern era* (BRILL, 2012).

Nelson, Debra L. & James Campbell Quick. *Organizational Behavior: Science, the real world, and you* (South-Western, 2010).

Neokleous, Christina Ionela. 'Accounting for Power: The history of an industry that shaped the world', *The Conversation* (online), 22 July 2016.

Nesmith, Susannah & Sophia Pearson. 'PwC Fights $5.6 Billion Fraud Trial Over Taylor Bean's Collapse', *Bloomberg* (online), 10 August 2016.

Nesmith, Susannah & Sophia Pearson. 'PwC Sued for Record $5.5bn for Negligence in Mortgage Fraud Case', *The Independent*, 15 August 2016.

Neville, Simon. 'British American Tobacco Drops and Sues PwC Over Pollution Scandal', *The Independent*, 3 March 2015.

Neville, Simon. 'Tesco Axes Pwc as Auditor After Accounting Scandal', *The Independent*, 11 May 2015.

Niemeier, Charles D. 'Independent Oversight of the Auditing Profession: Lessons from U.S. history', Speech delivered on 8 November 2007, German Public Auditors Congress of 2007.

Nigel, Richard Fitz & Constitutio Domus Regis. *The Establishment of the Royal Household*. Edited and translated by Charles Johnson with corrections by F.E.L. Carter and D.E. Greenway (Clarendon Press, 1983).

O'Connor, Sean M. 'Be Careful What You Wish For: How accountants and Congress created the problem of auditor independence', *Boston College Law Review*, Vol. 45, No. 4, 2004, pp. 741–828.

# BIBLIOGRAPHY

O'Halloran, Marie. 'Firms "Have Case to Answer" on Banks Crisis', *The Irish Times*, 5 November 2017.

O'Keefe, Brian. 'The Man Behind 2009's Biggest Bank Bust', *Fortune Magazine*, 12 October 2009.

O'Keeffe, Paul. *Some Sort of Genius: A Life of Wyndham Lewis* (Counterpoint Press, 2015).

Osborne, Alistair. 'Were Big Four Auditors Just Guilty of Failing to See Wood for Trees?', *The Telegraph*, 15 August 2016.

Ottaway, Joanne. 'Improving Auditor Independence in Australia: Is "mandatory audit firm rotation" the best option?' (http://law.unimelb.edu.au/__data/assets/pdf_file/0004/1709509/27-OTTAWAYJoanne-MandatoryAuditFirmRotationPaper2.pdf).

Paris, Dubravka. 'History of Accounting And Accountancy Profession in Great Britain', *Journal of Accounting and Management*, Vol. 6, No. 1, pp. 33–44.

Parker, Robert Henry. *British Accountants: A biographical sourcebook* (Arno Press, 1980).

Parker, Robert H. *Papers on Accounting History* (Routledge, 2013).

Parker, Robert H., Stephen A. Zeff & Malcolm Anderson. *Major Contributors to the British Accountancy Profession: A biographical sourcebook* (ICAS, 2012).

Parks, Tim. *Medici Money: Banking, metaphysics and art in fifteenth-century Florence, a work of history* (Profile Books, 2005).

Parks, Tim. *Medici Money: Banking, metaphysics and art in fifteenth-century Florence* (Profile Books, 2013).

Paul, Mark. 'PwC Claims €1bn Quinn Insurance Action "Poised on Cliff"', *Irish Times*, 7 May 2015.

PCAOB. *Annual Report on the Interim Inspection Program Related to Audits of Brokers and Dealers*. Public Company Accounting Oversight Board Release No. 2016-004 (PCAOB, 18 August 2016).

PCAOB Investor Advisory Group. 'The Watchdog That Didn't Bark ... Again', Presentation of the Working Group on Lessons Learned from the Financial Crisis, PCAOB Investor Advisory Group, 16 March 2011.

Pentin, Edward. 'Vatican Audit Suspended, Secretariat of State Announces', *National Catholic Register*, 20 April 2016.

Phillips, William D. *Slavery From Roman Times to the Early Transatlantic Trade* (Manchester University Press, 1985).

Pixley, Francis W. *Auditors: Their duties and responsibilities under the companies acts and other acts of parliament*, 8th edition (Henry Good & Son, 1901).

Politi, James. 'Vatican Suspends PwC Audit of Its Finances. Delay is a blow to Pope Francis's financial reform agenda', *Financial Times*, 22 April 2016.

Power, Michael. *The Audit Society: Rituals of Verification* (OUP, 1999).

Previts, G.J. *The Scope of CPA Services: A study of the development of the concept of independence and the profession's role in society* (Wiley, 1985).

Previts, Gary John, Peter J. Walton & P.W. Wolnizer. *A Global History of Accounting, Financial Reporting and Public Policy: Eurasia, the Middle East and Africa* (Emerald Group, 2012).

Price, Ilfryn & Tom Kennie. 'Leadership and Innovation Lessons from Professional Services Firms', Discussion Paper. London, Leadership Foundation for Higher Education, 2012 (http://shura.shu.ac.uk/5029).

PricewaterhouseCoopers. 'Our History', (www.pwc.com/gx/en/about-pwc/facts-and-figures.jhtml).

Pullella, Philip. 'Vatican Scraps External Audit Plan but Says Committed to Transparency', *Reuters*, 10 June 2016.

PwC. *Banking Industry Reform: A new equilibrium* (PricewaterhouseCoopers LLP, 2012).

PwC. 'Decision may support Section 199 eligibility for taxpayers assembling items from purchased materials', *PwC* (online), 6 October 2015.

PwC. *Effective Audit Committee Oversight of the External Auditor and Audit*, 19 July 2013 (www.pwc.com/gx/en/audit-services/publications/assets/pwc-the-role-of-ac-in-overseeing-external-auditor-and-audit.pdf).

PwC. 'Thrive in a Great Team' (www.pwc.com.au/careers/thrive-in-a-great-team.html).

PwC. 'Work Like a Start-Up' (www.pwc.com.au/careers/be-entrepreneurial-like-a-start-up.html).

'PwC faces record $5.5bn lawsuit over mortgage underwriter collapse', *RT* (online), 15 August 2016.

'PwC Glimpses the Ghost of Arthur Anderson'. *Viden* (viden.com.au/pwc-glimpses-ghost-arthur-anderson).

Quinn, Eamon. 'Auditors Cleared of Blame for Bank Collapse', *Irish Examiner*, 20 September 2015.

Quinn, Leslie. 'The Fibonacci Sequence', 12 April 2005 (math.ucdenver.edu/~wcherowi/courses/m4010/s05/quinnfibseq.doc).

Rappaport, Liz & Michael Rapoport. 'Ernst Accused of Lehman Whitewash', *Wall Street Journal*, 21 December 2010.

Rapoport, Michael. 'Role of Auditors in Crisis Gets Look', *Wall Street Journal*, 23 December 2010.

Rapoport, Michael. 'Deloitte Settles Suits Over Taylor Bean Audits', *Wall Street Journal*, 3 October 2013.

Rapoport, Michael. 'Crisis-Era Lawsuits Winding Down? Not for PricewaterhouseCoopers', *Wall Street Journal*, 29 July 2016.

Reich, Robert. 'Dear Mr. Corporation', *The American Interest* (online), 1 July 2010.

Reich, Robert B. *Supercapitalism. The transformation of business, democracy, and everyday life* (Knopf, 2008).

Reilly, David. 'Accounting's Crisis Killer: Tumult eases for PwC's Nally; Does he do his own taxes?', *Wall Street Journal*, 23 March 2007.

# BIBLIOGRAPHY

*re Kingston Cotton Mill Company (No. 2) [1896] 2 Ch. 279*, (U.K. Court of Appeal), per Lopes LJ at pp. 288–9 (https://en.wikisource.org/wiki/Re_Kingston_Cotton_Mill_Company_(No.2)_(1896)).

*Report of the Joint Committee of Inquiry into the Banking Crisis: 20/05/2015: John McDonnell – Partner PWC* (https://inquiries.oireachtas.ie/banking/hearings/john-mcdonnell-partner-pwc).

Riel, Sotheara & Carl TaNo. 'The Impact of the Global Financial Crisis on Audit Quality. A study of publicly listed Swedish firms', MA Thesis, Umeå School of Business and Economics, 2014.

Roberts, Dan. 'Senate Report Claims Caterpillar Avoided $2.4bn in US Taxes', *The Guardian*, 1 April 2014.

Rolnik, Guy. 'Auditors Take Investors to La La Land', University of Oxford, Faculty of Law blog, 12 March 2017.

Roscoe, William. *The Life of Lorenzo De' Medici, Called the Magnificent* (A. Strahan; T. Cadell jun. and W. Davies (successors to Mr. Cadell) in the Strand; and J. Edwards in Pall Mall, 1796).

Ross, Janet (trans. & ed.). *Lives of the Early Medici as Told in Their Correspondence* (Chatto & Windus, 1910).

Rovnick, Naomi. 'Hard Work Pays Off for "Vicious" Akai Liquidator', *South China Morning Post*, 6 October 2009.

Rovnick, Naomi. 'Ernst & Young Pays up to Settle Negligence Claim', *South China Morning Post*, 27 January 2010.

Rozvany, George. 'Oligarchs of the Treasure Islands', *Michael West* (online), 11 July 2016.

Russell, Raymond. *Sharing Ownership in the Workplace* (SUNY Press, 1985).

Samelson, Donald, Suzanne Lowensohn & Laurence E. Johnson. 'The determinants of perceived audit quality and auditee satisfaction in local government', *Journal of Public Budgeting, Accounting & Financial Management*, Vol. 18, No. 2, Summer 2006, pp. 139–66.

Sander, Peter. *Madoff: Corruption, deceit, and the making of the world's most notorious Ponzi Scheme* (Lyons Press, 2009).

Sanders, Deen & Alex Roberts. 'Professionalisation of Financial Services', White Paper: Professional Standards Council, revised edition (State of New South Wales [NSW Department of Justice] for the Professional Standards Councils, 2015).

Sansom, Ian. 'Great Dynasties of the World: The Medici family', *The Guardian*, 8 May 2010.

Sarbanes Oxley Act Section 301: 2: Public Law 107–204, 107th Congress (www.sec.gov/about/laws/soa2002.pdf).

Schellen, Thomas. 'Strategy & War – Part I: The Middle East's scarcity of qualified consultants is taking the competition for local talent to a whole new level', *Executive Magazine*, 3 February 2015.

Schellen, T. 'Strategy & War – Part II: Booz and PwC: It made sense on paper,' *Executive Magazine*, 4 February 2015.

Schellen, T. 'Strategy & War – Part III: Booz vs. Booz: An aggressive challenger', *Executive Magazine*, 5 February 2015.

Schreiber, Uschi. 'How Professional Services Can Disrupt Its Way Out of Automation', *Knowledge @ Wharton* (online), 5 November 2015.

SEC. Litigation Release No. 22911 / January 27, 2014, Accounting and Auditing Enforcement Release No. 3531 / January 27, 2014, Securities and Exchange Commission v. Deloitte Touche Tohmatsu CPA Ltd., Civil Action No. 1:11-MC-00512 (D.D.C. filed September 8, 2011) (www.sec.gov/litigation/litreleases/2014/lr22911.htm).

SEC. 'The Richard C. Adkerson Gallery on the SEC Role in Accounting Standards Setting', *Securities and Exchange Commission Historical Society* (www.sechistorical.org/museum/galleries/rca/rca07a-glossary.php).

SEC. 'Securities Exchange Act of 1934. Release No. 78490 / August 5, 2016. Admin. Proc. File No. 3-15168. In the Matter of John J. Aesoph, CPA and Darren M. Bennett, CPA. Corrected Opinion of the Commission. Rule 102(e) Proceeding. Grounds for Remedial Action. Improper Professional Conduct pp. 22–23' (www.sec.gov/litigation/opinions/2016/34-78490.pdf).

'SEC Charges KPMG with Violating Auditor Independence Rules', press release, *U.S. Securities and Exchange Commission*, 24 January 2014.

Segal-Horn, Susan & David Faulkner. *Understanding Global Strategy* (Cengage Learning, 2010).

SFC. 'EY's appeal over audit working papers discontinued', *Securities and Futures Commission* (online), 23 July 2015.

Sheehy, Clodagh. 'Commercial Property and Buy to Let Loans Caused the First Ever Overall Loss at EBS', *The Independent*, 20 May 2015.

Sheehy, C. 'Rules for Bank Auditors During Crisis Since "Found Wanting" – Banking Inquiry', *The Independent*, 20 May 2015.

Sigler, Laurence E. (translator). *Fibonacci's Liber Abaci: A translation into modern English of Leonardo Pisano's Book of Calculation* (Springer Science & Business Media, 2003).

Sikka, Prem. 'Audit Policy-Making in the UK: The case of "the auditor's considerations in respect of going concern"', *European Accounting Review*, Vol. 1, No. 2, 1992, pp. 349–92.

Sikka, Prem. 'Called to Account', *The Guardian*, 14 December 2008.

Sikka, Prem. 'Financial Crisis and the Silence of the Auditors', *Accounting Organizations and Society*, Vol. 34, Nos 6–7, August 2009, pp. 868–873.

Sikka, Prem. 'The Audit Industry Should Serve Society … Not Themselves', *The Herald*, 23 November 2009.

Sikka, Prem. 'The Predatory Practices of Major Accountancy Firms', *The Guardian*, 8 December 2012.

Sikka, Prem, Steven Filling & Pik Liew. *The Audit Crunch: Reforming auditing*, Working Paper No. WP 09/01, Essex Business School, January 2009.

'Singing River Health System Sues KPMG: "Colossal" Error': *The Washington Times*, 18 January 2015.

Simonetta, Marcello. 'The Medici Meltdown', *Forbes*, 30 October 2008.

Sitton, Robert. *Lady in the Dark: Iris Barry and the Art of Film* (Columbia University Press, 2014).

Skidelsky, Robert. 'Is Economics Education Failing?', *World Economic Forum* (www. weforum.org/agenda/2017/01/is-economics-education-failing).

Skinner, Chris. 'What Did the Medici Bankers Ever Do For Us?', Chris Skinner's Blog (online), (https://thefinanser.com/2014/04/what-did-the-medici-bankers-ever-do-for-us. html).

Skinner, Douglas J. & Suraj Srinivasan. 'Audit Quality and Auditor Reputation: Evidence from Japan', *The Accounting Review*, Vol. 87, No. 5, September 2012.

Smith, Kalen. 'China Orders Big 4 Auditors to Hire More Chinese Citizens', *Big 4 Firms Network* (www.big4.com/news/ china-orders-big-4-auditors-to-hire-more-chinese-citizens).

Soll, Jacob. *The Reckoning: Financial accountability and the making and breaking of nations* (Penguin, 2014).

Soll, J. 'First They Killed All The Accountants: How big banks, corporations and government made themselves unauditable', *Salon* (online), 4 May 2014.

Srinivasan, R. 'The Management Consulting Industry: Growth of consulting services in India: Panel discussion', *IIMB Management Review*, Vol. 26, Issue 4, December 2014, pp. 257–70.

Stacey, Nicholas A.H. 'The Accountant in Literature', *The Accounting Review*, Vol. 33, No. 1 (Jan. 1958), pp. 102–5.

Stempel, Jonathan. 'Clock Did Not Run Out on FDIC Lawsuit Vs Big Banks: U.S. Court', *Reuters*, 19 May 2016.

Stempel, J. 'PwC Must Face $1 Billion MF Global Malpractice Lawsuit: U.S. judge', *Reuters*, 5 August 2016.

Stevens, Mark. *The Accounting Wars* (Macmillan, 1986).

Stevens, Mark. *The Big Eight: An incisive look behind the pinstripe curtain of the eight accounting firms whose practices affect the pocketbooks of every American* (Macmillan, 1981).

Stevens, Mark. *The Big Six: The selling out of America's top accounting firms* (Simon & Schuster, 1991).

Stevens, Mark. *The Big Eight* (Simon & Schuster, 2010).

Stiglitz, Joseph. *The Roaring Nineties: Seeds of destruction* (Penguin, 2003).

Strathern, Paul. *The Medici: Godfathers of the Renaissance* (Random House, 2007).

# BIBLIOGRAPHY

*Strengthening the Professionalism of the Independent Auditor: Report to the Public Oversight Board of the SEC Practice Section, AICPA from the Advisory Panel on Auditor Independence* (Public Oversight Board, 1994).

Stringer, Andrew. 'Future directions in auditing', *Chartered Accountants Australia and New Zealand* (www.charteredaccountants.com.au/News-Media/Charter/Charter-articles/Audit-and-assurance/2012-05-Future-Directions-in-Auditing).

Subcommittee on Reports, Accounting and Management of the Committee on Government Operations, United States Senate. *The Accounting Establishment: A staff study* (U.S. Government Printing Office, 1976).

Sutton, Michael H. 'Auditor Independence: The challenge of fact and appearance', Speech delivered at the American Accounting Association 1996 Annual Meeting, Securities and Exchange Commission, 14 August 1996.

Sweet, Pat. 'US Regulator Attacks KPMG Response to Audit Quality Criticism', *CCH Daily* (online), 27 October 2014.

Syal, Rajeev, Simon Bowers & Patrick Wintour. 'Big Four Accountants "Use Knowledge of Treasury to Help Rich Avoid Tax"', *The Guardian*, 26 April 2013.

Task Central. 'Task Central' (https://au.linkedin.com/company/task-central).

Thomson, H. Byerley. *The Choice of a Profession. A concise account and comparative review of the English professions* (1857).

Thornton, Patricia H., Candace Jones & Kenneth Kury. 'Institutional Logics And Institutional Change In Organizations: Transformation in accounting, architecture, and publishing', *Transformation in Cultural Industries, Research in the Sociology of Organizations*, Vol. 23, 2005, pp. 125–70.

'Those Medici', *The Economist*, 23 December 1999.

Toffler, Barbara Ley. *Final Accounting: Ambition, greed, and the fall of Arthur Andersen* (Broadway Books 2003).

Tomasic, Roman. 'Auditors and the Reporting of Illegality and Financial Fraud', in Peter N. Grabosky (ed.), *Complex Commercial Fraud: Proceedings of a conference held 20–23 August 1991* (Australian Institute of Criminology, 1992; AIC Conference Proceedings No. 10), pp. 43–63.

Touche Ross & Co. *Employers' Accounting for Pensions* (Touche Ross & Co., 1983).

Treanor, Jill. 'Whistleblower at HBoS Attacks "Ludicrously Bad" City Regulation', *The Guardian*, 15 November 2015.

Treanor, Jill & Simon Bowers. 'I Was Sacked for Exposing Risks, Says Bank Whistleblower', *The Guardian*, 11 February 2009.

Trotter, David. 'A Most Modern Misanthrope: Wyndham Lewis and the pursuit of anti-pathos', *The Guardian*, 23 January 2001.

'Typical Fraudster Is an Experienced, Tenured Manager Or Executive With No Criminal History: KPMG Report', *PR Newswire* (online), 18 December 2013.

Unger, Miles J. *Magnifico: The brilliant life and violent times of Lorenzo de' Medici* (Simon & Schuster, 2008).

# BIBLIOGRAPHY

United Nations Conference on Trade and Development. *Corporate Governance in the Wake of the Financial Crisis: Selected international views* (United Nations, 2010).

United States General Accounting Office. *Report to the Senate Committee on Banking, Housing, and Urban Affairs and the House Committee on Financial Services (September 2003): Accounting Firm Consolidation. Selected large public company views on audit fees, quality, independence, and choice* (United States General Accounting Office, 2003).

UNSW Business School. 'Accounting Practices: Did fair value cause the crisis', *Business Think* (online) 2 March 2011.

Vatican Radio. 'Press Office: Statement on Vatican–PwC relationship', 10 June 2016.

Vaughan, Adrian. *Railwaymen, Politics and Money* (John Murray, 1997).

'Victoria's Secret case tests US manufacturing tax break', *Reuters*, 3 April 2013.

Villmer, Matthew. 'PwC Fails in Bid to Toss FDIC's $1b Negligence Suit', *Law360*, 10 September 2013.

Warner, Jeremy. 'Dereliction of the Big Four Blamed for Financial Crisis', *The Telegraph*, 31 March 2011.

Waterhouse, Edwin. *The Memoirs of Edwin Waterhouse: A founder of Price Waterhouse*, edited by Edgar Jones (Batsford, 1988).

Watts, Ross L. & Jerold L. Zimmerman. 'Agency Problems, Auditing and the Theory of The Firm: Some evidence', *Journal of Law and Economics*, Vol. 26, No. 3, October 1983, pp. 613–33.

Way, D. & R. Nield. *Counting House: The history of PricewaterhouseCoopers on the China Coast* (PricewaterhouseCoopers, 2002).

Weatherford, Jack. *The History of Money* (Crown, 2009).

Webb, Jonathan. 'PwC Sued for Missing $2.9 Billion Scam: Do auditors have a public responsibility to prevent fraud?', *Forbes*, 25 August 2016.

Webb, Nick & Roisin Burke. 'Were the Bank Auditors Conflicted?', *Sunday Independent*, 25 April 2010.

Weiss, Barbara. *The Hell of the English: Bankruptcy and the Victorian novel* (Bucknell University Press, 1986).

Weller, Patrick. *Kevin Rudd: Twice Prime Minister* (Melbourne University Publishing, 2014).

West, Michael. 'Oligarchs of the Treasure Islands', *MW* (online), 11 July 2016.

West, Michael. '"Tax Avoidance" Masters Revealed: Exclusive', *The New Daily*, 11 July 2016.

White, Anna. 'Deloitte Reveals Record Revenues as It Benefits from Financial Crisis', *The Telegraph*, 22 September 2011.

White, A. 'PwC Fined Record £1.4m Over JP Morgan Audit', *The Telegraph*, 5 January 2012.

Whittle, Andrea, Frank Mueller & Chris Carter. 'The "Big Four" in the Spotlight: Accountability and professional legitimacy in the UK audit market', *Journal of Professions and Organization*, Vol. 3, No. 2, 2016, pp. 119–141.

'Why I Wouldn't Be Gagged: The whistleblower who triggered the fall of a leading financial regulator reveals his full story', *The Daily Mail*, 14 February 2009.

Wiggins, Rosalind Z., Thomas Piontek & Andrew Metrick. 'The Lehman Brothers Bankruptcy: An Overview', Yale Program on Financial Stability Case Study 2014-3a-v1, 1 October 2014 (http://som.yale.edu/ypfs).

Wolmar, Christian. *Fire & Steam* (Atlantic Books, 2007).

WoodShedd: Web Hosting Master, in *Thread: Price Waterhouse – Donkeys*, 12 August 2002 (www.webhostingtalk.com/showthread.php?t=66696).

Wootton, Charles W. & Wande G. Spruill. 'The Role of Women in Major Public Accounting Firms in the United States During World War II', *Business and Economic History*, Vol. 23, No. 1, Fall 1994, pp. 241–52.

Zanki, Tom. 'SEC Suspends KPMG Auditors after TierOne Bank's Failure', *Law 360*, 30 June 2014.

Zayed, Yago. 'Agriculture: Historical statistics', Briefing Paper No. 03339, 21 January 2016.

Zeff, Stephen A. 'How the U.S. Accounting Profession Got Where It Is Today: Part I', *Accounting Horizons*, Vol. 17, No. 3, September 2003, pp. 189–205.

Zeff, Stephen A. 'How the U.S. Accounting Profession Got Where It Is Today: Part II', *Accounting Horizons*, Vol. 17, No. 4, December 2003, pp. 267–286.

Zeff, Stephen A. *Forging Accounting Principles in Five Countries: A history and an analysis of trends* (Routledge, 2016).

Zeff, Stephen A. *Insights from Accounting History: Selected writings of Stephen Zeff* (Routledge, 2010).

# Index

# INDEX

# INDEX

# INDEX

# INDEX